MW01039104

ON THE RUN

with Bonnie & Clyde

ON THE RUN

with Bonnie & Clyde

JOHN GILMORE

LOS ANGELES

Cover design by Ross Goza
Book design by Carson Gilmore
Copy editing by Nikki Bazar
Published by Amok Books
Los Angeles, California

First Edition

Bibliographic Information for Library of Congress
Cataloging-in-Publication Data

Gilmore, John, 1935-
On the run with Bonnie & Clyde
by John Gilmore

ISBN-10: 1878923226
ISBN-13: 978-187893226

1. Parker, Bonnie, 1910-1934. 2. Barrow, Clyde, 1909-1934.
2. True Crime-American History-Americana. 3. Criminals-Texas-Dallas-
Biography/Creative Nonfiction.
4. Depressions-1929-1934-United States. I. Title.

Amok Books are available to bookstores through our primary distributor: SCB
Distributors, 15608 South New Century Drive, Los Angeles, California 90248.
Phone: 800-729-6423, 310-532-9400. Fax: 310-532-7001.
Email: scb@scbdistributors.com
Web site: www.scbdistributors.com

UK Distributors: Turnaround Distribution, Unit 3 Olympia Trading Estate,
Coburg Road, Wood Green, London N22 6TZ. Phone: (0181) 829 3000.
Fax: (0181) 881 5088.

Non-bookstore Distributors: Last Gasp Distribution, 777 Florida Street, San
Francisco, California 94110. Phone: 415-824-6636. Fax: 415-824-1836

To view the complete Amok Books catalog, please go to the Amok Books web
site at www.amokbooks.com.

10 9 8 7 6 5 4 3 2 1

A certain ruthlessness and a sense of alienation from society is as essential to creative writing as it is to armed robbery. The strong-armer isn't out merely to turn a fast buck any more than the poet is out solely to see his name on the cover of a book, whatever satisfaction that event may afford him. What both need most deeply is to get even.

—Nelson Algren

In Memoriam:

Bonnie Elizabeth Parker

1920 - 1934

"If a policeman is killed in Dallas,
and they have no clue or guide
if they can't find a fiend,
they just wipe their slate clean
and hang it on Bonnie and Clyde."

—Bonnie Parker

Foreword
by Marshall Terrill

The bogeyman really does exist and his name is John Gilmore. How many writers today can you really say are badasses? John Gilmore doesn't know this, but he's my favorite writer. He has been ever since I cracked open his book *Laid Bare*, which is the best Hollywood memoir I've ever read. It's not one of those "warts and all" type books—John splays open his soul and puts it out there for all to see. He writes about the carnality of Tinseltown, the Boulevard of Broken dreams; those trampled underfoot.

Gilmore specializes in imploding Hollywood myths, and that, in my estimation, makes him dangerous. How many writers can you think of who are dangerous? So when John's publisher asked me to write a foreword, naturally I was thrilled. John is, in my humble opinion, the most talented noir/true crime writer on the scene today. His writing stuns. No one even comes close.

Did I say badass? The man is scary and I'll tell you why: he has witnessed evil up close. He knows where the bodies are buried; has seen the skeletons in the closet; understands everyone's strange peccadilloes. Gilmore is a literary surgeon whose pen is like a scalpel. He peers into souls, reads minds, and isn't afraid to crack open the cadaver to find out what's inside. He divulges the secrets of the rich and famous and cold-blooded killers alike.

What separates Gilmore from the rest of the great noir/true crime writers is that he was there. He befriended them all—the stars, starlets, has-beens, gangsters, pimps, hustlers, murderers—and strips away the glitz and glamour with the stroke of his cynical and merciless pen. He is comfortable in the darkness and writes from a very shadowy place. He is the sum total of his incredible life experiences: the son of an L.A. cop and a star-struck mom. He's been an actor, writer, director, teacher, painter, observer, confidant of legends, mythmaker as well as mythbuster. He has an angel on his shoulder and a devil in his prose. He has looked evil in the eye many times and never flinched.

He's from the *Mad Men* era where adults lived, loved and played hard; his literary voice comes from a life of gut-wrenching hardship, which, he'll admit, sometimes bordered on madness. He has lived an unrepentant life, that included plenty of beautiful women, booze, and dope. Most writers, including yours truly, secretly want to be loved by the public. Gilmore tells them, "Go fuck yourself." I kind of like that.

Gilmore gives a whole new meaning to the word "embeddedness." Off and on, he spent four decades gum-shoeing the story of the Black Dahlia, facing off with the likes of Charles Manson and his Family, and was the one scribe to whom murderer Charles Schmid chose to confess his hideous crimes. Gilmore spent several years in the Deep South, and the "heart of Texas" researching the now-mythic outlaws, Clyde Barrow and Bonnie Parker. Don't expect to read a tale of folk heroes who robbed banks to get back at the establishment during the crushing economic times of the Great Depression. Gilmore's version of the co-dependent, fast-running duo is raw, gritty and authentically American. He gives the readers perhaps the truest and best account of their lives on the run. But that is no surprise. No one does Babylon, noir, and true crime better than John Gilmore.

Marshall Terrill is the author of a dozen successful books, most notably **Steve McQueen: Portrait of an American Rebel.**

Introduction

Probing the Perverse
by Kurt Hemmer, Ph.D.

On the Run with Bonnie & Clyde is an astonishing undertaking by an author already renowned for true crime classics like *Severed: The True Story of the Black Dahlia* (1994) and probing exposés like *Inside Marilyn Monroe* (2007). John Gilmore presents Bonnie and Clyde from inside their stolen cars, and the result is the antidote to Arthur Penn's misrepresentative and exploitive film *Bonnie and Clyde*, a movie which has done tremendous disservice to those personages on whom it was based.

Gilmore attempts to rectify our image of Bonnie and Clyde and their associates through his mastery of the true crime genre. As with all of Gilmore's works, there is an element of the autobiographical. Having become fascinated with the story of Bonnie and Clyde as a child in 1943, he makes his depiction of their story a personal experience. "It doesn't matter what you do," Jack Kerouac would tell Gilmore over beers in New York's Kettle of Fish, "as long as you do it with every inch of what you've got individually." *On the Run with Bonnie & Clyde* is a passionate portrayal that hints at Gilmore's skills as a memoirist, fascinatingly displayed in *The Real James Dean* (1975), and later, in *Live Fast-Die Young: Remembering the Short Life of James Dean* (1997). Then *Laid Bare: A Memoir of Wrecked Lives and the Hollywood Death Trip* (1997), which Gary Indiana called "[Gilmore's] most astonishing work," and which Genesis P'Orridge described lovingly as "compelling, Baudelaireian repugnance." Gilmore also brings to the table the craftsmanship of a novelist, honed by his work on *Fetish Blonde* (1999), praised by William S. Burroughs as "[a] psychosexual crash"; *Crazy Streak* (2005), a twenty-first-century *Lolita* of Southern Californian depravity; and *Hollywood Boulevard* (2007), which crawls into the subterranean murk of Tinseltown. His skills as a true crime researcher are marvelously on display in *The Tucson Murders* (1970), revised as *Cold-Blooded: The Saga of Charles Schmid, the Notorious "Pied Piper of Tucson"* (1996); *The Garbage People* (1971), revised as *Manson: The Unholy Trail of Charlie and the Family* (2000); the gut-wrenching collection of enthralling putrefaction called *L.A. Despair: A Landscape of Crimes & Bad Times* (2005); and the unforgettable *Severed*— "satisfying and disturbing," said David Lynch; "[t]he best book on the Black Dahlia—in fact the only reliable book," echoed Colin Wilson, while Marilyn Manson fantasized about morphing it into his unrealized directorial debut.

None of Gilmore's previous works could be characterized as "love stories." *On the Run* is an outlaw love story, but not a Hollywood romance. The 1967 movie's director and the star got it terribly wrong, portraying Clyde—bafflingly—as impotent, and presenting the couple as naïve, adorable scamps. Gilmore will show you that there is nothing adorable about Bonnie and Clyde. Their certain death would be imminent and violent—and they knew it. Clyde Barrow was not fucking around. Whether friend or foe, if you made Clyde's acquaintance for any significant amount of time, chances were something bad was going to happen to you eventually. Bonnie and Clyde were dangerous people to know, though for decades since the film the outlaw paramours have been icons of romantic love. Listen to Serge Gainsbourg and Brigitte Bardot's duet "Bonnie and Clyde" (1968)—"La seule solution / C'etait mourir"— ("The only solution / Was dying")—musically the most interesting of the Bonnie and Clyde songs. In Gainsbourg's video you can see Bardot do her best Faye Dunaway impersonation. She is quite stunning and demure, but she is not Bonnie Parker—not Gilmore's Bonnie Parker.

On the Run is dark love, not adolescent bedroom fantasy, though it has become irresistible to view the lawless lovers as the quintessential icons of tragic love. There are dozens of songs that reference Bonnie and Clyde. In songs performed by country stars Merle Haggard, David Allan Coe, and Travis Tritt, to hip-hop idols Tupac Shakur, Eminem, and Jay-Z, Bonnie and Clyde have become empty signifiers waiting to be filled with the romantic musings of songsmiths and their devotees. When Desmond Dekker sings, "I don't want to end up like Bonnie and Clyde" in 1967's "Israelites," used with great effect in Gus Van Sant's *Drugstore Cowboy* (1989), the understanding is that we may want to be like Bonnie and Clyde while they were alive; we just do not want to die like them. PJ Harvey expresses the romantic yearning to identify with the doomed outlaws when she sings on "Good Fortune," from *Stories from the City, Stories from the Sea* (2000), "Like some modern-day / Bonnie and Clyde / On the run again." This sentiment is echoed by Mike Ness of Social Distortion on "Reach for the Sky," from *Sex, Love and Rock 'n' Roll* (2004): "You can run, you can hide, just like Bonnie and Clyde / . . . And I thank the Lord for the love I have found / and hold you tight 'cause tomorrow may never come." The bond between the tattooed lovers, Bonnie and Clyde, is all the more appealing because it is tied to imminent, violent death.

Death in an automobile, John Gilmore will tell you, is a particularly American death: James Dean, Jackson Pollock, Jayne Mansfield. When you add guns, like JFK, Tupac Shakur, or the Notorious B.I.G., it is even more romantically American. In the perverse American psyche, sex, guns, and cars swirl around in one intoxicating cocktail.

The stimulating saga of Bonnie and Clyde, like most crime stories, is an incomplete puzzle, but even more so. For this reason Gilmore's talent as a researcher was put to the test. The historical facts have as many holes as the Cordoba gray Ford V-8 after the final ambush.

As a matter of fact, when examining the various published accounts of the Barrow Gang, one finds that even basic details are disputed. Accounts vary from the self-serving to the downright ridiculous. Though some writers will state otherwise, there is no evidence that Clyde was a child molester, homosexual, bisexual, impotent, or a drug addict. Authors making such claims probably have their own issues to work out.

With his skill as a researcher and novelist, Gilmore gives his reader the sensation of being in the car beside Bonnie and Clyde. His years of expertise in the writing of true crime offer the best creative nonfiction account we could hope for. As a lifelong denizen of the shadows of notoriety, Gilmore may have an advantage when trying to capture the essence of characters like Bonnie and Clyde.

Just read Gilmore's other books and you will see that he feels as alienated from society as the troubled souls he writes about, and after reading this book a first time the emotional impact will compel you to read it again. Gilmore's Bonnie and Clyde revel in their perverse boil of passion. It is not perverse because it is foreign to us but because we so rarely allow the purity of our feral propensities to surface. The word "perverse" comes from the Latin *pervertere*, "to turn." To be perverse is to turn away from society's mores—and maybe inward to our own desires. It is this perverse relationship with the world—simultaneously attracting us and repelling us from the people who exude it—that we see in Gilmore's Hollywood icons. The outlaws are not like the movie stars as much as the movie stars are like the outlaws. They are living dangerously emotionally. Gilmore probes the perverse personalities of celebrities and criminals—the famous and the infamous. We recognize them. We want to get closer to their incandescence even as we turn our heads from the burning light. They show us what we do not see in the mirror smoldering beneath the surface.

In the hands of another writer, Bonnie and Clyde's story may have been used as a moralizing tale warning us against the pitfalls of intemperate behavior. But John Gilmore is not a moralist, and *On the Run with Bonnie & Clyde* is bereft of words of wisdom. It is brutal.

Author's Note

On the Run with Bonnie & Clyde is by necessity part documentary, part memoir, part narrative and reportage, plus a personal account that arrives *ipso facto* as a portrait of the American outlaw. The long haul of tracking the serpentine trail of Clyde Barrow and Bonnie Parker, as a means to understand them, to walk in their shoes, so to speak, fixed my focus to those two individuals, proving to me the only true way to share their tale was to shed my own shoes and ride with them.

Consequently, this offering rarely strays from Clyde and Bonnie in reconstructing a saga that narrowly includes situations in which they were not present, or events that lay beyond the windshield of their lives. In offsetting the obsession with their deaths, I have attempted to illuminate their lives, how they birthed emotionally, bonding in their youth to the inevitable, violent outcome of their union. The only way to offer what I've learned is to reconstruct what was lived.

My sincere thanks to William Daniel Jones, in memoriam, for talks shared in Dallas in the early 1970's. A rare, close associate of Clyde and Bonnie, "W.D.", as he was called, held valuable memories of the two this book specifically focuses on.

Apart from Texas, I journeyed through Missouri, New Mexico and Arizona, spent time in Oklahoma and other states, and lived four years in Louisiana. It's now seventy-nine years since Bonnie and Clyde were ambushed and murdered on that lonely road in northern Louisiana, neither having left personal records or diaries. Apart from Bonnie's long poems, *Suicide Sal* and *End of the*

Line (published before her death, a remarkable prediction), plus the many personal "on the run" snapshots and the scraps of bullet-riddled clothing snipped from their bodies, there is almost nothing. Whatever dreams they possessed went up in gun smoke.

To many others whose names appear throughout this text, I remain indebted for their sharing with me often objected-to or overlooked points of view. I confess that years ago I lacked the confidence to set down an account from my obsessive note-taking, kicked off in 1949 by my interest in 1930's Depression crime. Yet fueled by that same boyhood passion, the idea festered until I knew I'd eventually do it—rob a bank or write a book. I chose the latter, as my father was a member of the Los Angeles Police Department.

If one finds this tale a jerky, nonlinear narrative, or a string of scattered episodes with no discernible arc as that is the truth of Clyde and Bonnie's story—a disjointed, interrupted subject about a shapeless, chaotic existence broken into non-matching, unrelated facts few agree upon—they may be right. I never bothered to argue because I've embraced this history as the closest to an accurate picture of who these individuals really were.

The sporadic hunt has been like opening a Chinese puzzle box or filling a jigsaw with missing pieces, always seeking something other than a quasi-documentary guess at what might've been. So much of the "history" one finds in books, archives, old newspapers or past offerings by so-called authorities or scarce survivors, even relatives and dubious one-time associates, has piled error upon error, camouflaging gaps with moralizing rhetoric or confusing issues with make-believe, self-serving conviction. Each new presentation tends to opinionate the previous—many even borrowing from the 1967 Hollywood melodrama manufactured solely for exploitation and thus burying any genuine grab at truth beneath an avalanche of slapstick misinformation.

Answers to real-life questions about Clyde and Bonnie are lost to the past. The deeper one digs, the more discrepancies are found. This has created an alternate reality which most have and will subscribe to.

Two other books have pieced together an approximation of what might've occurred, and I salute the efforts of James R. Knight and Jonathan Davis for their *21st Century Update*. I also thank Winston G. Ramsey for his *On the Trail of Bonnie & Clyde Then and Now*, both works offering detailed explorations of that time and what remains—graves and broken headstones, highway pavements widened over once dangerously narrow dirt roads which Clyde would maneuver at near top speed. One sees the rotting bridges, empty washes, and weathered shacks collapsing in desolate fields. The authors present detailed portraits of what might have been, and what's largely forgotten or gone.

In offering this personal narrative of Bonnie & Clyde's run across a now-disappeared American landscape, I have sought to bridge a gap of irresolute time and distance by bringing them to life through their language; without it they are but silhouettes. I've attempted to reflect the essence of these beings—bad, good, wildly in-between, without grace or blessing. My goal has been to grasp a hoped-for truth in portraying them as their desperate lives revealed, hopefully breaking the stereotypical shadows stemming from the excuseless errors in previously published or filmed accounts.

My thanks to my publisher, Stuart Swezey, for taking on this unconventional book and showing again the faith he has demonstrated for years in creating a remarkable history in alternative publishing, enabling such an author as myself to explore two fringe lives beyond the status quo.

John Gilmore

One

With a tight grip on the steering wheel, the pretty girl in red slowed the four-door Ford V-8 to a stop before the small Louisiana bank. Behind the rimless sunglasses her bright eyes turned to the man alongside as he leaned to kiss her. He buttoned his jacket to hide the butt of the pistol, tucked an empty canvas deposit bag against his left side, and got out of the car.

Keeping the clutch pressed to the floor, Bonnie Parker jerked the shifter into neutral, waiting, the engine idling as she watched Clyde Barrow walk casually into the bank.

Looking dapper as a door-to-door salesman, his tan suit pressed and white shirt starched, his silk tie knotted precisely and shoes shined to a glossy finish, Clyde walked directly to the teller window. Adjusting his brown felt hat, he glanced around the practically empty bank, then presented a ten-dollar bill to the young man behind the bars. Clyde said, "I need change, please."

Smiling and reaching for the bill, the teller said, "Good morning—" but fell silent as he looked at the muzzle of the half-hidden .38 pistol aimed at his stomach. He froze, his eyes locked on the gun.

"This is a stickup," Clyde said calmly. "Don't raise your hands or do any talkin'. Put the paper money in this bag and nobody's gonna get hurt."

Stunned and shaking, the teller stuffed currency from the cash drawer into the canvas bag. He pushed the bag across the counter to Clyde, who said, "Stand right there and keep your mouth shut till you don't see me no more. You open your trap, I gotta come back and shoot your ass full of holes." Concealing the gun against the bag, Clyde turned and casually walked out of the bank.

Her foot floored on the clutch, Bonnie shifted into low gear as Clyde came briskly across the sidewalk. He climbed into the car, tucking the revolver into the waist of his trousers as Bonnie let out the clutch, the car pulling quickly from the curb. Shifting fast into second, she steered sharply around a corner, then jammed down on the gas.

Clyde tipped back, the momentum pulling him into the seat as the Ford jumped ahead. "Take it easy," he said, reaching for the shotgun at the foot of the seat. He placed the weapon between the edge of the seat and the door, and sat back as Bonnie wheeled into an alley behind a grocery store. Another two blocks, then slower, angling north onto a narrow dirt road sloping into a creek of black, dirty water. The air was wet, thick with mosquitoes, and Clyde rolled up the window. Seconds later he opened the canvas bag.

"How'd you do?" Bonnie asked.

Digging into the bills, Clyde said, "Not too bad."

"I love you," she said.

He smiled. "I love you too, sugar."

The road forked west, running beneath an overpass where a southbound train rumbled overhead, blowing its whistle. Pressing the fingers of one hand against her left ear, Bonnie raced beneath the bridge. Clyde said, "Loud noises still hurtin' your head, aren't they?" She nodded. He reached across her skirt and tucked his hand between her legs.

"Now I don't hear any sounds," she said. "Just my heart beatin' with your hand parked where it's at."

Like a narrow path of dirt through a field of weeds, the road bordered a stretch of woods where Clyde had concealed a new Ford roadster he'd stolen that same morning. He'd already switched the roadster's Louisiana license to an Oklahoma plate.

Bonnie maneuvered between tree trunks, stopped, killed the engine and climbed out of the car. She opened the truck and Clyde removed two rifles. Together they gathered from the still-creaking car three handguns, a second shotgun, two cardboard cartons of ammunition, a stack of out-of-state license plates and a pile of Hollywood movie magazines. Except for the shotgun and one rifle, the rest of the load was placed into the trunk of the roadster, along with two suitcases Clyde pulled from the rear seat of the sedan.

"Wait!" Bonnie said, opened one of the suitcases and dug through a cache of clothes. She brought out her camera.

"Hold on till we get across the border," Clyde said, climbing behind the wheel. He adjusted the shotgun against the armrest and the edge of his seat for a fast reach. Leaning forward, he fumbled beneath the dash and the engine kicked over. Grinning at Bonnie getting into the car, he said, "Sweetest picture God ever made." She pulled the car door shut and set the opened bank bag between her blue, size-three shoes. Closing her eyes, she took a few deep breaths and braced herself as Clyde maneuvered the car out of the woods and onto the dirt road.

Bonnie opened her eyes and said, "Guess what I'm gonna do, honey."

Clyde said, "What're you gonna do, angel?"

With a bright smile, she said, "I'm goin' to buy a pair of pretty red shoes to match my dress and I'm goin' to get my hair curled like Joan Bennett's."

Clyde grinned, pushing for speed, a whipping funnel of dust blowing behind the car as he left the dirt road. The speedometer needle climbed fast into the danger zone as he raced onto the highway heading west for the Texas border.

Forty-eight years later, I was driving to St. Louis to marry my son's mother, though the boy, Carson (as in Kit), wouldn't arrive for another four years. It was 1981, and instead of heading towards the Mississippi River, my fiancée and I got a motel room in Joplin. We lounged around the city I hadn't seen in two and a half decades, since 1957, when I was an actor on my way to New York. That first time, I hung around Joplin for a spell and met a pretty girl named Edith. She worked at a drugstore where I was getting coffee, and because of an old "Wanted Dead or Alive" poster on the wall, we got to talking about Missouri history. Edith said her mother had a bunch of "real" newspaper clippings about the "Barrow Gang" and a gunfight at a Joplin apartment building.

"The people who own that building," Edith said, "are acquainted with my mother. They go to the same church and are vegetarians."

A day later, I was picking through a pile of old newspaper clippings and photos that hadn't been rubber-cemented into a five-and-dime scrapbook, but just cut out of the papers to clutter an old pie safe.

Later, with a bag of bananas and a wax paper ball of walnuts, Edith's mother drove us to a building by Thirty-Fourth Street and Oak Ridge Drive.

Two garages occupied the lower half of the structure, with an apartment overhead, the windows facing the street where twenty-four years earlier hell had erupted, bad as a quake that could've shook a devil out of the ground. She showed us what she said were scars in the stones from bullets that had struck the walls that spring day in 1933.

Clyde Barrow, twenty-four at the time, and Bonnie Parker, twenty-two, had holed up above the garages for almost two weeks, Bonnie nervous, complaining, "We're here too long with people looking for us everywhere…" She meant even in a town like Joplin, back then known in certain circles as giving a Good Housekeeping seal to characters on a breather from the law.

Clyde's older brother, Buck, and his wife, Blanche, shared the quarters with Bonnie and Clyde, along with a pimple-faced, determined sixteen-year-old named William Daniel Jones—called W.D. for short.

Edith's mother arranged for us to see the apartment Bonnie and Clyde had occupied for that brief time. The kitchen, living room, two bedrooms and even the floors and walls seemed permeated by a presence other than the current occupants. Edith whispered, "Ghosts."

"It's what you know that makes it so," said her mother. "You ever hear of silent echoes? You listen carefully and maybe you'll hear Bonnie washing dishes and humming a tune. She could sing, you know. She had a good voice.…" Edith's mother said she could imagine the smell of chicken roasting, red beans cooking and even butter melting on salted corn. If you tried hard enough, she said, getting your ear against the floor, you could maybe hear footsteps coming up the stairs. "Or in the bedroom," she said. "I've smelled the aroma of Bonnie's perfume… Someday," she said, "if you listen hard enough, you might hear the bedsprings creaking, 'cause they got to creaking when the two of them were in the same bed—no matter what these know-it-alls say. Maybe you can even sense Bonnie standing beside you, looking at you with those haunting, blue eyes."

At that same time, I was introduced to Miss Johnson, an elderly, gentle lady who walked with a crooked bamboo cane and claimed to have witnessed the 1933 shoot-out. "The air," she said, "was full of smoke from gunshots, and I only saw silhouettes runnin' and shootin'. I hid on the ground beside an automobile. Thought I'd never be able to get up with those bullets whistlin' in the air, or ricochetin' every which way, makin' sparks and terrible plunkin' noises when they struck the automobile. More police were on the way," she said, "but the gang escaped, leavin' two of the officers shot down. It was the worst thing I'd ever seen."

Miss Johnson told me she had spoken to Bonnie Parker. "It was only days before that awful event, I was at the grocery store, and Bonnie was hidden in a big hat and sunglasses. She had a chicken she was wantin' to roast, a load of corn, and red beans. I didn't know who she was at that time, only a wee tiny girl I hadn't met before, except for knowin' they'd rented. I introduced myself because I enjoyed meetin' new neighbors, and she said her name was Elizabeth. She didn't volunteer much to say, and she seemed eager to be on her way with the chicken and groceries. She was polite and pleasant, and fashionably dressed, wearin' a pair of red shoes I admired, though she said one was pinchin' and she was walkin' on a blister.

"I lived but a short ways and invited her for tea and macaroon cookies. Some time when it would be convenient for her, I said. She replied she'd be delighted. Such a pretty smile when she said she would enjoy that, but a little sad, too, a sadness about her that I'd recall but had no understandin' of. She said she didn't know anyone in Missouri, though they were due in St. Louis at some time. Somethin' about travelin' on business. She hinted at being homesick and missin' her mother who was not with them. I didn't know who she meant by 'them.' The girl didn't say where she was from, only that she'd be honored to visit as it would warm her heart. Those were her words—warm her heart."

Only briefly had Miss Johnson seen the others occupying the stone house with "Elizabeth." "There was a couple," Miss Johnson told me. "A man and another woman, and I did see Clyde Barrow drivin' one of the cars. A boy was with him, and as they drove past, the man who I'd find out was Clyde smiled at me and touched the brim of his hat. I didn't know his name, and had no way of knowin' he was a wanted criminal. I believed that Elizabeth, who I'd be told was Bonnie Parker, must have mentioned to him about us speakin' at the market, and must have pointed me out. Also I had no way of knowin' he was not her husband, or who any of them were."

Miss Johnson claimed she baked macaroons for the occasion, but Elizabeth never came for tea and cookies. "It was so soon," she says, "that the awful shootin' happened, and afterwards I prayed for the two policemen who had been shot that day, and I also said a prayer for the girl, wherever she might've gone—wherever she was... After knowin' what I was to learn, I knew there would be no end to my rememberin' her."

Fast forward to 1981, when I was about to marry the mother of my son to come. Back in Joplin, I learned that Edith, the girl I'd known, had married a soldier and moved to Wyoming. Then I learned she'd died from ovarian cancer not long after her mother had been shipped from a Missouri nursing home to the care of relatives in South Dakota. The Joplin house Edith had lived in with her mother was gone, replaced by a fast-food drive-thru.

The stone house the three of us had visited years before stood practically unchanged. Then, on a second visit to that building, I seemed to experience what Edith's mother had suggested: an odd but not uncomfortable sense of the long-gone Bonnie Parker. It was as though at any moment I might turn to see her standing behind me, those blue eyes focused upon the back of my head.

From that last encounter with the bullet-scarred stones, I left Joplin not only to get married in St. Louis, but eager to explore the lives of the by-then dubbed "star-crossed lovers," catapulted to icon status by the 1967 movie *Bonnie and Clyde*. Disregarding fact, the motion picture nonetheless gained success as "shoot-'em-up" entertainment, while many critics described it as being nothing more than "a soapy melodrama." *New York Times* critic Bosley Crowther labeled the movie "a cheap piece of bald-faced slapstick comedy."

Much of the so-called historical data on Bonnie and Clyde—abstract dribbles of half-truths and manufactured information jumbled together over decades—left me cold. I wanted to know Bonnie and Clyde. I wanted to reach into the past and touch what it was propelling the violent rush of their lives.

Four years later I was sitting in a greasy diner in Big Spring, Texas, eating macaroni with a handicapped old man. His name was Henry Edwards, an ex-bank robber who'd changed his surname to erase a past he couldn't escape. The town of Big Spring looked almost empty of inhabitants. Half the main drag struck me as literally a ghost town, and the same kind of emptiness seemed reflected in the sad face of the man with eyes as blue as Bonnie Parker's.

Henry told me he'd been convicted once, and had done time. "Convicted only once," he said, though he didn't have enough fingers to count every joint he'd hit. I understood and asked what it was like robbing a bank. "Boils your piss first time around," he said, "but you get the hang and a charge like a shot of moon." He shrugged, saying, "Nothin' to it."

My now-pregnant wife and I had been offered an empty, multi-storied department store for $750 a month. We'd stayed up half the night laughing over how to furnish a gutted department store.

"You could rob the bank," Henry said, showing a crooked smile. Later in the diner, with strips of yellow flypaper waving overhead, Henry said, "Clyde sat across from me same as you're sittin', and said his father's name was Henry—same as my name. He said he didn't know if it was good luck like a four-leaf clover, or bad like a black cat walkin' behind you, but either way, he said it worried him."

Clyde didn't talk like I was talking, Henry told me. "He wasn't a sociable guy, but he was smooth and had beady eyes like an Indian. Maybe wonderin' how your scalp'd look hangin' on his belt. He could've had some injun blood mixed in," Henry said. "Always packin' a load of guns and his squaw, and watchin' every door or window…

"But, hell," he said, "it isn't fair my callin' Bonnie a squaw. I mean she wasn't like that, other than Clyde bein' the apple of her eye. He was her religion, you could say, and there wasn't even a way somebody'd get a tin shim between the two of them.

"I gotta say I couldn't see any charm in Barrow. He was a smart-lookin' kid, but he was sure as hell hard-nosed to the business, even as he was so unduly worried about mistakes. He was nervous about makin' any, and didn't want to get in that position since he had murder warrants on him, and more warrants the further he went. Whatta they call it—a paper trail?

"Not that mistakes don't happen—they're always a hazard of the business. I can't in truth say Barrow got a kick outta pluggin' someone for its own sake, like idiots do today. Contrary to what's portrayed supposedly about Clyde, that sort of shit never happened with him, though he showed cold when we talked about a job in Louisiana, and then another one in Jasper—in Texas. He had more interest in the Louisiana job than in Jasper, which I was entertainin'.

"Clyde knew dealin's in the parish," Henry said. "I've always figured that's where they were headed, up in the upper Louisiana. I wasn't partial to gettin' back in Louisiana 'cause Texas was bad enough if they nailed you. Half the country was lookin' for Barrow—and Bonnie too, though havin' nothin' on her except bein' with Clyde. All that accessory hog-shit. They had to give the devil his dues 'cause they couldn't get Clyde. He was a rattlesnake in high grass and in high gear, and didn't give no howdy to see you comin'. So the law didn't know how to stop him, didn't know where he was or where he'd pop up next. Maybe right under their noses and they wouldn't even know it until he'd already been there and gone. That's where the ambush ideas came from—shotgun him when he wasn't lookin'."

The bad angle, Henry said, was Clyde being a little fast on the trigger. "Not that he set out that way," he said, "and told me as much. But if he'd get cornered, and again it's a part of the job that happens, as the law's there with the same idea—same occupation. You took your chances. A guy couldn't get work, so you stole a hunk of cheese. You stuck up some smart-ass fucker, and soon you saw the profits they're makin' and you say well, so what the hell, let's join the party if you got the stomach for it.

"I wasn't comfortable with puttin' down the law," Henry said. "In the end you get the same ride for pluggin' a John Doe, except for a cop they're on your ass like it's never goin' to get easy. Their whiskers'll reach past their balls as far as forgettin' about you, and any chance of walkin' away clean on a job is messed if the law's on your neck.

"Clyde was looking at me and sayin' he wasn't goin' down. He said he'd stand up to the end of it. Understandable he'd get a lot of mileage with the artillery he was haulin', like he wasn't as keen to hit a bank as startin' a war."

Henry ate soft-boiled eggs and drank buttermilk. He said an ulcer was gnawing through his stomach like "a badger in a box." He blamed the condition on a life of looking over his shoulder to see if a shotgun was aimed at his shoulder blades.

He said he knew Clyde's brother, Buck, after the older Barrow busted out of Huntsville prison. "He'd married Blanche and was hidin' out, hopin' nobody'd miss him. He was easy to figure, but Clyde— and Bonnie, too, she was like a little vaudeville actress—always actin' but she was a thinker, too. Both of them were hard to know and that made it tough.

"They stayed in a shed behind a garage owned by a guy Buck knew, and were headin' to Abilene for a job—wasn't goin' to be Jasper. When you look right at it, what Clyde said, more or less he had you like a dog chasin' its tail because he was cagey. Not lettin' you know where you stood.... You had to have trust, but he had Bonnie, you see, and the others who came and went didn't count. You could get a straight deal out of Buck, though he wasn't smart. Clyde was the smart boy, and wouldn't say anythin' you might piece together and get ideas he hadn't figured out. When we got together about a job," says Henry, "he must've had half a dozen killin' warrants on him. I had to say I never shot at nothin' but cans or beer bottles, and for that they don't stick you on the hot seat."

Henry told me, "Him and Bonnie were eatin' in a little joint when we talked about the parish and Jasper. Bonnie lookin' half-asleep, but eatin' chicken like a last meal. She had a big wad of mashed spuds and a mess of gravy she slopped around with a spoon. Clyde wasn't eatin' until she broke off a hunk of the chicken. He ate in a dainty way, pickin' while she shoveled it in like she hadn't eaten in days, and maybe she hadn't. Livin' out of cars they'd swipe. Imagine that? Maybe two cars or three a day, and if they weren't sleepin' in them, they'd shack out in sheds or on the ground in woods, or empty cabins where nobody saw who they were. After that Joplin shootout, though, newspapers all over the country had so many pictures of them you'd be hard-pressed not to see you were lookin' square in the face of Bonnie and Clyde....

"So she ate the potatoes and gravy while I fished information out of Clyde. I gotta say I wasn't as sharp as he was. He talked about what he wanted but he wasn't sayin' any facts, see, and in the middle of it he put his hand in Bonnie's lap right down at the bottom of her belly, and kept lookin' at me. I knew he was figurin' how he'd take that parish bank on his own, Bonnie with him, swipin' another car, she'd drive and he'd take it all like a king on his own man-made mountain—his queen right beside him and him showin' what he owned....

"You could see he was tickled by Bonnie and how he got a bang out of what she did. It was like they didn't hardly have to talk. More like a mind-readin' act, each knowin' what the other was thinkin' or goin' to say. When you got right down to it, you had to figure they were two of a kind, twins with a pair of aces, and a spooky language they'd be speakin' when they weren't even usin' words like you and I are doin'."

When Bonnie told Miss Johnson her name was Elizabeth, she was telling the truth. Elizabeth was her middle name—Bonnie Elizabeth Parker, born in a sun-bent, pot handle of a Texas town named Rowena, some two hundred dusty miles from Dallas. By the time of Bonnie's birth, October 1, 1910, the town of Rowena had boomed to over six hundred residents—mostly Czechs, Germans, and railroad refugees. Her father, Charles Parker, a bricklayer and an avid Baptist, spent every Sunday bringing his wife, Emma, to Rowena's First Baptist Church, along with the three children—a boy called Buster, and Bonnie, then little Billie Jean.

Bonnie would later tell a waitress friend that her sharpest memories of her father always spiked when she got a whiff of cement or wet mortar.

Charles Parker once said that working in an undertaking parlor promised a more prosperous profession than laying bricks. Bonnie was four years old when her father "kicked the bucket," as she said, also remarking, "My mother cried and said he'd lost faith when he thought he was dyin' and God wasn't going to save him to see his kids grow big enough to tie their shoes."

His death left widowed Emma broke. She needed work, but who would take care of the children? Could she earn enough to pay someone to watch after three kids?

With little or no employment offered in Rowena, Emma packed up, gathered the kids, and made the trip to her mother's in West Dallas.

Mary Krause lived in a runoff area called Cement City. Chalk, limestone, and shale half-formed the ground upon which puddled the town, supported by Portland Cement workers who lived in houses owned by the company. While the few stores and markets were owned by Portland Cement, a post office that had opened in 1907 shut down the year Emma brought Bonnie, her brother, and her sister to settle in with their grandmother.

Her father's death would linger as a mystery to Bonnie. At age eight, she'd attended a funeral in Dallas with her grandma and brother Buster. The deceased in the open casket was an elderly acquaintance of Mary Krause, remotely resembling Bonnie's father. His hair seemed white while his mustache looked almost black. Bonnie asked her grandma why the man's mustache was "the color of tar," yet his hair pale as gauze. Buster spoke up, saying, "Somebody glued a mustache on his face so he won't look so dead!"

Both children giggled. Their grandma said, "He was a nice man and this is a sad occasion. A funeral is no place to giggle like a pair of fools."

"It isn't sad for you when you're dead," Bonnie asked, "is it?"

"Not if you're in heaven," the woman replied. "There's no sadness in God's house, but for us on the earth it is sad, and you can't laugh at somebody's funeral."

Bonnie said, "What happens if you go to hell?"

Her grandma looked at her, shaking her head. "I imagine it's sad for everyone," she said, "especially yourself if you're visitin' with the Devil."

The words of her grandma about dying would simmer in the secret corner of Bonnie's "private thinkin'," as she called it. Early in her life, she'd started writing details of her private thinking in a small kind of notebook she called a diary. "She'd imagine herself in a coffin with silk and satin all around her," said Billie Jean years later. "Seein' she was lookin' beautiful as the evenin' sunset."

At twelve, Bonnie visited a Dallas undertaking parlor and ran her fingers along the shiny linings of expensive caskets. She then wrote a poem about a coffin floating like a cigar-shaped boat "on a body of bright blue water." Billie Jean says, "Bonnie read in the newspaper about a man in Niagara Falls who got inside a barrel and went over the falls, livin' to tell about it." Bonnie wondered if it was true, and if someone could go over the falls in a coffin. "That kind of thinkin' was disturbin'," said Billie Jean, "but that's how Bonnie amused herself."

Entitling her poem "Forever," Bonnie gave it to her teacher, who asked if anyone was inside the coffin. Billie Jean says, "Bonnie told her it was herself inside the coffin, that she'd written a self-portrait with the lid shut down. Some people said she had a peculiar streak of humor that didn't fit in with the way everyone usually thought, but Bonnie persisted in jokin' or teasin' people, half the time gettin' their back-hairs risin' up...."

Two

Jennifer Harris worked as a waitress in Dallas during the Great Depression, and says she'd met Bonnie in a café. "She was still in school. A sweet girl with a beautiful smile that lit right up." As a waitress, Bonnie was liked by people, and regular customers thought highly of her.

"One time we were talkin' about the food being served, and she told me how her grandmother had fixed meals special, even though there wasn't much to go around. She'd taught Bonnie how to fix a stew they'd fill full of bread instead of meat, and seasoned to taste like lamb. Bonnie told me how much she loved her grandma but wanted to be more with her mother who'd worked whatever jobs she could find, accordin' to Bonnie, so the kids were taken care of.

"Boys were always tryin' to get Bonnie's attention," says Harris. "She'd smile and you could see them melt in their tracks. Her smile was like that flash you get when you first strike a match. She was fast-thinkin' and smart, she'd write stories and give speeches, excellin' in school where others asked her opinion or even tried to get her to write papers for them.... Then sometimes like it was the other side of a coin, she'd be scrappin' with bully kids bigger than herself, and plain determined not to show fear. You wondered if she didn't care if she got socked or hurt because she wouldn't let go.... Then all of a sudden that switch in her nature and she'd be sweet as pie."

Unlike her brother or sister, Bonnie's personality seemed "scrambled underneath the surface," according to Harris. "A few times when we were workin'," says Harris, "she and I got to talkin' about boys we'd known, and Bonnie was sayin' they'd confuse you. She talked about one she'd chased—admittin' she ran after him, knowin' he was a troublemaker. 'Everyone knew it, includin' me,' she'd said. Bonnie couldn't help chasin' him in spite—or, rather, because—of people sayin' he was bad. She said he stole a motorcycle, got kicked out of school, and then got in trouble stealin' a car. Last she'd heard he'd been locked up in prison."

At sixteen, Bonnie got involved with "another sour apple," says Harris. "Roy Thornton was older than Bonnie. She got tattooed on her leg, showin' a heart with their names linkin' together like weeds. I suppose Roy was a charmin' show-off—in and out of trouble same as the boy she'd chased in school—the kind Bonnie seemed to fall for. They were no good. She married Roy, and he'd take off for a week or two weeks, then finally seemin' to desert her, gone practically a year...."

Bonnie wanted romance, and wanted excitement. She wanted someone to love her and pay attention to her. She'd do whatever she could to gain their attention but then they'd be gone. Harris says, "Bonnie was sick of Roy's ways and when he finally showed up after nearly a year, she chased him out, yellin', 'Get out of here!' She didn't want him in her life even for one night on the couch. She tossed out what he owned, threw it right in the road, and after that he got arrested for robbin' or burglary and sent to prison."

Bonnie's mother coaxed her to divorce Thornton. She'd say, "You can't bind the rest of your own life to someone careless as Roy." She had to set herself free.

"Only Bonnie couldn't do it," says Harris. "She said he'd been knocked down by fate, and even though she didn't love him anymore, and maybe it was only infatuation from the start, she couldn't kick him while he was down. Emma, her mom, tried to shed light, sayin' Roy had showed her no respect, and he'd knocked himself down by his own hand. Nothin' to do with fate. Bonnie had no call to share a part of Thornton's personal unhappy consequences."

Although the devotion Bonnie showed for her mother seemed unshakable, she extended little of what she felt in her heart. She couldn't cut herself free from Thornton by divorce because something more than a sense of fairness had tied her to the situation.

"Some sort of bond," says Harris, "that Bonnie had little control over. Some part of her deep nature had little to do with the world around her, as if Bonnie was chained to this bond—tied hopelessly without even knowin' it. Someone could be bad and wild as a dog, even with somebody havin' to get a gun and shoot the beast, but Bonnie could get all worked up about that person, even someone she'd see in a movie, like Billy the Kid or Jesse James, and they could have her shinin' with excitement, like a little tyke tellin' you she'd just got all she dreamed for, even though she was seein' the guy on the picture show screen and it had nothin' to do with real life."

Billie Jean remembered a time when Bonnie brought home a cat that had been hit on the street. "Too far gone to live," said Billie Jean, "but Bonnie placed the injured animal on a wad of rags in a box and surprised me—I guess shocked me—tellin' me and Buster she was keepin' the cat so she could watch it die."

Harris says, "A lot of folks couldn't imagine Bonnie doin' that—bein' so keen on the process of dyin'. That cat had to be so torn up there wasn't anythin' to do except maybe bury it, or put it out of its misery. Billie Jean said Bonnie fooled with that sort of talk, and I was reminded of Bonnie's notions about Jesse James and Billy the Kid from picture shows and the stories she'd read, and wantin' to write them herself."

Outlaws—train robbers and gunmen—held a fascination for Bonnie. "She once told me she'd dreamed about marryin' Billy the Kid," says Harris. "He gave her a spotted horse and she rode along-side him, even fancied packin' a sidearm and a rifle in this dream. I asked, 'What're you dreamin' about pistols and rifles for? You got ideas of shootin' up the town?' She laughed and got a look her sister said was a piece of her 'private thinkin', and she said she wasn't goin' to shoot up the town, though half those she'd meet, she said, deserved a bullet between the eyes. No way of knowin' back then that what would happen wasn't too far in the future. And though she didn't do any shootin' or robbin' herself, she got as attached to it sure as wings on an angel."

Bonnie was nineteen when laid off from her waitress job. The business folded as the bottom fell out of the country. She watched things turn bad—then worse, as the Depression washed across the nation like a plague. Thousands upon thousands of citizens fell into despair and loss unprecedented in American history. Industry ground to a standstill. Small businesses collapsed. Evictions and foreclosures rampaged, devastating families. People were going hungry. "Brother, can you spare a dime?" became the new national anthem. The American Dream became yesterday's newspaper, flushing away in a downhill gutter.

Meanwhile, not everyone considered suicide a viable option. Not everyone walked the streets on "Hoover leather" (cardboard wadded into shoes to cover the holes), or gulped a cup of "Hoover soup" (boiled water with a root or weed plucked from the road). The bankers and their Washington cohorts sat comfortably in amassed wealth while hordes roamed the streets below, refugees without homes, without jobs, turning into bums on boards or boxcars or sleeping in the mud of a hobo hollow.

Ralph Mendoza, an elderly Fort Worth resident managing a motel, recalled his younger years during the Depression as "nothing but pain and anguish. I was raised in Louisiana, spent half my life workin' my ass off in Texas, then windin' up in a Dallas breadline that doubled around a city block. I walked six miles for a doughnut and cup of coffee at a Salvation Army stand. My wife was sick, the kids were hungry, and I walked back with half the doughnut wrapped in wax paper, lookin' for butts on the street....

"Instead of things gettin' better as Washington was sayin', the breadlines tripled. We got kicked outta the two-room flat because we couldn't pay the rent. I had a college degree. My wife had run a bakery. The law came and put us out on the sidewalk. Killin' myself and my family crossed my mind more than once. Other guys told me they thought of killin' themselves, and some did. I saw a lady with a little baby throw herself in front of a garbage truck. She got tangled up in the wheels but the baby was bounced ahead into the street, squallin' and cryin'. Some other lady picked the baby up and went off with it. One pal I'd worked with jumped off a bridge into a train yard.

"I wasn't alone in thinkin' how bad it could get that you didn't want to live. Not that killin' myself or the family was somethin' I could do, but thinkin' it out made me feel at least I'd hold out another day. Maybe by the next mornin' somethin' would happen that'd change things. Only what happened was nothin' happened the next day, and the day after that just promised that things would get worse than they were the day before.

"I was a veteran who'd fought in the war to make it a better world. They took our furniture and what little we had. The church turned us away, sayin' they had too many others lookin' for help.

"Folks without homes or jobs or places to go gathered in vacant lots and parks on the edges of towns. Sometimes right in the middle of the city, and cops would come and bust you with clubs to get you out of the public parks." The unemployed squatted in makeshift shacks made of cardboard and hunks of wood, or scraps of metal, rags, and squashed cans to shim out the ice. Sorrowful pits of humanity called Hoovervilles—in dishonor of then-president Herbert Hoover, who Mendoza says, "kept tellin' us everythin' would be fine! All we had to do, Hoover kept sayin' to a country which couldn't find wages anywhere no matter the beggin', was we had to spend money to get the economy on its feet. Buy houses! he'd say. Invest! Invest? We couldn't scrounge a half buck to feed our family. People looked bewildered as hell when you heard Hoover talkin' like a crazy man. You asked, 'Is he livin' on the moon? Is he talkin' to Wall Street or a people goin' hungry?' Sayin' how everythin''s gonna be fine as long as we do the impossible!

"One thing was for sure," Mendoza said, "Hoover and his pals weren't waitin' in breadlines. They weren't out on the street beggin' a dime to feed a hungry kid. None of the rich boys lost fancy homes or were thrown out. The business boys and banks were busy showin' profits, but not a cent was sneakin' through their grubby hands to people sufferin' in the steerage of Hoover's sinkin' ship—the United States of America—the land of the free. Our kids were hungry and sick. A lot were dyin', and all the workin' people no longer had jobs and were drownin' in misery.

"John Dillinger? Sure, I knew all about John Dillinger. Everybody did. He hit the bastards where it hurt. Not in their kids' empty bellies, but in the bankers' swollen billfolds. An awful lot of regular folks who'd lost all they'd worked their lives for weren't faultin' John Dillinger for stickin' up banks. I'd have done it myself if I'd had the nerve of a Dillinger or Pretty Boy Floyd or Clyde Barrow, dishin' out hard times to the bastards starvin' my family. Shootin' cops? You talkin' about the guys whackin' your head with a club when you're yellin' you can't get a job or enough to eat or feed your family? They forced an honest, hard-workin' vet to scrounge in garbage cans for a hunk of potato so my sick wife and kids wouldn't starve. Nobody born since then really knows what livin' in hell was like.

"Cops were stooges for the Washington hotshots. They caved your head in or locked you in jail for stealin' a pickle or a loaf of bread. My youngest, a little two-year-old, was sick and we couldn't get help. The law came and threw us out on the street. Just plain shoved us out of where we'd been livin'! They threw our clothes and beddin', our books, on top of us. Wouldn't even let me back in to get the radio. Pulled out handcuffs and said I'd go to jail if I tried it.

"An old black family took us in, fed us, but my little one had pneumonia bad and we couldn't get help. They said she was too far gone. They didn't even get her to a hospital to die under medical supervision, so she died on a mattress in a little room off the kind black folks' kitchen... Her little cheeks were all kind of pinched in.

"I didn't care how many stooges ready to bust a guy's head for wantin' to keep his kids from dyin' got his ass shot full of holes by John Dillinger or Clyde Barrow or any of them others runnin' contrary to the so-called protectors of the law. I'm only sorry they didn't take their war to that fool Hoover's front door in Washington and put a bullet where it'd do the most good for the workin' man."

With the Oklahoma plates put on, the roadster slowed to a crawl and rolled off the highway south of Lufkin, Texas. Bonnie opened her eyes and gazed through the dusty windshield. "You think they have a hotel dinin' room where we can eat off real china?"

Clyde said, "We won't find any nice hotel just yet, angel." Off the highway, he drove slowly along a west-heading dirt route until he came to a gas station. He pulled in and shut off the motor. Bonnie took a deep breath and nodded as Clyde got out. "Fill it up with your ethyl," he told the attendant, "and wash off the windows so I can see through 'em." He then strolled to the small station office.

Because Bonnie was rubbing her legs, it took the attendant longer to clean the windshield than to pump the gas. She was smiling at him on top of it. He then turned away when she slid behind the wheel and started the engine. She slid back into the passenger's seat as soon as the attendant entered the station office where Clyde was studying an unfolded Texas state map. Wiping his hands, the attendant was about to say something when he glimpsed the revolver Clyde was holding beneath the map. "Open the drawer," Clyde said. "I'll take what you got in the drawer."

Eyes wide and mouth working to form a smile, the attendant unlocked the cash drawer, gathered the few bills and handed them to Clyde who said, "Don't do any hollerin'. I don't want to do any shootin'."

"No," the attendant said. "I got my mouth shut tight as a clam."

Clyde said, "I don't like pluggin' guys young as you."

Nodding quickly, the attendant said, "I understand that, sir!"

"You got a safe in that floor over there?" Clyde asked.

"No—other guy—the boss, he comes and gets the receipts.... You got 'em now, sir...." He managed a smile. "I'm doin' just as you say. You're the boss right now."

With the bills stuffed into his jacket pockets, Clyde returned to the driver's seat in the car. He adjusted the shotgun at his left side as Bonnie waved goodbye. The attendant waved back, holding the same smile he'd fixed for Clyde.

Less than a mile north, Clyde went off the highway onto a rural road lined with wood frame houses. He stopped the roadster across the lane from a Ford sedan parked by a small Baptist church. While Bonnie again slid behind the wheel, Clyde crossed the street and quickly got the sedan started. He drove away from the church, heading south, Bonnie following close behind.

Near a small industrial area, Clyde left the highway and pulled behind an abandoned one-story warehouse. He stopped the car, Bonnie edging in close alongside. She climbed out and quickly the two unloaded the roadster, packed the sedan, and deserted the smaller car.

Inside the sedan, Bonnie said, "It's got a radio, honey! We can listen to the radio!"

Clyde said, "I get only the best for you, baby."

Several miles northwest, Clyde left the highway and drove behind a roadside café, leaving the engine running. He handed Bonnie a few bills, and she hurried into the building. Clyde leaned back, shutting his eyes.

Minutes later, Bonnie returned with sandwiches, cupcakes, a half-dozen hardboiled eggs, and four bottles of flavored soda. She said, "I got the bottles with screw-on caps so we can fill 'em with water."

A half hour later, nestled in a dark, pine-wooded patch, Clyde changed the license plates from Texas to Louisiana. They spread a blanket and each ate a sandwich, a hardboiled egg, and drank flavored soda. Clyde said, "What is this I'm swallowin'?"

"That's grape," she said. "This one's cherry. You want the cherry?"

"This is alright," he said. "Tastes more like raspberry than a grape soda."

"Well, it's grape," she said. "It says so on the cap."

"Gimme a kiss," Clyde said.

"I'm eating my egg," she said.

"Then gimme somethin' else."

Bonnie stood up, stepped out of her shoes, pulled up her skirt and stepped over Clyde, straddling him, looking down at him as he chewed his egg and stared up the length of her legs. Taking hold of her calves, he eased her forward until she came down onto his chest, her knees at his sides. He said, "Tell me what you told me before about suckin' on the cupcake paper."

Smiling, she said, "I told you the flavor of the cupcake gets all sunk into the wax paper, and I gotta suck on it and scrape on it with my teeth so the flavor gets sucked away from the wax paper...."

Three

An old truck belonging to Conrad Richards, formerly of Hot Springs, Arkansas, suffered a breakdown on the highway south of Dallas. Richards left the truck on the side of the road and walked several miles before he reached a store. "I went to see if I could get help," he says, "but I didn't have any money and these folks in the store told me to get out. So I turned around and was gettin' out, and a young fellow in a hat and suit of matchin' clothes was comin' in the doorway. We were blockin' one another from him comin' in and from me goin' out. He looked like one of those federal investigatin' fellas, but that wasn't who he was. I can tell you that. It took me only two seconds to know that face, and I saw the gun stuck in his belt, so I reckoned he was about to do some robbin'. In a hushed-up voice, I said to him, 'Please don't shoot me, Clyde Barrow. I don't work here—I don't work nowhere, and you wanna shoot someone in here I got no objectin' to it.' He says to me, 'Who are you?' So I told him I'm a farmer who's got no farm no more 'cause the bank took it. They stole it from under me. My wife fell dead with a stroke and I can't get her grave moved off the farm that isn't my land no more. Said they'd shoot me if I trespassed, so I've been livin' in my truck that's busted down the road a piece. I can't get no help, can't even get me a Royal Crown Cola from these folks in this store to quench my thirst from walkin' for miles. 'Rest of my family's gone west,' I told him. 'My son and his wife and their kids have gone and I've got nothin' left, but I guess to keep on livin'....'

Richards says, "He was starin' right at me while I was doin' all the talkin' and tryin' to squeeze myself outta his way, and what he did was give me the ten dollar bill he had in his other hand. He told me get on my way as he had some business to attend to. I thanked him and gave a look back at those holier-than-thou folks behind the counter as Clyde Barrow was diggin' in his coat pocket and pullin' out another ten dollar bill he crumpled up in his fist, and came past me. I said to him, 'You can attend to some of the business for me, too, Mr. Barrow....'

"Soon as I walked outside I saw that big pretty-as-a-picture Ford sittin' there with the motor goin' and the exhaust kickin' up, and behind the steerin' wheel I saw another pretty picture—just about the prettiest face I'd seen since the last picture calendar I'd looked at—and who was I seein' in that Ford? It was Bonnie Parker herself, and she gave me a smile like a ray of sun through a cloud. I said, 'How do you do, ma'am,' and as fast, I said, 'I'm gettin' right outta of your way quick as these old legs're gonna carry me.'"

Like Conrad Richards of Arkansas, the Morgan Taylor family went bust on a Texas road, and soon found themselves beneath the Houston viaduct near the West Dallas railroad tracks. The area was called "the campgrounds," a makeshift village of wanderers, hobos, a melting pot of drifters, boomers and unemployed strays with nowhere further to go. Some, more industrious than others, cobbled together shelters to shield themselves from the hard sun and harder rain.

Everson Taylor, fifteen at the time, says, "We were lost and had nothin' to do except curl up and die. None of my family was about to do that. My folks had lost the home, and with my uncle and my sister, we went to El Paso to try and get work. We'd planned stayin' with my dad's other brother, but he was losin' his property and already had two people livin' in the house that wasn't any bigger than a garage. We tried lookin' for work back east across Texas, but couldn't find anybody hirin'. We settled down on this campground, my mom and sister sleepin' in the car while the rest of us slept on the ground.

"You'd have to steal a mattress and wooden boxes from the junkyard where there must've been a hundred people wanderin' through the rubbish. I got a spade, a fan blade, and found a mattress that looked like somebody died on it. That night, three of us slept on half the mattress, layin' crosswise, with our butts on the cardboard that we'd spread on the ground."

Taylor says he got to know some kids around the park and the river. "There wasn't anythin' to do except see what you could steal or put to use. That's when I was talkin' to old man Barrow and his older son, older than me, who they called Buck. We swiped a load of pipes, Buck and me, sold some and stuck others in the ground to put up walls so we'd have some shelter. We almost got caught pinchin' some boards, but Barrow wasn't worried so much and said to me, 'Well, what the hell, they feed you in jail, don't they?'"

To Taylor, old man Henry Barrow looked "run down, like he'd fallen out of a truck and got run over himself. He was skinny and draggled like he didn't sleep none too good. But he was tough, and he was a man who wasn't layin' down and dyin'. He was holdin' up best he could under the crap we were all in, stranded in the middle of a dung heap. Or maybe forgotten's the best word."

Henry Barrow had never learned to read or write. He'd spent a life following harvests through the South, his own father having died when Henry was eleven.

While picking cotton, Henry met and then married Cumie Walker, a slim, square-jawed, wiry woman from Nacogdoches, Texas. The union bore Barrow seven children between 1894 and 1918; the firstborn was named Elvin Wilson Barrow, then came Artie Adell, followed by Marvin Ivan, nicknamed Buck. Next was Nellie May, followed by Clyde Chestnut, then L.C. and little Lillian Marie. Clyde, the fifth child, was born in 1909 in Telico, Texas, thirty miles southeast of Dallas. He was often left in the care of his sister, Nell, five years older than Clyde.

The children worked alongside their mother and father in the fields, the youngest attending various schools for short spurts, often splitting up to work the harvest migrations or parceled off to relatives throughout Texas.

Sometimes the kids would be able to go to the movies, though popcorn and candy were luxuries. Years later, Marie Barrow would say, "Gettin' candy was like findin' chunks of gold." With a laugh, she said, "Lookin' back on my life, I know that I eat so much candy now that it'll probably kill me, but seems like it hardly matters long as I'm fillin' up with what I missed the most."

They gave a nod to their mother's insistence that they stay in school, as well as attending a church. Cumie believed in laying a solid religious foundation in their lives. She prayed daily and taught the children to pray, but the kids pretended for their mother's sake to show an interest in "gettin' educated" or an introduction to a "good Lord in the clouds."

"Times were just too goddamned tough," says Stanley Crowell, a one-legged, onetime indigent Depression refugee who remembers Marvin Ivan. "Buck came and went and never on any particular occasion." Buck told Crowell he'd faked an interest in whatever teaching he'd been offered, more concerned in getting what he could for as little as it would take. He'd eventually learn that with a gun in his hand, it would take very little. Most of the Barrow offspring split from the family to find work in the city—away from living as their parents did. "They never had anythin' better," Marie once said. "Being a sharecropper gave no future except to wind you up with less on your plate than the little you had to begin with—killin' yourself to make someone richer than they were already."

Henry, his wife, and the two children remaining with them, L.C. and Marie, lived in a tent on the campgrounds, attached to the old wagon they had brought, creating shelter close to the Texas and Pacific railroad tracks. The area spread out as a long plain bordered on one end by the Trinity River, across which offered a Dallas skyline of tall, gray buildings.

West of the river, "the Devil's Back Porch" spread over dirt streets, shanty shacks, and shotgun hovels. The so-called residents of the unincorporated squalor were mostly an unemployed mixture of drifters, boomers, good-for-nothings and "nickel" whores. Clyde avoided them—he said he had no use for "bums and hobos," nor was he going to associate with any "doughnut-sniffin' sob sisters."

While Clyde complained, groaned, slept, or admired himself in downtown Dallas store windows and coffee joint mirrors, his father continued with his daily scrap runs, the wagon wheels creaking and his old horse slowing down. One afternoon while Henry was gathering a pile of dumped iron stakes, a car collided with his wagon, running a length of metal torn from the vehicle into the horse.

Nell, often considered the most practical if not the brightest of the Barrows, coaxed her father to hire a lawyer and sue the driver. Reluctant at first, intimidated by the law, Henry was encouraged by the rest of the family to forge ahead, and with Nell's help, he eventually won a settlement. The victory allowed him enough money to move the three-room shack from the campgrounds to a lot obtained by Nell, located on Eagle Ford Road. She had deeded the lot to her mother and father, saying, "They worked hard all their lives, and had so little to show for it, except the love and gratitude we gave them. A lot of heartache came in to boot, but you have to take them as lessons in gettin' tough."

Clyde's younger brother, L.C., later recalled Clyde rarely staying on Eagle Ford Road. "He was always hangin' around at a couple fellas' places and figurin' ways of gettin' money."

Sylvia Nolan, seventeen years old when she met Clyde, says, "He was workin' at the cracker company, and then he was missin' work all the time because he'd run off with his brother, Buck. They were stealin' stuff they'd take to the house where his folks were. Not that their folks knew what they were doin'. His mom and his dad were very carin', generous people."

For a short time Clyde was employed by Procter and Gamble, but was laid off for reasons that remained vague. "I didn't like what he was doin' and he didn't last long on that job either," says Sylvia. "I heard that later on the company was sayin' they didn't have any employment records for Clyde Barrow." He tried another job, working as a glazier for the United Glass Company, and though telling Sylvia he was going to quit, "Sayin'," she says, "he didn't like the work any more than at Procter and Gamble, he stayed longer at United Glass than any other place he'd probably ever worked."

She says, "He'd fuss over his clothes, so concerned with how he looked, but lackin' the money to look as dapper as he probably thought he should. Clyde was a very vain person, though he could present himself in a soft-spoken, friendly way, and he always acted like a gentleman. His brother Buck wasn't like that. Clyde had a way of thinkin' highly of himself, and wanted to break off from his past— how poor his family had been, how they'd struggled to keep goin.'"

Sylvia believed Clyde wanted to be more than what he thought was reflected by his upbringing. "He was afraid he couldn't change the way fate had put on him. He had talents and he was smart, but it seems he was caught in a trap and wanted to free himself, and this battle overrode any opportunities he might've faced to improve his life, along with improvin' the way his folks had been livin' most of their lives." Remaining convinced that such a force was "like a fire inside of him that he couldn't put out," she says, "he needed to be someone other than what the powers that be had made him.

"He stole clothing from shops. He'd go into a shop, have a chat with a salesman, then steal a pair of fancy socks or a necktie or some expensive, fancy wallet or a belt, or even a hat—just puttin' the hat on his head and walkin' right out of the store as though he'd been wearin' it walkin' in. He'd put cufflinks in his cuffs, stealin' them because he'd go in the store without the cufflinks, and later he'd brag, makin' a joke of it, givin' his brother Buck a laugh over all of it. Clyde would look so dapper and he'd parade down the road like a peacock struttin' his feathers."

Clyde and Sylvia once talked about getting married, but for Sylvia the uncomfortable situation persisted, convinced as she was that his stealing wasn't a rash of boyish pranks but a serious fault that would land him in jail. "Then," she says, "he'd never be able to escape the past, and he'd be swallowed as sure as that big fish gulpin' down Jonah."

In Clyde's personal view, the "recklessness" and problems his woebegone girlfriend foresaw amounted to nothing more than a supplementing of his income, a gradual opening of chances that led him to the conclusion that it was far easier to steal money than the goods one used the money to buy. Cash could carry him farther than the length of a necktie, and any allegiance to "what was right," as voiced by Sylvia, quickly soured the touch-and-go dating; and along with that, her rosy picture of marriage and "a little cottage in Dallas" with kids squabbling underfoot fell apart like a picture made of smoke.

Besides, Clyde had already become enamored with another girl. Eleanor Bee Williams, a high school student, was about the same height as Clyde—at least, according to Clyde, she wasn't any taller than he was. He'd told his younger brother, L.C., "I don't want any long, drawn-up girl lookin' down at me."

Eleanor found his mild, "whisperin'-like" voice and intense, dashing eyes irresistible, proving, as Clyde believed, the permanence of her attractiveness for him. He'd meet her after school, buy her a soda pop or dessert "like a hunk of huckleberry pie with a mess of chocolate syrup dribbled all over the top of it." Or they'd sit in the park where she kept asking about his job.

"Still workin' nights," Clyde would tell her. "Still sluggin' away. I don't sleep anyway 'cause I'm too jumpy and got a lot to do—a lot of what one's gotta do." Then he'd stare off at the trees and wouldn't say anything further.

But to show how much he cared about her, Clyde had Eleanor's initials tattooed on his forearm. She was thrilled that he'd done that, then more pleased when he gave her several gifts, including a fancy boudoir mirror and a ring he'd stolen the same day from a jewelry store.

Eleanor said, "My desire is to get married someday."

"Is that so?" Clyde said.

Nodding, she said, "Certainly. I want to have a family of my own."

"Hungry mouths to feed," Clyde said.

"That's why I want a husband who can afford a family," she said, raising her hand so the sun sparkled on the ring. "We could afford a family, couldn't we, Clyde?"

Later, his sister Nell asked him, "Do you love this girl?"

"Oh, sure," he said. "Why not?"

"I mean, do you want to marry her?" Nell asked.

"That's what she's thinkin'," he said. "You got married and you're livin' alright, aren't you? I haven't made up my mind."

He wanted to see more of Eleanor. He told her to quit school so they could spend more time together. He said, "I don't think what you're learnin' is doin' you any good."

She said she'd like to spend more time with him, but the only way to consider such a situation was if she was getting married and ready to have a baby.

That shut him up. She wasn't sure how it happened—the falling apart of their relationship. "A lot of little things," she said later, "like wakin' up one morning to find you're in a different room." She believed some other part of Clyde was incongruous with his charm, as though he pretended the well-meaning intentions, but didn't really believe in them. She felt pressured by his insisting on things with an almost "fierce kind of independence" she said she couldn't understand. He didn't seem to appreciate "the notion of settlin' down." Talk of getting married proved a hodgepodge of "contrary notions" and intentional slights that spurred disagreements.

Artie Barrow, Clyde's other sister, was told by Eleanor that it was impossible to get Clyde to see another's point of view. According to Artie, Eleanor said, "He doesn't listen no matter what you say—half the time it's the same as talkin' to a deaf man." She cared about him, yes, but he was proving too difficult to understand. "My mother told me when Clyde and I first dated that he was a dreamer who lived by rules he'd make up as he went along. She thought he was the kind of fella that didn't pay attention to the rules everyone else lived by." Needing time to think, Eleanor told Clyde she'd be visiting her aunt in Broaddus, a distance from Dallas, and they'd talk about things when she returned.

Clyde didn't want her to go. He said whatever her aunt'd think about him while he wasn't there to defend himself could never be in his best interest. She closed the discussion by saying, "It's not your best interest I'll be particularly thinkin' about."

What he wanted to know, he said, was if she knew some other guy in Broaddus? An angry Eleanor asked him to leave.

Clyde's mother cooked him a bowl of oatmeal while he scribbled a note to Eleanor, a soft-pedaled apology for upsetting her. He stressed that since he still considered them to be engaged, they should "go away for a time," get away from everyone else. Then things would be alright, he said.

He decided not to mail the note to her. He reasoned that the smartest thing would be for him to hand-deliver the note, visit her aunt's in Broaddus where a demonstration of his feelings would convince Eleanor to take a trip with him. He'd tell her, "Let's get on the road," just the two of them, as though striking out on a brand new trail of life. He realized his plan could be foolproof. He'd rent a car and go in style. To bolster his presentation, he'd invite Eleanor's mother to accompany him as far as Broaddus. He'd tell her mother, "You'll be able to see your sister and all enjoy yourselves."

His expressed devotion to his own family impressed Eleanor's mother. She believed the sincerity of his "inspired" plan to visit Broaddus, while to Clyde taking Eleanor's mother seemed the reasonable thing to fortify his position with Eleanor. He believed she'd be equally impressed with the importance he placed on his own family closeness, and upon that understanding she'd be convinced of his devotion to her. He'd take her walking in the country, hold her in his arms and show her how much he desired her. He even pictured taking Eleanor to Oklahoma City—or St. Louis, Missouri.

Though the one-day contract on the car Clyde rented from a Dallas auto dealer restricted the vehicle to the local area, he neglected to say he'd be driving out of town and possibly for longer than a day.

Eleanor's mother would later say that while driving to Broaddus, Clyde not only drove too fast, but did all the talking. "Important notions about himself," she said, "that were very uncomfortable to behold.... There was also a sticker on the car that said it was from an automobile rental agency, though Clyde said he'd borrowed the car from a friend. I said he certainly had generous friends, and when I asked how soon he had to return the car to his friend, he waved his hand a little and said oh, he didn't know—the friend was in California and was gonna write him—maybe weeks, he said...."

While Eleanor was alarmed at Clyde's arrival in Broaddus, her aunt was pleased with her own sister's visit. Away from her mother and aunt, Eleanor read the letter Clyde presented to her, then handed it back to him. She'd needed time to "sort out feelin's," she said, and his showing up unexpectedly—with her mother—not only confused but made her angry.

Clyde repeated almost everything she'd just read in his letter, adding that he wanted to marry Eleanor in St. Louis, "or maybe Oklahoma City," he said, if she didn't want to go to St. Louis. He said, "We'll take your mother back to Dallas, then we can head north and get married."

For moments she stared at him in disbelief. "I don't have any urge to run away somewhere and leave my mother," she said, "any more than you wanna be away from your folks." Then she said she wasn't even sure if she wanted to get married after all, and if she did it certainly wouldn't be to Clyde.

"Well, then," Clyde said, "we don't have to get married, but we can drive to St. Louis." Eleanor said she didn't want to hear any more "crazy talk." He stopped insisting, smiled, and said he wanted to make love to her. She said no. He said yes.

Back at her aunt's house, Eleanor told her mother what Clyde had proposed, and the woman said, "You are not goin' anywhere with him. He has no rights tryin' to talk you into such a scheme!"

The following day when the auto failed to be returned to the Dallas company, the dealer contacted Clyde's mother. Without knowing the restrictions on Clyde's rental agreement, Cumie said her son had gone to Broaddus to visit a relative of his girlfriend. Suspecting unlawful intentions, the dealer notified the sheriff in Broaddus to check on the girlfriend's relative and to locate the car.

Late that same afternoon, the Broaddus sheriff and a deputy paid a visit to Eleanor's aunt. "We're lookin' for Clyde Barrow," the sheriff said, and explained the circumstances.

When Eleanor told the lawman that Clyde had gone off on business, her mother cut in. "He is not on any business! He was here a while ago." She advised the sheriff she had traveled to Broaddus in the car the law was looking for, and Barrow told her he'd borrowed it from a friend.

Meanwhile, the deputy located the car, got it started and drove off for the sheriff's garage. The Dallas rental company would arrange to have the car returned.

As soon as he'd spotted the sheriff, Clyde disappeared, only to surface again when the law had departed. Eleanor's mother, angry that he had made her "an accomplice," accused him of being a liar and causing the law to "barge" into her sister's home. She said she didn't want Clyde to bother Eleanor further and insisted he leave— immediately. Eleanor's aunt said everyone should calm down, and that the Christian thing to do was send Clyde packing the next morning, avoiding the roads in the dark.

That night, Clyde sat in a shed behind the house, bothered that Eleanor had blabbed to her mother about his plans. When the woman and her sister were asleep, Clyde made his way back into the house to tell Eleanor how much he cared for her and that he didn't think he could live without her.

She told him to get out of the room—she'd call her mother! But he looked so sad, so "crumpled down," she told him he could stay with her for a while. He remained in her room the rest of the night. Early the next morning while he was asleep in Eleanor's bed, the sheriff was again at the front door. He was there to arrest Clyde.

"You'll have to hide," Eleanor told him. Before climbing through a crawl space leading into the attic, Clyde told her to tell the sheriff that he'd taken off during the night.

The sheriff said he still had to search the house, but failing to find Clyde, he left, saying the law would no doubt grab Barrow back in Dallas. As soon as the sheriff left, Clyde snuck out the back door.

It took him a day and half to reach West Dallas. He explained to Cumie the rental misunderstanding, that he thought he'd have to pay for extra time when he returned the car. His mother said she understood. She heated bean soup for him, and buttered a slice of cornbread. He was sick to his stomach, he said, and hadn't slept in three days. Cumie told him to lay on the couch, take a nap. She placed a damp wash cloth on his forehead and within minutes he was asleep, a smile on his face.

He was still dreaming when two Dallas policemen showed up to arrest him. They dragged him outside, stood him against the wall, frisked him, then placed him in handcuffs. "What are you doin' with him?" Cumie cried.

Clyde was hauled to jail, fingerprinted, photographed, and charged with auto theft.

"They're nuts," he said. "I never stole that car. I rented it plain and legal and I thought I was gonna be charged extra for getting back late."

Believing Clyde had intended "no criminal action—just foolishness and irresponsibility," the agency declined to press charges. The dealer said, "It will cost us a hundred times more than the water to hose off the vehicle."

"You're makin' a mistake," the police warned, reluctantly releasing their prisoner.

Back on Eagle Ford, Clyde changed his clothes, donned a tie and vest, looped a silver watch chain without a watch, brushed his shoes and teeth and headed for downtown Dallas to steal a watch.

Days later his folks convinced him to return to his job at United Glass, which proved a "nightmare," he told his sister. He wrenched through the days, frequently pulled away from work by lawmen showing up to question him about various car thefts or driving him to the police station, badgering him to confess to thefts. He was beaten several times—the cops claiming he'd fought with them during an interrogation, even that he'd attempted to flee through an open window.

Clyde told his sister, "They don't even have a window in that room, they drag me in and lock the door." He tried to see Eleanor but was turned away. Bruised and limping after another interview with the cops, Clyde hobbled back to work to find he was being replaced. "We can't have police harassin' employees," he was told, and "where there's smoke there's bound to be fire."

Not long after joining the unemployed, Clyde was arrested again and questioned about a Dallas burglary.

Nell said later, "He was hurt and injured from being pushed around, and didn't go to Mom's. He stayed in our house and kept peekin' out windows, scared the police were comin' to beat him up him again. They'd knocked his teeth loose, cracked a rib, and cops weighin' twice his size punchin' him black and blue. It's not any wonder he'd sit there sayin' he wanted to kill the cops that kept knockin' him to hell and back."

Sidney Moore, a pal of Buck's, told Clyde, "You're not alone with those sentiments, brother, but they got a fancy chair at 'the walls' all hooked up with a high-voltage wire that'll fry you straight outta this world, 'course that's after they've busted your bones."

Clyde said, "Maybe it's a better place you get fried to visitin' that hot scat."

"Not a whole lot's gonna argue with you that."

Clyde left his sister's, but didn't go back to his folks. He moved in with Sid, also a pal of another young man Clyde knew, named Ray Hamilton.

Billy Simms lived near Eagle Ford, "Right in the Devil's back porch," he says. "I knew Ray Hamilton and his brother, and they were pretty bad eggs. Ray was considered a tough character and they had some wild ways that were headed to gettin' wilder. Girls and a lot of boozin' in Dallas. Even though Clyde had been hooked up in bustin' into some places and maybe a little small-time hijackin', this was the time things were changin' for him—in my opinion, y'understand. He was smarter than the Hamilton boys and the others hangin' around. A few of them went to Mexico, havin' big times there drinkin', though Clyde wasn't any real boozer, wasn't that taken to alcohol, but he was carryin' a gun, had an automatic pistol tucked down back of his belt, and Hamilton was totin' one as well, a revolver he'd show you, but I never saw Clyde do that, showin' off like Ray did.

"They busted into a service garage and stole a bunch of tires and other auto parts, both of them armed when they did it, and I thought, 'What're they doin' with the guns? Gonna shoot someone who might've caught them swipin' tires?'

"Clyde said they sold tires and stuff in Mexico, and said they had a mess of girls down there. He was sendin' postcards back to his folks and sisters, showin' him in a sombrero, alongside a half-assed horse, with a Mexican gal on each arm. You could see the butt of that gun showin' above his belt, and he'd signed the postcards 'Kisses from your Poncho Barrow.'

"I figured somehow in some way that was a turnin' point and nothin' for Clyde was ever goin' to be the same again."

Four

Back from San Antonio in early '29, Buck began dating a West Dallas girl but broke it off when he met Blanche Caldwell, a cute eighteen-year-old. At the same time, Buck was "boostin' walls," as he put it. "You boost the wall," he'd say, "by goin' under it." He'd laugh like he had you thinking he was some kind of gopher, but what he meant was burglary—but not only burglary.

Clyde said his brother had a sense of humor "fit for a pig's appreciation." He said Buck ought to keep his mouth shut about walls and "boostin'" before somebody a lot smarter started adding two and two with the law. Clyde's secret concern was that if under a lot of pressure, Buck would spill the beans about what they'd been doing—"boostin' walls"—for more than three years, Clyde going side by side with Buck.

The two had hot-wired cars in Dallas, getting the trick down to a few-second task. They'd cracked a couple safes, stuck up a few grocery stores and service stations, Ray Hamilton joining on more than one "trip." They roamed the roads from Dallas to Abilene, from Austin and halfway to Houston.

One night, without Hamilton, Buck and Clyde picked up Sidney Moore, stole a Buick, and headed northwest. Buck was bragging he knew a spot in Wichita Falls for easy pickings, but when they got to Henrietta, Clyde said, "I can feel the law breathin' on my neck in this Buick. I don't like Buicks—cops're always lookin' at a Buick."

Sidney said nobody was looking, but Buck said he had to trust his kid brother's "sense of smartness," since he had a knack for "smellin' things out like a trackin' hound." They quickly swapped the Buick for a Ford, then prowled the night streets looking for action.

In a short time they found a house that seemed unoccupied. Breaking in was easy, but the score turned sour. Only a few dollars turned up. Clyde uncovered a box of jewelry and back in the car they split the booty three ways, each stuffing his pockets with trinkets.

Sidney was nervous. "Let's take off," he kept saying. He wanted to get back to Dallas. Clyde drove, keeping a fast pace, but slowed as they cruised the town of Denton. Buck suggested they look around, but Sidney complained, "In this dead goddamn place?"

Buck said, "That means somebody's got a stash stuck up their ass."

"I don't like it either," Clyde said. "We're the only live ones on the street."

Pointing to an auto garage, Buck said, "There it is, boys. That's what we're lookin' for, and I tell you somethin' sweet's gonna happen."

Clyde turned onto Oak Street, eyeing the Motor Mark Garage, a lightless scene as quiet as a mausoleum. He slowly entered an alley and drove to the back of the building. Minutes later, with Sidney shining a weak flashlight, Buck managed to force the rear door. Inside the garage, they quickly made their way to the narrow office and the small, free-standing safe.

Buck made several attempts to open the steel safe but couldn't. Clyde tried without success. "We need a goddamn torch," he said, but Buck claimed to have a better idea—move the safe out of the building, load it into the car and torch it open later.

Sidney said, "You been readin' too many funny papers. This sucker's not big but weighs a goddamn ton."

"Come on," Buck said. "We'll rock this baby right outta here, and buy us a filly mignon."

The three struggled with the safe, rocking it back and forth, from edge to edge, and with much effort, cursing and sweating, managed to load the safe half into the back of the car which sunk beneath the weight. "Let's get outta here," Clyde said. "Dump this fuckin' safe right here and let's get outta here. We can't drive with this damn barn smashin' us to the road."

Buck refused to abandon the safe. He said, "We can make it, I'm tellin' you. Leave it here and someone's comin' to grab what we busted our nuts over."

The car wobbled as they slowly drove south out of Denton. Looking into the rearview mirror, Clyde saw the car behind them. "Laws—" he said. The car kept following though Clyde drove faster. Then the car behind veered to the left to pull alongside the Ford, but Clyde pushed the gas, jumping ahead and cutting the car off. The chase continued for half a mile until Clyde swerved sharp on a turn, accidentally rammed the curb, and heard the axle snap.

"Run!" Buck yelled, jumping from the car. Sidney dashed out in a different direction until one of the cops started shooting. Halting abruptly, Sidney threw up his hands and cried, "Don't shoot! Don't shoot! I give up!"

Chasing Buck, the second cop kept yelling for him to stop until he wounded him with a bullet in the leg.

Clyde kept running. He'd heard the shot that dropped Buck, and knew the cop was chasing him. A shot was fired, missed, and failed to slow Clyde. He ran several blocks, dashed between two houses, dropped to the ground and pushed through a screened crawl space. He quickly covered the opening with the screen, curled on his side beneath the building, and listened as the cop ran between the houses and kept going. Clyde hunched as small as he could, holding his breath, waiting.

He didn't sleep. Huddled beneath the house the rest of the night, he waited for dawn, and soon as the sun was up, he squeezed out from beneath the house, brushed the dust from his clothes, and walked towards the highway. He told himself he'd catch a ride or two, maybe a straight-through to Dallas. He began to whistle as he walked, his eyes shifting quickly for any sign of the law.

The safe's stash came to less than thirty dollars. Shot through the leg, Buck was tended to medically, and then jailed with Sidney. Both had managed to unload the jewelry from their pockets before the cops had made their search. Both said they couldn't identify the third runner. Buck kept saying, "I don't know who the hell he was.

Just some dumb kid hitchin' a ride that we picked up. Scared the crap outta him seein' the law on our ass."

Laying low at his folks on Eagle Ford, Clyde helped his father tarpaper the outhouse. He did chores and read the newspaper to the old man and Cumie, both worrying about Buck, who, along with Sidney, had been indicted and swiftly tried.

Both pled not guilty but were convicted by a jury within minutes. The Barrows believed Clyde had been with Buck on the ride, and knew he'd escaped only by his swift thinking and "the seat of his pants." Weeks later, Buck and Sidney were sentenced to four years each and transported to Huntsville prison. Meanwhile, Clyde was hanging around Fred Kramer's Auto Repair, talking motors and keeping an eye on the road for signs of trouble. He knew the cops were looking for him, though he hadn't been charged along with Buck and Sidney.

Several times the cops cruised past the Barrows, slowing for any sign of Clyde.

Dapper as usual, a silver watch now hooked to the end of his chain, Clyde paid a visit to an old friend, Clarence Clay, to talk about Buck's troubles and what the prison was like. A few younger people were at the get-together, laughing and kidding, one being Buster Parker, who Clyde knew only casually. Parker's younger sister, Bonnie, was also at the party, nineteen years old, blonde and blue-eyed, a bright, contagious smile. Buster told Clyde that Bonnie had been married to a fellow who was doing time in Huntsville prison.

Clyde kept looking at her. She seemed alone, like she wasn't even really at the party—fiddling with a piece of cake or looking out the window. Then he realized she was looking at his reflection in the glass. Clyde asked Bonnie if she was still married to the guy in prison. She said yes, she was, "legally," but didn't feel personally married at all.

"I've never been married," Clyde said. Bonnie said she knew, and Clyde asked how she knew. She said, "People talkin' all around here. They talk about your brother and they talk about you."

Clyde said, "This place is sure stuffy. They could use a fan in here. I feel like I'm gonna fall over it's so damn hot. You wanna go for a walk?"

Bonnie said, "I have to get home to my momma pretty soon."

"I'll walk you there," he said. Together they left the party, both exiting out the kitchen door. He asked about her brother but she said, "Seems he comes and goes how he wants."

Clyde walked beside her, listening to whatever she said. When they reached her house, Clyde said, "I sure don't feel like I wanna say good night to you, Bonnie...." She asked if he'd like to come in and have a cup of hot chocolate. They went in through the back door, and Clyde stayed in the kitchen holding her left hand while she stirred the chocolate with a mixing spoon in her right hand.

Laughing a little, she said, "You're not very tall, Clyde. I'm a short person and you're not a whole lot taller than me."

He said no, he wasn't too tall, but said she looked no bigger than a kid, and perhaps that was just the right size for him. She was looking right into his face and he said, "I feel like givin' you a kiss on your lips." She said she wouldn't mind that.

He went to her house the following night for another walk, and as they strolled along the river's edge, Clyde threw an empty beer can into the water. He said he didn't care about anybody but himself. "You standin' here with me is nice," he said, "and I care about you, but I don't care about the rest. I don't give them any more carin' than that tin can I just tossed in the river. My folks—okay, I care about them, and my brothers and sisters, but I don't care about the people out there in Dallas or everywhere else any more than thinkin' about a bunch of squirrels in some tree."

Bonnie laughed a little, and squeezed Clyde's hand. "Long as you care about me, that's what I care about."

"I do care about you," he said. "I don't include you in all the rest of the people."

The following week they went to the movies, ate peanuts, popcorn, and shared a chocolate bar. Clyde held Bonnie's hand, and they kissed a few times. He said little as he walked her home, but she sensed this was the one person, just her size, "small and pretty-looking," she'd say. There was something about him that reached into her that she couldn't clearly understand, something bound in with his smiling, self-confident manner that at the same time masked some impenetrable cloud—an idea of danger lurking, moving with him as he went.

He was a risk-taker who spoke at times in a grandiose way, saying he'd never follow "anyone else's route." Yes, Bonnie said, she understood. He wasn't stamped out for an ordinary life, or the "God-fearing" path or so-called "righteous way." She said she knew because she sensed that in herself.

Struggling for wages was a waste of time in a country on the brink of disaster. Clyde told Bonnie flat out that his brother Buck was a thief and he said you could say he was one himself. He'd never work "some stuff-shirt job" again, even if he got it on a "silver platter." He'd done that, he said, "but without any platter," and gotten fired time after time—so it was clear to him who the enemy was. There'd never be any doubt in his mind.

Bonnie admired that and couldn't hesitate giving her affections to Clyde. "Like you snap your finger," Harris said. "It was that quick they got romantic, and no matter what he said she believed him. He believed everything she said. She didn't know he'd had as much trouble with the law as he'd had, only that they were 'sniffin' around' for him and eager to nail another Barrow if they could." That didn't appear to matter to Bonnie. Who he was—what he was—struck every chord in her.

At the same time, some part of Clyde's nature recognized that streak in Bonnie. You could call it wild, or something untamed. She said to Clyde, "I dreamed you were Billy the Kid, and you claimed me for the rest of my life." Could she call it true love? Or call it "crazy love"—and did it make any difference either way?

Her sister, Billie Jean, looking back at Bonnie's attachment to Clyde, said the two were "like hunks of a picture puzzle that fit as though made that way, and once you got the pieces fitted there wasn't any way they'd get taken apart, and nothin' anybody could do about it."

Each evening after dark, Clyde would leave Kramer's garage and make his way to Bonnie's house. He'd stay late drinking coffee or hot chocolate, sometimes eating red beans and soda crackers, holding Bonnie's hand and waiting for her mother and Billie Jean to go to sleep. Instead of heading back to his folks, Clyde began sleeping on the couch in Bonnie's front room, using a pair of pajamas Buster had outgrown.

In the middle of the night, Bonnie would sneak out of the bedroom she shared with her sister, and nestle under the blanket with Clyde.

Knowing he had to get out of West Dallas if he wanted to avoid the cops, he'd leave the Parkers' before daybreak. He gave Bonnie a small gold ring, telling her if he got put in jail, or if they wouldn't let him go, he wanted her to know that no one else in the world mattered to him, and he'd spend every day thinking about her and every night dreaming of the day they'd be together again. He said, "So you can say it to yourself that we're like married folks and nothin' is ever goin' to change it."

With the ring on her finger, Bonnie told him she knew she'd loved him the moment she first saw him. She'd been on dates and had boyfriends "here and there," but she'd never been in love with "a single one of them." She didn't know why she married Roy Thornton, and said, "It just was the next thing that had to happen, same as when he ran off—it was the next thing that had to happen...."

She wasn't sorry she'd done it, marrying like she had, but told Clyde, "You're someone I'm never gonna let go of. I'm gonna carry you in my heart same as if it's grown that way and nothin' else's ever goin' to matter." Everything he'd told her–even the "bad" about himself, only convinced her she'd found someone she could die for. She'd found Billy the Kid and Jesse James all in the hide of Clyde Barrow, and she said, "It isn't even any choice I could make. It's like it's been written on the sky."

One morning, Bonnie shook Clyde awake. He opened his eyes and sat up from the couch. Someone was knocking on the front door hard enough to split the wood. Emma Parker hurried into the room wringing her hands. "There's a policeman at the back door!" she cried. "He's got a gun in hand. They're gonna break down the door!"

Emma had no choice but to let both the lawmen into the house. Both rushed Clyde, who'd managed to get his feet to the floor, and told him, "You're under arrest, Barrow!"

"Can I put my pants on?" Clyde asked.

His trousers were seized and the pockets searched, same with his shirt, and when he'd gotten into both, he was handcuffed and frisked again. "Let's go!" he was told.

"I'd like to get my feet in my shoes," he said. One cop picked up the shoes while the other steered Clyde out the house barefoot. Bonnie was standing in the open doorway of the house, watching Clyde being loaded into a waiting wagon. He kept looking back at her, silently saying, "I love you—I love you!"

She cried out, "I love you!"

Confronted with several warrants for his arrest, Clyde was fingerprinted and photographed, then logged into the Dallas jail, only to be transferred to Denton to face charges for the Motor Mark burglary. "What burglary?" he said. He claimed he had nothing to do with it. "I was in West Dallas and my folks and other people'll tell you so."

In support of her son, Cumie was setting out for Denton. When Bonnie learned from Cumie that additional charges were piling against Clyde, she asked Cumie if she could go with her.

When they got to Denton, Clyde told Bonnie and his mother, "I don't know what's gonna happen with all this. They're tellin' me I'm headed to prison for a long time." Already brokenhearted over Buck being confined in Huntsville, Cumie said it would practically kill her to have two sons in the penitentiary.

Clyde asked Bonnie if she was going to divorce Roy Thornton, and she sighed. "My mom's coaxin' me to do just that, but there's time for it. I can't even think about that. Whatever's goin' to happen right now," she said, "your mom and I are here and we're with you."

By the end of February, the attempt to build a case against Clyde on the Motor Mark charge lacked sufficient evidence. The case was dropped, but Clyde's elation at the prospect of being cut loose collapsed when told he was being transported to Waco to face charges for jobs he'd pulled earlier. Clyde told Cumie and Bonnie, "I suppose they're gonna run me all over like chasin' a goddamn turkey and not bein' happy till they got my butt in Huntsville."

Bonnie told him she had a cousin in Waco. "Your mother and me can stay there if there's gonna to be a trial, 'cause I'm not leavin' you at all. We'll be there every day," she said, "and wherever they send you, I'll be there. If you go to prison, honey, I'll pack up what I've got and live as close as I can to wherever you are."

It didn't take Clyde long to see it would go easier in Waco if he played along with the law. Facing seven felony counts, and with the courts bogged down and time pressing in, he was told it would be to everyone's advantage for a bargain to be struck. To Cumie, he said, "They're tellin' me to plead guilty to the burglaries, and no contest on the car theft. They wanna give me two years on each count, and work it out so that's all the time I'll do—those two years. If I don't do as they say, I'll be locked up for the whole fourteen years. You know, Mom, I'd just as soon be dead than doin' that." The only way he could see out was doing what they suggested, and "gaggin' on sayin' what they're askin.'"

Five

Minding the law in a hole like Huntsville wasn't Buck Barrow's idea of living at an easy pace. He wrenched through each day as if dragging through a swamp, the picture in his mind of Blanche the only thing keeping him moving. He told her, "I gotta get out of here. I ain't sleepin' or eatin' and pretty soon I'll be dyin' if I can't get out.…"

One brisk, cold afternoon in the middle of March, while working on kitchen duty, Buck and another prisoner walked away from the pots and pans. They got out through a side door, hot-wired a guard's car parked behind the building, and in minutes the two men were off the prison grounds.

Staying clear of the highway, Buck drove north to Dallas, sweating each mile of the ruts and back roads. Splitting up with his kitchen pal by dropping him off in Dallas, Buck then headed for West Dallas. He hid the car off Eagle Ford and hurried on foot to the Barrows'.

Henry was proud of his son for "bustin' out," but what in the Lord's name was he going to do? "Tell me, Buck," he said, "what're you gonna do, 'cause they're after your hide for sure. Soon they're gonna have us all locked up."

"Don't worry," Buck said. "Nobody's gettin' on my tail. Me and Blanche are headin' outta Texas pronto. I'll let you know where we are once we get there." He changed his clothes, told Cumie he loved her, and by nightfall was driving out of West Dallas.

He abandoned the guard's car, met with Blanche, hugged her, kissed her, and boarded a Dallas bus—the safest way to go. By dawn the next day, Buck and Blanche had vanished from the state of Texas.

Staying with her cousin Mary, in Waco, Bonnie paid daily visits to the McLennan County Jail where the guards nicknamed her "the chilly little filly."

Clyde was sharing the steel-hatched holding cell with another prisoner, William Turner, who faced the same judge as Clyde. Convicted of burglary and auto theft, Turner had twenty-five charges against him, wound up sentenced to only four years but told Clyde he wasn't sticking around to be sent to Huntsville. "No one's keepin' me hangin' in 'the walls' for four years," he said.

"What're you plannin' on doin'," Clyde said, "killin' yourself?"

Turner shook his head. "You're only doin' two years, fella. I got four and that's far more than I'm willin' to do."

Thinking for a moment, Clyde said, "Well, pal, two's more than I'm gonna spend in a goddamn cage. You know some way of gettin' outta here?"

"If I had my gun I'd get out fast," Turner said. "That's the key, y'know. I got the gun but it's not where I can get it. You know what I mean? If there's a way I can get a gun we'll be walkin' right now."

"Maybe there's a way," Clyde said. "Let's talk about it...."

The next morning, Bonnie's small hand reached through a slot in the cell's steel straps and held Clyde's hand as she told him that as soon as he was sent to prison she wasn't going back to West Dallas. "I'll be stayin' here," she said. "I'll find a job and be waitin' for you."

Lowering his voice, Clyde said, "Possible we'll be together sooner than you sittin' for two years waitin'. Turner's been talkin' about us takin' off, but first we gotta get someone on the outside to do somethin' for us."

"Well," Bonnie said, "I'm on the outside."

Turner came closer, stood next to Clyde, and almost whispering but smiling, told Bonnie he had a gun in a house in east Waco. "It's hidden," he said, "but if you can get it, your boy here'll be in your arms a hell of a lot sooner."

Clyde squeezed Bonnie's hand. "It's the way of me gettin' out," he said. "I can't go to prison, sugar. Buck's busted out and I don't wanna fill his shoes in Huntsville. That's all there is to it."

She stared at Clyde and said, "I don't want you goin' to prison. I'd rather die than see you bein' locked up like this. It hurts me. What can I do?"

Turner said, "You find my gun and get it to me, and we'll be the hell outta here. There's no other way." Using spent matches, Turner had sketched a little map of the east Waco house and made a square mark where the gun was hidden. "It's loaded," he said, "so you be careful. Nobody'll be in the house most of tonight." He told her where to find the key to the front door.

Folding the little pencil-sketched map, Bonnie stuck it into her blouse and turned to leave. Clyde said, "Wait a minute." Thinking Clyde wanted to kiss her, Turner turned away as Clyde took Bonnie's hand again. He said, "You've never done nothin' wrong, honey."

"I know it," she said.

"Except maybe marryin' that guy," he said. "Law won't lock you up for that, but if you get Turner's gun and get yourself caught, you'll be in jail same as me."

She stared at him, withdrew her hand then reinserted it through a slot to touch his face. "I want to do it," she said.

"If you get it, hide it in your clothes—somewhere they won't frisk you, and come back visitin' tonight. Tell 'em your momma needs you and you're catchin' an early train."

"I'll find it and be back," she said, her eyes bright. "If they catch me, it won't matter none since bein' without you is the same as gettin' locked in jail." She tipped her head to kiss him through another slot.

Bonnie enlisted her reluctant cousin Mary on the "secret mission." No longer was it a "private thinking place," like when she was little. Driving anxiously through the Waco streets, Mary finally found the neighborhood, and said, "How come the street's named Turner, too?"

"A coincidence," Bonnie said, climbing out of the car. "They sure didn't name it after him." With little effort and a small flashlight, she located the front door key hidden beneath a painted rock.

On the porch, Mary said, "Isn't this goin' to be considered breakin' into somebody's house and bein' a burglar?"

Holding up the key, Bonnie said, "What's this look like—a crowbar?"

"Looks like a key," Mary said, "but this isn't anyone's place I got knowledge of."

"You don't need to and neither do I." Bonnie opened the door and stepped into the living room. Using her flashlight, she studied the map and moments later was in the small bedroom where Turner indicated the gun was hidden. She searched a chest of drawers, a trunk, a wicker laundry basket, Mary fidgeting anxiously in the doorway, swearing they'd be arrested.

"Hush up!" Bonnie told her, rummaging in a closet. She dragged a chair across the room and stood on it, feeling over the shelves. On her hands and knees, she hunted beneath a daybed and was about to give up, then realized the square shape Turner had sketched wasn't a chest of drawers, but a window box. The scribbled location of the window had confused her. He hadn't indicated a window seat, just a box against a wall.

Bonnie removed cushions and newspapers from the lid and lifted it. She was reaching beneath a stack of magazines, old newspapers and clothes, when her fingers touched the cool steel of a gun barrel at the bottom of the box. She felt over it, gripped the butt and lifted the gun out of the window box. Using her flashlight, she could see the lead tips of bullets in the chamber of the .32 caliber Colt.

They hurried out of the house, locked the front door, and replaced the key where they'd found it. As they drove from the neighborhood, Bonnie wondered how she'd get the gun past the jailers— what part of her clothes could she hide it in? At night there were two guards, one upstairs and another at the downstairs desk. Talking it over with Mary, she said the only way to do it was to hide the gun on her body. "I can't walk with it between my legs," she said, "and no way to get it loose when I get to the cell."

"Why are you doin' this?" Mary said. "It's crazy. If they find out, you'll be in terrible trouble and I'll be in trouble for helpin' you!"

"Be quiet!" Bonnie told her. "I have to think." She decided to use a long, thin scarf to secure the pistol against her bosom, partly between her breasts and the separation of her ribs. She could hunch herself slightly, keeping her arms close to her breasts. It was cold out, wasn't it? Could she get past the jailers?

Turner was pacing back and forth in the cell while Clyde lay on the bunk, his eyes closed. "How can you sleep right now?" Turner said. Clyde opened his eyes. He said he wasn't sleeping. "What do you think's goin' on?" Turner asked. "You think she got what she went for?"

"You'd know better than me," Clyde said. "It's your house. If your drawin' is right, she's got it."

Less than forty minutes later, Clyde sat up, listening to sounds outside the cell. Bonnie had returned to the jail.

It was past visiting time, but she told the downstairs guard, "I'm sorry, but I gotta go back to Dallas come sunup. I'm catchin' an early train...." With Turner's gun hidden against her chest, her eyes and lips sweet-talking the guard, she said she had to see Clyde again—speaking all the while with a smile and the ease of serving free coffee like she'd once sugared her customers in the café. She said, "It won't take me more than a minute that's no bigger than a little mouse?"

The guard said, "Go on upstairs, filly."

Clyde was clutching the steel slots, watching Bonnie as she reached the head of the stairs. She was gasping a little to show she was out of breath, leaning slightly forward as the jailer approached her. With a side glance to Clyde, her eyes told him she'd done it—she had the gun. Clyde nodded to Turner who mumbled to Clyde, "She don't look scared at all." Now she had to move it out of her clothing and get it through the slot in the bars into Clyde's hand.

The jailer said, "Well, go on and see your boy and say good night."

"I'm gonna kiss him if you're not lookin' at me," she said. With a grunt, the jailer turned from the cell as Bonnie moved against the steel, puckering her lips. It was fast, Clyde bending down a little to kiss Bonnie while she in the same movement pushed the gun from between her breasts, out of her blouse, through the steel slot and into his hand. Waiting behind Clyde, Turner took the gun that was passed to him in a sleight-of-hand move. He tucked the gun into the waist of his pants beneath his shirt.

Bonnie said, "Well, sweetheart, I'll be back to see you sometime soon...."

"All done smoochin'?" the guard asked.

Bonnie stepped back, eyes wide and dancing with the crime she'd just committed. Later she'd tell Billie Jean a thrill ran through her "from feet to ears and back again," an excitement few can know except those pushing the limits of danger. Walking into the jail to sneak a loaded gun to a prisoner had quietly vaulted Bonnie across an unseen boundary into an arena beyond law and order.

"Go back home now, honey," Clyde said. "Whatever happens is gonna happen, and soon as it's okay, I'll be comin' for you."

Trembling with the strange, unfamiliar sensation, and with the jailer escorting her to the stairs, Bonnie glanced back to blow Clyde a kiss, then descended the stairs as Turner hid the gun. "Is it loaded?" Clyde asked.

Turner nodded and said, "We gotta figure this fast. Any delayin' they're gonna find what we got. We'll go tomorrow?"

"I'm ready," Clyde said.

Six

Early the next morning, another prisoner swaggered into the holding cell. Bigger than Clyde or Turner, Emory Abernathy had been charged with bank robbery and bragged to his two new cellmates that he was facing "a hundred years in the jug." Clyde's ears perked up. He wanted to hear more about "stickin' up banks."

Laughing about the burglaries Clyde and Turner had been convicted of, Abernathy said, "If we ever get outta here and run into each other, I'll show you boys how to take one down in six minutes flat."

Clyde said, "I'll do it in four minutes."

Abernathy grunted, looking a little sour. "I'd lay you odds, but you aren't outta here, are you, sonny? Easy to say from where you're sittin', ain't it?"

"Maybe sometime I'll show you," Clyde said, "but not this minute. Me and Turner got us a way out."

"How the fuck you got a way outta here?"

"He's got a key to the door," Clyde said.

Squinting at Turner, Abernathy said, "What sort of key is he talkin' about?"

Turner rolled over and carefully let Abernathy have a fast glance at the gun. Surprised, the big man smiled. He said, "That's the best kind of key anybody's got or can ever get a hand on."

Nothing was said the rest of the morning, but by the afternoon they were talking fast—setting a plan into motion. Abernathy had joined the party as a "blessin' from the hand of the Lord," he said

Later, Turner complained to the jailer that his stomach was "on fire." He was having an "attack of ulcers—sick as a dog," he said, groaning painfully. He asked for milk to ease his guts.

The three sat anxiously, waiting for the jailer to return with the milk. "What'd he do, go to sleep?" Turner said.

Minutes later the annoyed jailer opened the cell door to hand a tin cup to Turner who suddenly bolted forward, wedging his body into the opening of the door. At the same time, Abernathy grabbed the surprised jailer, shoved the muzzle of the gun into his ribs and said, "Yell and you're dead."

Turner pushed the jailer into the cell as Abernathy warned him, "You stay quiet 'cause you don't want to lose your head off your jawbone." They locked the cell, and the three men made their way to the stairs. The second jailer was at a desk on the ground floor, and Clyde motioned for Abernathy to keep him covered. Waving the gun, Abernathy told the jailer, "Get your hands up!" The man stood, looking up, his hands in the air as the three hurried down the stairs. Clyde grabbed the keys to unlock the main jail door while Turner removed the steel crossbar, and Clyde then unlocked the door. Abernathy told the jailer, "Stand here with your hands up and don't move 'cause I don't want you boys comin' after me for a killin'."

The three bolted from the building, hitting the street at a run. They were approaching the corner when Abernathy hollered, "He's comin' after us!" Two shots were fired as Clyde and Turner darted into an alley. Abernathy had slowed, turned around, and sent two shots in the direction of the jail.

Clyde was sprinting ahead as the three ran out of the alley, the jailer's shots going wild. Another block and Clyde suddenly stopped at a parked green Ford coupe. He opened the hood as Turner climbed into the car. "Stick it in neutral," Clyde told him, then crossed the wires. The engine kicked over, Clyde locked down the hood and told Turner, "Move over—I'll drive." He slid onto the seat, shoving Turner, as Abernathy squeezed onto the passenger seat.

A mile away from the jail, Clyde slowed to a crawl. "We gotta get rid of the car," he said. "Get us another one right now." A few blocks away, the three climbed out and approached a vehicle parked in front of a small house.

In a moment the engine was running, Abernathy grinning. He said, "There's your minutes, pal. We'll see how it goes when we gotta eat."

Turner laughed. "I'm starvin'. Don't forget my ulcers, boys."

A short time later, Clyde drove off the road behind a service garage. He said, "One of you get some money, a screwdriver, and pliers and what you can. We'll get over the line into Arkansas."

Abernathy said, "I'll go in. You drive around back of this dump so we're headin' to the road." He got out, Turner's gun in hand.

Clyde said, "Don't shoot anybody." They waited while Abernathy strolled to the front of the building. Slowly, Clyde inched ahead, gravel crunching under the tires. He nosed close to the north side of the building, waiting until Abernathy came out of the station, bills in one hand, the gun in the other. He jumped into the car a second before Clyde sprung ahead, bounced at the shoulder, then raced onto the road.

"Looks like thirty or forty bucks," Abernathy said. "He was just about to stick it in a hole in the floor." He brought a screwdriver and pliers out of his pants pocket, saying, "The guy asked if I wanted a crowbar. I told him, 'I got my hands full, pal.' He said, 'Thought you'd like a crowbar and you're sure welcome to what you got.'"

Turner laughed. Clyde said, "First bunch of cars you see, give a holler so I can get rid of these plates."

Out of Texas and into Arkansas, Clyde stopped at a roadside diner to remove the Texas license. He told Turner to get some grub on the run. "Don't stick 'em up so we don't have any laws crawlin' around here." While Turner went for some food, Clyde removed the Texas plate and unscrewed an Arkansas license.

Time seemed to race with Clyde behind the wheel as they swapped another two cars and roamed as many states, stopping along the way to stick up a couple of gas stations, fill the tanks, rob a market and two roadside cafés. Before they reached Middletown, north of Cincinnati, Ohio, they were out of money.

Abernathy had bragged about his Ohio connections, but they didn't pan out. Clyde was annoyed with the bouncing back and forth of what he felt to be nothing but hot air on the part of Abernathy, while Turner played second fiddle to the more experienced of the trio.

Clyde kept thinking about Bonnie—what she'd done, setting him free, like she'd flung open a window. Now he was chasing a blind trail into Ohio—far from what he knew or felt easy with, and eager to make the trip back to Texas as soon as possible.

It was the middle of March, stranded in downtown Cincinnati, when the three entered a café. After sharing stew and pork and beans, Clyde said, "I don't wanna to stick around. You boys might have other stuff goin' on, but I gotta get back to Texas."

When the trio stopped at the Baltimore and Ohio depot in Cincinnati, Clyde went in, casually roaming from baggage to postcard rack, finally asking for a train schedule. He looked around carefully, taking in what he saw. After a few minutes, he left the depot and made his way back to the car where Abernathy and Turner were waiting.

Clyde climbed behind the wheel. "We can do it," he said. "We'll come back later." He drove away from the depot, finally slowing beside a creek. He stopped, cut the engine, and put his head back on the seat.

Abernathy dozed while Turner twisted restlessly, curling on the seat, unable to get comfortable, groaning that his legs were cramped and aching. He said, "I got some kind of problem—some fever in my leg bones."

Neither Clyde nor Abernathy said anything. The rest of the afternoon they spent dozing by the creek or waiting for the dark to set in.

By sundown they were on the move. They stuck up a gas station, Abernathy going in with the gun while Clyde sat behind the wheel, engine humming, his left foot holding the clutch to the floor.

Bonnie knew he'd be coming back. Her heart raced at the thought of his closeness. She'd received a telegram from Indiana. He said he was okay. She knew he was on the run and couldn't show. But what was he doing in Indiana?

She knew the law was watching her house—watching the Barrows' as well. Bonnie'd catch sight of the cops driving past, slowing, snooping, looking around. She kept waiting for Clyde but he didn't show. He'd be hiding, she knew it. Even miles away, she knew he could sense what was happening. She believed he shared a bond with her that couldn't be broken, something formed of some hot metal like an iron ring that held the two locked in an irreversible union. At times the thoughts made her dizzy. She never believed such a thing could happen to her. It didn't matter that her body was not in his presence, because she swore to herself that her soul was clenched with his as securely as his arms had been around her.

Bonnie Elizabeth Parker.

"I'm going to be a writer 'cause I got lots of imagination."
—Bonnie Parker

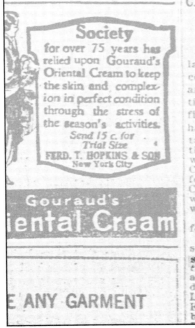

CEMENT CITY WINS COUNTY LEAGUE LITERARY CONTEST.

Cement City won the annual Dallas County interscholastic literary contest in Dallas Saturday, it was announced yesterday by W. C. Martin, in charge of the event. It was first announced that Highland Park had won the meet, by reason of its taking a majority of first places in the events, but a check of the points won by each school shows Cement City has 71 points. The cup offered for highest score goes to Cement City. Lancaster won second place with 63 points and Highland Park was third.

The Cement City winners are as follows:

Wilma Emmons, first in senior spelling; Bonnie Parker, first in subjunior spelling; Gladys Meadows, third in essay writing; Minnie Jones and Alta Coppinger, second in girls' debate; Travis Hamby and George Lunday, second in boys' debate; Keith Brandenburg, second in junior boys' declacamation contest; Elva

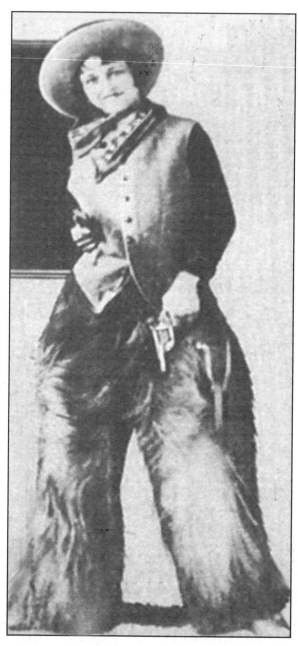

Pre-Clyde Barrow, Bonnie poses as Billy the Kid.

Bonnie was married at age 15 to Roy Thornton, September 1926. He was later arrested for robbery and sent to prison.

Bonnie working in Hargrave's Cafe, Dallas, Texas, before joining Clyde.

Bonnie and her sister, Billie Jean.

Clyde with Eleanor "Bee" Williams, in hat, on his right, and Eleanor's cousin, Lela Heslep, 1926.

*The Barrows' Star Service Station served as the family home
as well; on Eagle Ford Road, West Dallas.*

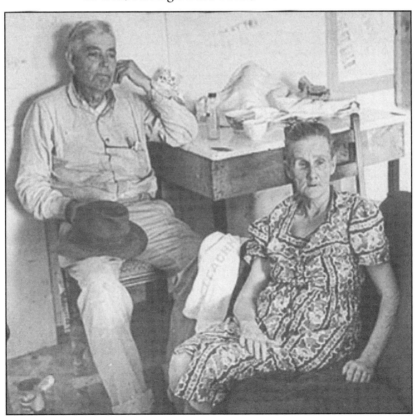

*Henry Barrow and Cumie Barrow, father and mother of the
Brothers Barrow and their sisters.*

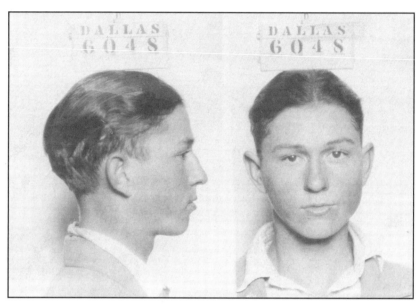

1926. Mugshot of Clyde after his first brush with the "laws"; charged with Grand Theft Auto.

Clyde shows his tattoos and white cat.

Clyde with sisters, Nell and Artie Barrow.

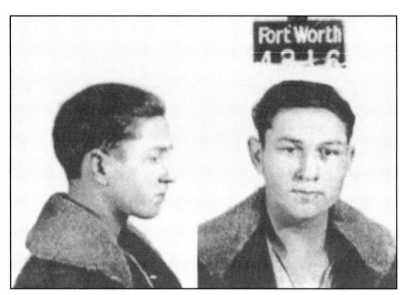

Arrested in Fort Worth, Clyde's "trail" begins.

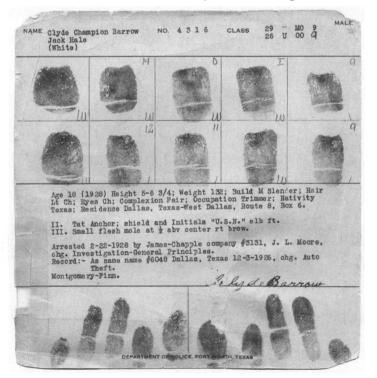

NAME Clyde Champion Barrow   NO. 4 3 1 6   CLASS   29 - MO 9   MALE
Jack Hale   26 U 00 q
(White)

Age 18 (1928) Height 5-6 3/4; Weight 132; Build M Slender; Hair
Lt Ch; Eyes Ch; Complexion Fair; Occupation Trimmer; Nativity
Texas; Residence Dallas, Texas-West Dallas, Route 8, Box 6.

II. Tat Anchor; shield and Initials "U.S.N." elb ft.
III. Small flesh mole at ½ abv center rt brow.

Arrested 2-22-1928 by James-Chapple company #3131, J. L. Moore,
chg. Investigation-General Principles.
Record:- As same name #6048 Dallas, Texas 12-3-1926, chg. Auto
Theft.
Montgomery-Finn.

DEPARTMENT OF POLICE, FORT WORTH, TEXAS

*Captured in Middletown, Ohio, after his escape from the Waco jail
in Texas.*

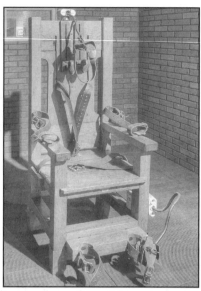

Clockwise from above left: Ted Rogers, one of Clyde's partners in crime, would get away with murder; electric chair at Huntsville State Prison; Ralph Fults, friends with Clyde in prison, later joins Clyde and Bonnie on the "outside"; Raymond Hamilton, Clyde's on-again, off-again partner, would die in the Texas electric chair.

On the run, Clyde stole over 700 automobiles.

Bonnie, on the run with Clyde.

Fun and games on the road. Note cigar stub in Clyde's hand. As a joke, Bonnie uses the cigar for her next picture.

Pretending to chomp the cigar she snatched from Clyde, Bonnie poses as the "gun moll," a joke she'd later regret.

Seven

Clyde cruised slowly, at moments killing the headlights so the car would be swallowed by the dark. Abernathy and Turner said little as they roamed the night streets of the town. They drove past a gas station, a café, then the Gough-Lamb cleaners on Charles Street, at last pulling in outside the Baltimore-Ohio railroad office. Opening the car door, Abernathy said to Turner, "Okay, buddy, let's get this show on the fuckin' road."

The robbery went swiftly, but netted less than sixty dollars.

Clyde sped to the outskirts of town, the asphalt soon turning to dirt. The roads seemed to wind and drift, one branching from the other. The car came to a stop, Clyde turning off the headlights. Shaking his head, he said, "Which of these goddamn roads is gettin' us outta here?" Abernathy didn't know. "It's too dark to see," Clyde said. "Our headlights are cuttin' damn near across the town."

Turner said, "Leave 'em off before anyone spots us."

"Nobody's gonna see us," Clyde said. "We're in the middle of nowhere. Damned if I know which way's out."

Abernathy said, "We'll lay low out here. Pull off the road and we'll wait till it gets light." He opened the door and got out of the car. "Let me get in the back," he told Turner. "You get in front."

Turner climbed out, slid onto the seat next to Clyde and smoked one cigarette after the other. He finally slumped to the right with his head against the window ledge while Clyde sat staring over the steering wheel into the night.

He didn't know when he dropped off, but when Clyde opened his eyes daylight was flooding the windshield. Turner was crumpled asleep and Abernathy was snoring. Clyde twisted around to nudge Abernathy. "Wake up," he said. "We gotta get movin'. We're sittin' in the middle of someone's property." Clyde started the car. It grumbled, sputtered, then rolled smooth after he pushed the gas, clearing the engine. He shifted gears and made a turn on the road that looked as confusing as it had in the dark. In moments, he realized they were heading in the same direction they'd traveled the night before—heading straight past the Baltimore-Ohio office.

Turner said, "Shit, the cops're right there!" Two uniformed officers came running out of the railroad office—looking at the three men in the car traveling past.

"Get us outta here!" Abernathy cried. "We're in a fuckin' trap!"

Downshifting and hitting the gas, Clyde raced ahead as the cops climbed into the police car. "They're comin' after us!" Turner said.

Clyde cranked for all the speed he could get, but the cops were right behind them. They almost cornered the Ford, but Clyde swerved onto a side street. The cops screeched around the same corner, firing at the car. Bullets pinged against the metal. Left side. Trunk lid. The roof of the car. Clyde pulled to the curb, grabbed the gun from Turner, threw open his door and shot at the law's windshield. He then made a run for it.

Abernathy and Turner bolted from the car and were running. One cop chased Turner into an alley, fired a shot that missed but brought Turner to a standstill. "I'm done runnin'!" he yelled.

Clyde and Abernathy broke off in opposite directions, Clyde quickly managing to lose the cop by disappearing behind a building and climbing through a basement window. The cop then took off after Abernathy who was still in sight.

An alert went out and within an hour, Abernathy was caught on the east side of Middletown, heading north on the highway. It wasn't until late afternoon that Clyde climbed out of the basement through the same window he'd entered. He figured he'd stroll to the railroad yards, catch a ride, but the alert for the armed holdup suspects had saturated the area, and Clyde was spotted by a cop patrolling on foot who immediately unsnapped the holster at his side.

Clyde made a dash straight at the cop, charging him and almost knocking him down. The man hadn't yet got his gun in hand, and stumbled back, then gave chase. He later said, "I wasn't sure if he was one of the gang but I wanted to find out, but he ran at me—almost knocked me down gettin' past me. No one had ever done that to me—charged me like a bull. He ran faster than I could, and on a main street where he was keepin' close with a bunch of people. Smart, knowin' I wouldn't fire into a crowd. He jumped around so fast like damn lightnin' and zigzaggin' every which way. I fired in the air and hollered at him but he outran me and ran around a corner. By the time I got to where I'd seen him, he wasn't there. But I kept lookin', something tellin' me I'd get him."

Running far enough from the cop, Clyde bought enough time to grab another car and sped off onto another street, the exhaust blowing from the car. He saw the cop still hounding him, and the cop saw the car—and saw Clyde. He raised the gun but Clyde made a screeching turn onto a narrow street, then racing ahead he suddenly found he'd plunged down a dead-end street—a stupid predicament, the cop plodding right behind him, fast cinching the distance between them. Rattled, Clyde bumped the car across a yard between two houses, almost crashing into the rear of one of them.

There was nowhere to go. He was at the edge of a hydraulic canal, with no way out. He jumped from the car to run again, but the cop was about to fire, hollering, "Halt!" The cop had the best of him, he knew it. He threw Turner's gun as far as he could into the canal. It didn't even make a splash. Raising his hands in the air, he turned to face the sweating and hard-breathing cop with the gun shaking in his hand. "Don't make a move!" the cop ordered.

With a smile, Clyde said, "It's okay. I'm not gonna give you any trouble."

The laws at the Middletown jail pushed Clyde around as a tough, snot-nosed punk who said his name was Robert Thomas, a seventeen-year-old who'd hitchhiked from Indianapolis. "Those two guys who picked me up wanted me to drive," he said. "Told me they were bushed. When you guys rode on us, they said you'd shoot us."

However, the law's records from Waco established Clyde's identity, and he finally admitted he'd escaped from the Texas jail. He also admitted being the third member of the "gang," as the cops put it, but maintained his age was only seventeen.

Jailed separately from Abernathy and Turner, additional charges soon mounted against Clyde. Multiple counts of car theft, interstate flight, armed robbery, burglary, and forcible recapture.

He was transported back to Waco, where Cumie was waiting. His mother told him that any chance he might've had for the court to be lenient had gone up in smoke. Cumie said, "There was a gun used when you escaped from here with those other fellas."

Clyde said, "I know it. I don't know where the boys got the gun. Surprised the hell outta me. They talked me into bustin' out with them."

Cumie said, "Unless the Lord sends us down a miracle, they're gonna send you to the same place your brother's run from, and I'm prayin' Buck'll see his way to comin' and give himself up."

"I have to see Bonnie," Clyde told his mother. "I wrote her and I need to see her."

His mother said, "I talked to her and she understands you were runnin', so she knows you couldn't come for her." Cumie had encountered the newsmen who referred to Clyde as "Schoolboy Barrow," and the three as "baby bandits," and "baby thugs." She tried to tell them that Clyde was a "good boy" who'd gotten mixed up with a bad crowd in Waco. She said Clyde had no reason to escape or be on the run, since he'd had such a short sentence to serve. Now, since he'd escaped, the court would be dead set to "bring him right down to his knees." As God was her witness, Cumie told Clyde, "I'll do all I can, but you've shoveled up yourself a pile of trouble."

Very few would understand the inner revelations Bonnie rarely revealed in the tiny tips of an iceberg jutting through the flatness of her life: a short road paved with hardship and near poverty, a youthful marriage to a convict she'd never loved though she still couldn't bring herself to divorce him while he was still behind bars. She told her sister, "Let Roy tell himself he has me on the outside, so he still thinks there's the possibility of a life if he's ever free," though for

Bonnie there was a blank, faceless side to that coin.

In her "heart," which she said belonged to Clyde, Thornton had ceased to exist. The only face she could see was Clyde's.

The seven two-year sentences handed down previously to Clyde to run concurrently now stacked up to the full fourteen years of pending imprisonment in "the Walls"—Huntsville prison—and under this threat, an exchange of letters between Bonnie and Clyde accelerated.

In April 1930, Clyde was processed into the Texas state prison system as number 63527. He learned that he would eventually be sent to Eastham farm, called "Hell's Hole," but due to the existing charges against him he'd remain in Huntsville to be transported to answer the multiple warrants in other jurisdictions. Clyde told a fellow prisoner, "I'd rather do my time in the Walls from all I'm told about Eastham." The other prisoner, heavier than Clyde and over a foot bigger, said, "I bet you would, boy. Little and lookin' like you do, Eastham's gonna turn you inside out—if you even live that long. This joint figures the less they gotta feed, the more money's in the boss's pocket."

Clyde said, "I'll kill any son of a bitch who lays a hand on me."

The convict laughed. "That's about what you're gonna be doin', killin' one prick-sucker after the other, or else get yourself some muscle."

Eight

Clyde's circuit of answering charges fared poorly for the law. "Insufficient evidence to prosecute" kept cropping up, leaving Clyde only with the long prison sentence to serve. He told Cumie, "I don't wanna spend fourteen years locked up—I'll do the same thing as Buck, and I'll bust out. I'll go on the run and keep runnin' if it takes the rest of my life."

His mother said, "I'll do all I can to get you outta jail sooner than they're plannin' on holdin' you."

"How you gonna do that?" he asked.

She said, "I mean by goin' to them and pleadin' my case."

Clyde changed the date of his birth to make himself younger on the records, believing hard time would go easier. He also listed his middle name as "Champion" instead of his birth name of "Chestnut," thinking it was sissified enough to have others breathing down his neck. He insisted to the board that Bonnie Parker was his wife, which allowed a greater exchange of communications between the two. She had written to him in Waco, saying, "I love you, Clyde, and no matter what happens, wherever they're going to send you, I'm going to pack everything and be there as close to you as I can get. It's like I told you, if you're locked away from me, I might as well be locked up the same as you, because my life won't mean anything without you."

In the middle of September, Clyde was being delivered back to Huntsville when he met another young convict, Ralph Fults, riding the same prison-bound wagon. Two years younger than Clyde,

Ralph had already been in and out of lockups since he was a kid. He had just spent almost a year at Eastham farm, Camp One, escaped from solitary with other prisoners, and was later captured in St. Louis. "They got special treatment for guys who wanna run," Ralph told Clyde. "If they don't take you behind a buildin' and shoot your ass, they got somethin' called a 'tune-up,' where they beat the livin' shit outta you with clubs while they're tellin' you it's always good for you to be learnin' your lessons."

Some miles north of Huntsville was the town of Weldon, and Eastham Camp Two. Ralph Fults had made his break from Camp One, where they'd housed many prisoners in solitary. Camp Two lacked solitary accommodations, but instead had small sheet-iron boxes in which prisoners were locked to roast. "In the summer," Ralph said, "you can smell the hide of these cons cookin' in them tin doghouses."

Clyde's survival at Eastham was to prove a miracle. More than once he was selected to "ride the barrel," a form of punishment in which a prisoner's hands were handcuffed behind them, then they were forced to stand on an upended barrel until further notice. Hours later, with legs blue from numbness, a prisoner would topple to the ground, only to be beaten for failing to do what he was told. This form of "instruction" was engineered to make "adjustments" in the prisoner's attitudes and thinking. The alternative, of course, was suicide—or escape, which was considered by convicts to be another method of suicide.

A first escape attempt was rewarded with beatings that lasted for hours. Ralph had proved a candidate for the beating, as a reminder of an earlier escape attempt. With Clyde now as a witness, Ralph was pistol-whipped and clubbed while Clyde stood by under guard to witness the instructions. On a second escape attempt, it was understood that the prisoner would be shot. Ralph had told Clyde, "They walk you behind the buildin', put a shotgun to the back of your neck or a pistol to your head. Then this screw comes around the other side of the buildin' and says the prisoner made a run— even though what's left of his head's black as a nigger from powder and his brain's stickin' to the wall."

Clyde said if he ever got out of prison he'd make it a point of coming back to Eastham, "not to be visitin'," he said, "but blowin' down the walls, and gettin' as many guys outta there as I can."

Ralph laughed. He said, "I never heard of anybody bustin' into a prison. Once you get your ass outta here you're gone!" Clyde said once he busted in, he wouldn't be staying for very long.

Within a short time, Clyde was transferred back to Eastham Camp One where they could "keep a closer eye on him." Fults believed Clyde was moved because the two had been getting too chummy, with word getting around that Clyde was bragging about somebody busting into the prison to free as many prisoners as he could.

One guard said, "The son of a bitch is crazy." It wasn't long in Camp One before Clyde was "bought" for a few packs of cigarettes. The prisoner who bought Clyde was called Big Ed, a six-foot-one, 210-pound mass who showed an insatiable hunger for raping younger, smaller men. Big Ed, it was said, made his arrangements with the guards to purchase Clyde for the cigarettes—the usual prison tender. Big Ed told other prisoners, "You pay for somethin', you do whatever the fuck you like."

For a short time, Clyde lived in a nightmare of pain, abuse, and illness from loss of weight. One day, while Clyde and a prisoner named Harry were working at a wood pile, he told Harry, "I think I'm gonna die in here. My soul's rottin' in me." Harry, experienced in all matters penitentiary, muttered to Clyde that he should have a talk with a prisoner named Aubrey. He said, "Aubrey's doin' life and he's got no kind feelin's for Big Ed. You talk to Aubrey. See what advice he's got to tell you."

Clyde was able to slip away long enough to find Aubrey, who was already well-acquainted with the situation. He looked at Clyde and said, "You're gonna die soon if you don't do somethin' about it. What do you wanna do? I hate that stinkin' tub of lard, and he'd be no loss to anybody." Clyde didn't say anything. Aubrey said, "I'll tell you what to do. You get his ass alone somewhere in that fuckin' latrine, and we'll take care of him."

Clyde asked, "What're we gonna do?"

"Well, we're gonna kill the son of a bitch." Aubrey said, "You got qualms about killin' a queer son of a bitch?"

"No," Clyde said. "How're we gonna kill him?"

"First off, I don't see no point in wastin' time about it," Aubrey said, "seein' as what you're goin' through. So just go on in the crapper tonight, and use somethin' to hit the son of a bitch in his head."

"That's it?" Clyde said. Aubrey said he'd take care of it from there. Clyde said, "Why're you gonna do this?"

"I don't mind none," Aubrey replied. "I'd like to see a queer son of a bitch dead, wouldn't you? I hate queer sons of bitches."

Clyde said yeah. "What am I gonna hit him with?" Aubrey stared at him, and shrugged. Quickly, Clyde said, "I know where's a hunk of pipe—an inch pipe maybe a foot'n' a half long—"

"—that'll do," Aubrey said. "Now, you hit him hard like you're gonna bust somethin'. You don't want him gettin' up, you know."

That night, Clyde found Aubrey and told him he'd hidden a length of pipe in the latrine. He said, "It wasn't easy findin' anywhere to hide a chunk of pipe." Later, while Aubrey watched, Clyde got out of his bunk and walked slowly out of the barracks into the latrine. The pipe was where he'd hid it, and moments later as he stood facing a urinal, Big Ed approached him from behind, unaware of the length of pipe in Clyde's hand. The big man was already breathing hard as Clyde jerked around, swinging the pipe with all the strength left in his arm. The pipe hit hard against the left side of Big Ed's head and across the temple.

With a groan, the man dropped to his knees, rocked back and forth for a moment, then fell forward against the floor. Quick and sure, Aubrey was right there, a freshly sharpened shank in hand. They rolled the big man over onto his back. Clyde said, "Is he already dead?"

"No—we're fixin' that now," Aubrey said, and stabbed Big Ed hard in the chest, the blade sinking to almost the tape-wrapped handle. Aubrey used both hands to pull the shank out of the thick body, then straightened up. With the same shank, he quickly cut himself across the shoulder, then said, "Now get outta here and get rid of that pipe!"

With dogged determination, Clyde's mother hounded the law to reverse her son's sentences to concurrent status, as when he'd been first convicted, with the possibility of early parole. She was repeatedly told it was impossible, but with an almost superhuman inability to take "no" for an answer, Cumie hammered at the task relentlessly to the point where her request was taken into consideration.

Clyde was aware of what was happening, but admitted to his sister Marie and to Bonnie that when he brought up that his sentence might be reduced to two years, he was laughed at. "They say it's crazy," he wrote to Bonnie. "Maybe they're right."

No one mentioned Big Ed. The law understood that Ed had attacked Aubrey in the latrine, cut him with a shank, and tried to kill him. They knew Big Ed had always bragged he'd put Aubrey in the ground. They'd struggled for seconds before Big Ed slipped in his own piss, fell, hitting his head, the shank in hand sinking into his chest. Over in seconds. Though it made the newspapers, nobody cared. Eastham farm was worse than hell—the work details kicking off before daylight, prisoners squinting to find their way to the fields, then shutting down only near dark. Despondent, sick, plagued with fever and lack of sleep, Clyde was denied medical attention and quickly learned that the only way to get out of Eastham and sent back to the Walls was if something disabled him, losing a leg, a foot or an arm, or if he suffered such an infection as to be near death.

Riddled with hopelessness and despair, believing Cumie's crusade had stalled or was being turned down, Clyde decided to amputate a part of his foot. He needed his hands, his fingers, and he still had to drive a car, so he couldn't lose a leg or a whole foot. Toes were a different matter. He could lose toes and still walk. Maybe he'd have a kind of limp, but he could force that—make it worse. He'd be taken off work details and sent back to the Walls.

He struck a deal with a fellow convict, asking that part of one foot be chopped off with an ax blade. He'd claim he had done it himself by accident. The convict said, "Gotta take the shoe with it," then gave a hard fast blow with the ax, severing two toes from Clyde's left foot.

Nine

Sadly for Clyde, the amputation took place before he learned that a pardon was, in fact, in process. He'd later say it didn't matter. He could walk, run, and once clear of the Walls and "nine hundred miles from Eastham," he'd dance a jig on eight toes instead of ten. A "stupid accident," he wrote to his mother, that maybe if he'd known his pardon was on someone's desk, he might've been able to be somewhere else—doing something else instead of getting his foot in the way of an ax.

He hobbled out of prison on crutches, rode a bus from Huntsville north to Dallas, and sat for an hour in the Dallas bus depot waiting for Nell to meet him. He said little on the way to West Dallas, and once in his family's Star Service Station, he sat with his bandaged foot propped on an orange crate, eating doughnuts and listening to the radio. He'd later tell Bonnie, "I was just sittin' tryin' hard as I could to not to be thinkin' about anythin'."

Things had changed. The West Dallas shack they'd lived in had spawned two extra rooms and a canopy over the front of the structure. Gasoline pumps has been installed. And Henry Barrow told his son that oil was everything. "Everybody will be operatin' an automobile," he said. "Everybody will be buyin' gasoline." Whispering, he said, "Oil's takin' the place of God Almighty." Then he said, "This here where we're livin' is not so bad, son, and while you were gone locked up, I sat outside on a box like your foot's restin' on, and I was countin' automobiles drivin' on the road. I figured your mother and I can be taken care of by what we're gonna earn from the gasoline that's sellin'."

What was once the small front room in the Barrows' shack had been made into a shop for selling doughnuts, soap, different kinds of candy, coffee, and soda pop.

Clyde confessed the grub in prison hadn't been too good, and once he'd been shipped from Eastham, the only thing he'd thought about was sitting down to a meal made by his mother.

He was still on crutches when he went to see Bonnie, apologizing for his lameness. She silenced his words with her lips. She said if they'd cut off his legs she'd have carried him in her arms the rest of her life. Clyde said, "You're too little to do that," and picked her up in his arms, throwing all his balance to the foot with five toes.

"From the minute he got home," his sister Marie said later, "him smilin' and sayin' nice things, I had the feelin' he was fakin' the good thoughts he was comin' up with. He'd get a look—you didn't know what he was thinkin'—the next minute his face'd be hard as a skillet bottom, the same way he'd look when sayin' something' about bein' locked up those two years. Mostly he wouldn't wanna talk about it, and wouldn't let you know what he was thinkin'."

He said he wasn't ever going to prison again. He'd rather be dead, he said. When Cumie and Marie spoke up, saying to be dead was the worst that could happen, the worst you could possibly be, Clyde remarked, "Like hell it is. Unless you've lived in a rat hole where I have, you can't know what I'm sayin'. Dyin' is what we're all gonna do one of these days, you just get it over with one time. But bein' back there you're dyin' every day, and knowin' it when you wake up from bein' dead the day before."

Marie told Cumie she believed Clyde had changed, "and not for the better." She said, "Whatever they'd done to him in there, they might as well've poured him full of concrete as far as anyone shakin' it loose. They made him a different person who can't see nothin' except the bad side of everythin'. How's he gonna live a life that way?"

Days later, in an attempt to cheer him up, Cumie and Marie took Clyde to downtown Dallas to shop for some new clothes. Marie would recall Clyde being "finicky and particular. Wantin' a silk shirt like a rich man wears, then wantin' kid leather gloves that cost more than an entire box of work gloves…." Half the day was spent, she said, "goin' from store to store, and Clyde on those crutches, lookin' for what he wanted, like hungry as a dog wantin' his dinner, but nothin' seemed to suit him except the fancy stuff he said he had to have."

Dressed in his suit, a silk shirt, and fancy silk necktie, he took Bonnie into Dallas for a Chinese dinner. Over chop suey, he asked if she'd been out with other guys while he was locked up. She said she'd dated a couple fellows, "just someone to talk to or see a movie," maybe for a chance to turn her head from the misery she felt over Clyde's absence. She said, "I got to thinkin' you'd be gone a long, long time, and my life would just be over if that were true, honey. There's nobody but you that's ever comin' close to being anythin' to me—only you and no one else...."

Clyde told Bonnie he'd thought of her every day, every night, despite each tomorrow that was nothing less than being shoved into a torture chamber. "It's the worst place in the world," he said. "Somebody gets murdered in there, they shrug it off—no one cares, 'specially if the son of a bitch deserved to get himself killed. What I'm gonna do someday is get fellas outta there by bustin' into that hole." She looked surprised. he laughed. "I'm not jokin'. I'll free as many as I can 'cause they're livin' in a graveyard—just haven't had the dirt tossed over 'em yet." He stared at her and said, "Sugar, I've never seen it so clear in my mind—bustin' into Eastham and gettin' them guys free."

After a moment, Bonnie said, "As long as I'm with you, I'll do whatever you want to do. That will be my life. My life bein' with you."

Clyde's sister Nell told him, "I got Buck's wife a job at the beauty parlor. Blanche likes workin' there and is gonna be doin' more." Nell had a friend on a construction job in New England, she said, if she talked to him he could probably put Clyde on the payroll.

Staring at her, Clyde said, "I can hardly walk, Nell. How am I gonna be doin' much construction work?"

There was no plumbing in the Barrow house. The family used an outhouse and newspapers or a roll of paper hanging from a sink chain. On the inside of the wood slat door was a tin crucifix with Jesus nailed to it with cotter pins.

Sitting on the crapper, his crutches propped against the door, Clyde was tearing off hunks of newspaper when his eye caught the mention of Simms Oil Refinery, a short distance from where Clyde was sitting. The ad talked about the increased demand for gasoline, the success of Simms refinery, and the increase in their payroll. More employees meant more payroll.

Alvin Sinclair, an employee of Simms, occasionally stopped at the Barrows' pumps to fill the tank of his Ford coupe. He'd say hello to Marie, giving her a wink, and he'd ask Blanche about Buck, still "cooped up" in the Walls. Late one afternoon, Clyde hobbled to Sinclair's car and the driver said, "How's it feel wakin' up to find you're outta hell?" Clyde shrugged. Sinclair said, "You got anythin' planned for what you're gonna do?"

"I'm not nursin' any plans," Clyde replied. "My sis's got some ideas on me workin' up in Yankee country. Some contractor she knows up there."

Sinclair said, "Soon as you're off those crutches, you oughta come over to Simms and see about gettin' to work."

"You must be makin' a lot of money, buyin' yourself a new Ford," Clyde said. "I can see myself in one of these—except I'm an ex-con."

"Shit," Sinclair said, "Simms has got a con or two workin'—givin' guys a break. They're hirin' right now. You oughta go see 'em."

"How often you get paid over there?" Clyde asked. "I got no bank account, you know."

Sinclair said, "The dough comes in every other week, and most get paid in cash."

"Sounds like a good deal," Clyde said, nodding. "Guess we'll see what happens."

Soon as he was off the crutches, and to please Cumie, he reluctantly accepted Nell's idea of going for a job in Worcester, Massachusetts. Her friend had relocated to operate a company, and guaranteed he could get Clyde a job. "Of course," Nell was told, "with the understanding your brother can give us a good day's work."

During another Chinese dinner in downtown Dallas, Clyde broke the news to Bonnie about the trip to Massachusetts. Bonnie panicked, saying the thought of another separation was too painful to consider.

"It's Nell's idea," Clyde said. "I don't wanna go do any damned job." He said while his sister had talked Cumie into appreciating the plan, the "plain truth" was that he didn't want to be away from Bonnie or his family, his mother in particular, since she'd worked so hard at getting him out of prison. "I'd still be locked up," he said, "if she hadn't done what she did."

Bonnie said, "But I don't know what I'm gonna do if you're gone. I've only been countin' each day until you got here."

"Maybe you can go with me," he said. "Can't go as my wife since you aren't divorced, but you could get some work in the town maybe—wherever the hell it is."

"Honey," she said, "I'd go if I could, but my momma'd be so worried she'd be jumpin' outta her skin." Hugging him, she said, "I love you, you don't even wanna go away...."

"You're right, but I'm doin' it for Momma and so they don't think I'm just plain loco," he said. "I don't reckon I'll be stayin' long up there anyway since you can't be with me. It's not doin' me any good seein' you here and bein' off somewhere else without you."

"I'll be here waitin' for you," she said. "I won't be goin' anywhere without you."

With as much interest in construction work as an alligator in a desert, Clyde found himself in Massachusetts, unable to shake his longing for Bonnie or the ideas he toted to do with Simms Oil Refinery, and that fat cash payroll waiting to be plucked like feathers off a chicken.

Avoiding as much work as possible, Clyde quickly arrived at his plain truth: Massachusetts was a stupid mistake. It was a stupid place to be. Since the long bus ride to Worcester, his lack of sleep had intensified his visions of Bonnie. He could smell her hair and her skin as clear as if she lay naked against him, and all he had to do was touch her—his fingers gliding down her back and around her waist.

There were other pictures rotating in his head of a raided Eastham burning to the ground. Torch it! He could see charred bodies, skin sizzling and bones turning black. The cons would have crashed out—free—thanks to Clyde Barrow, though he knew he'd only be able to round up a few. Half asleep, he'd wonder where the hell he was. Massachusetts? Where the hell's that?—and to hell with it anyway.

Ten

In less than two weeks Clyde was on a bus heading back to Texas and breathing easy.

To convince his family of the difficulties he would've faced by remaining in New England, he claimed he couldn't take the eastern weather. He'd freeze to death, plus his teeth were killing him. He'd developed "impacted molars," he said, and the pain was as bad as his foot with the missing toes. He said sometimes he could hardly stand.

Despite his mother and Nell's concern, his quick decision to dump the job and get back to Bonnie unnerved them. Nell said, "Trouble's written all over Clyde, and he ain't never gonna straighten it out."

The reward for Clyde's abandonment of New England was Bonnie's open arms. She'd stayed awake, she said, every night he'd been gone. She'd suffered awful pictures in her mind. She said, "Once I dreamt you'd fallen into quicksand and I couldn't get you out of it.... They threw a rope but it turned into a snake. The only thing to do was jump into it myself."

Clyde said he hadn't slept either. "I felt like I was back in the jug. I'd wake up thinkin' I was gettin' pushed around, thinkin' I hadn't got outta that rat hole—none of it bein' true that I was here. I was still there—dreamin' I was here, but I'm not ever gonna be locked up again. They'll have to shoot me first and bury me in a garbage can or that quicksand you're dreamin' about, long before they're gonna get me into any cage."

"Any door they're gonna lock on you," Bonnie said, "they'll be lockin' on me at the same time."

Except for his folks, he said, Bonnie was all that made any sense or meaning to him. The rest of the world meant nothing. "It's crap," he said. There was no hope in any way, except by doing what you had to do. No hope except to get all you could as fast as you could get it.

Bonnie squeezed his hand and said she understood.

Two of Clyde's past pals were especially glad to see him. Ralph Fults, released from prison, had returned home to McKinney where another associate of Clyde's—Ray Hamilton—was jailed on car theft. He'd soon cut his way clear by using hacksaw blades supplied by Fults, who'd hidden them in the spine of a magazine.

Clyde got together with Ralph and passed the news about the oil refinery down the road. There was money in a safe every two weeks for a big payroll. As they walked along Eagle Ford, heading towards the refinery, Clyde said the guy who worked at Simms, and who bought Cokes and gas at the Barrows' station, had recently "got to talkin'. He told me he's got a cousin in the can who'd stuck up a joint downtown. This cousin's belly-achin' about bein' in the joint, and this guy wants to know what I'm gonna do. I told him nothin' except lookin' for some fast scratch. He got all bushy, his eyes poppin', and says he knows of a score and would I be interested. So I said, 'Sure, whatcha got in mind?' He says there's a payroll put in a safe before it's doled out. He says the safe's no Fort Knox—just a straight tumbler deal, and says it's old."

"So we get into the place," Fults said, "and crack the safe. That's it? What's this guy want?"

"He doesn't want nothin'. He's showin' me what he knows—hotshot. That's why I think it's maybe a lot of bunk."

"But what if it ain't?" Fults said. "A payroll? That could be a lot of damned dough."

"He says there's folks workin' the graveyard shift," Clyde said. "This guy's not sayin' it's an easy score, but could be enough to go around for everyone workin' at Simms. He ain't withholdin' the information."

"You don't think it's some setup?" Fults asked.

"He's too dumb for that," Clyde said. "He used to chew the fat with Buck. Practically pointin' to it and lookin' like a smart guy—a hotshot. I'm thinkin' we get Ray and that's three of us for the job. See if it's crap or not."

"What about the people workin' in there?"

"It's only three or so, and one of us holds them off while we crack the safe."

"Whoever's holdin' them has gotta have a gun," Fults said. "I haven't got one."

"Blanche's got Buck's gun," Clyde said. "Used to be Buck's. I'll get it. We've got all the tools we'd need right at the station."

"A heavy hammer and cold chisels, dependin' on what kind of safe it is," Fults said.

"He's sayin' it's a big cash payroll, Ralph. Not somethin' to walk away from."

"I hear you," Fults said. "Let's meet tonight. I'll get Ray. The laws're lookin' all over for him, and talkin' about that, you got your butt just about a stone's throw from this refinery."

"I figure we go in fast and get out," Clyde said. "Head north and out of the state. The three of us can knock off a bank or two, and get raidin' Eastham laid out. Get enough guns and ammo and bust that joint open. I get sick every time I'm thinkin' about the wallopin' we've had, brother. Maybe we'll even wind up shootin' a couple of those sons of bitches."

"I'd like to go through there," Fults said, "shootin' every bastard that laid a club on me or givin' me a goddamn whippin'."

Clyde smiled a little. "Would you do that, Ralph? You think you'd go shoot them screws?"

"Makes me madder'n hell," Ralph said. "That it does."

Clyde kept smiling. "I know what you mean, partner."

Years later, Sinclair would say, "I never told Barrow about a cousin in jail or how Simms could be robbed. He made that up. Barrow got all clever over us talkin', and him askin' me right out how the Simms payroll was delivered and what they did with it until handin' it out, 'cause guys with kids must've been eager as hell to get paid. I told him far as I knew it came in a day or so before payday and was kept in a safe in the company office. I had an idea of what he was thinkin' and I had qualms about passin' to him what I'd heard. I knew about him from his sis and younger brother—even used to see him on Eagle Ford, and I didn't give a damn what he did. I admired him. Clyde was a slick guy and smart, and fancied himself a notorious outlaw. He was smarter than his brother Buck, and I knew he'd never be changin' his ways. Neither of them. I never liked Buck so much, a runt and lookin' like a rat with him seein' you straight on, his narrow eyes squintin'. He wasn't smart. Clyde was different—he was smart. I knew the Parkers, and Bonnie Parker's sis, and I'd say hello to her mom like I'd say hello to Clyde's mom, a skinny old lady tough as any man. She could take a shovel to you. I felt bad for the Barrows, but I knew neither Clyde nor his brother were ever gonna make their folks happy or proud because both of them were born crooks who weren't ever gonna get cured, and Clyde, bein' the smartest one, was bound to kick up the most trouble. I knew what he had in mind about Simms. Only they got a hell of a surprise for all their trouble."

Ralph wanted to know what kind of safe it was, but whatever it was wasn't going to make much difference since he'd bust it either way—chisel or blow it.

Ray Hamilton confessed he knew nothing about breaking into a safe, but was taking on the job as long as he could get enough to get out of Texas. His eyes lit up when he saw the gun Clyde borrowed from Blanche, and he said, "We're splittin' three ways, aren't we? An even split, I take it?"

"Like the fuckin' holy trinity," Ralph said.

"We're poolin' for the raid on Eastham," Clyde said. "This job's for financin' the raid."

"Should be plenty for what we'll need," Ralph said.

Though nodding, Ray didn't look convinced. "Just that I don't know about this raid you're talkin' about. Why are you gonna get a bunch of guys out we don't even know?"

"'Cause that's what we're gonna do," Clyde said. "We'll have us an armed posse that's on the other side, and operatin' like a team. You don't wanna do what we're gonna do? Nobody says you gotta do it, Ray."

"That ain't it," Ray said. "Just no damned money like we should be gettin' for bustin' a safe. I don't even know nothin' about this safe-crackin' business, and we don't have any guys for the team."

"I've told you what I got planned," Clyde said. "You don't have to know any more. Just hold the fuckin' gun on who's there—if anyone's there."

"They'll be there," Ralph said. "We'll take care of them when we get there."

The three struggled cutting the chain link at Simms, sweating until Ralph finally broke through. Clyde felt dumb about the wire cutters, not the grip he intended. The rest of the tools for the job would do.

"What're we gonna do with these people?" Ray whispered.

"We're not gonna do anythin'," Clyde said, "unless they wanna get shot full of holes."

Ray carried the bag of tools through the fence. The car he'd stolen was hidden off Eagle Ford by the tracks, and the three made their way across the refinery grounds.

Once inside the building, they tied bandanas across the lower halves of their faces. Heading to the company office, they encountered a watchman, and Ray said, "Don't move, pop. We got guns." Clyde told the watchman to walk ahead of them as they moved to the office.

Three employees were working the night shift as the three men entered the office. "This is a stickup!" Clyde announced. "Let's open that safe."

One lady cried out, "There isn't any money in here!" She protested opening the safe, told Clyde they couldn't, that only the manager was able to open the safe and that he wasn't due until morning. "But there isn't any money in there tonight."

"You're payin' people tomorrow, right?" Clyde said.

The lady said, "The payroll doesn't come in till morning."

Clyde and Ray tied up two of the hostages and gagged them with hand towels and tape around their faces, while Ralph went to work on the safe, quickly chipping at the tumblers.

Ray, sweating and nervous, made Clyde uneasy. "Stand still and quit peein' in your pants," Clyde told him.

Fifteen minutes later, Ralph had opened the door to the safe and was digging into it. Pulling back, he blinked and said, "It's empty! That lady's right."

Clyde said, "What do you mean 'empty'?"

"Papers and shit. No cash. Not a goddamn dollar."

The bookkeeper cried, "I told you there wasn't any money until tomorrow!"

Clyde peered into the safe. "Let's get outta here," he said.

In the car, Ralph said, "If we gotta shoot anybody, it better be the fuckin' fool tellin' you about a payroll that isn't there. Now we'll have the laws on us and we're broke!"

They drove north, heading for Sherman. With Clyde at the wheel, the car would be in Oklahoma in less than two hours. They needed money. Ray talked about hitting banks. "If Floyd can do it, we can do it."

"Pretty Boy's got a few guys with him," Ralph said, "like what Clyde was talkin' about, and he's got a hell of a lot more ammunition."

"There's three of us," Clyde said. "We'll get all the ammo we need."

"I'm okay with a bank job," Ray said. "I've had enough of petty ante crap, and at least a bank's got money in a fuckin' drawer."

"And a lot more in a safe," Clyde said.

Grunting, Ralph said, "One that ain't empty."

Ray laughed.

They drove all night.

Near dawn, the three abandoned the car in a private driveway, stole another vehicle and crept down an alley behind a hardware store. While Ray sat waiting behind the wheel, Clyde and Ralph entered the store through a rear window.

Within minutes, the trunk of the stolen car was being loaded with shotguns, pistols and boxes of ammunition. They even lifted hunting hats and three mackinaws. By morning they were driving slowly on the icy Missouri streets. The roads proved wrong for a fast getaway. "Ice—snow," Ralph said. "We bog down in here, we'll be back in the joint. Maybe they'll get us sent to Texas and we'll be back in Eastham."

Clyde said. "We'll be goin' there just one more time, and we'll be on the outside of that stinkin' hole—not inside."

"Whatever we're doin', we're splittin' three ways," Ray said. "I don't know what you're expectin' cuttin' loose a bunch of cons that's got no business with us."

"They're gonna have business with us," Clyde said. "We'll get a handful of banks and be sittin' pretty. Should be plenty for what we'll need, and plenty goin' around between us. We get a few guys out you'll be sittin' on that mountain you're always dreamin' about."

An old ex-convict who claimed he knew Ray Hamilton in the Walls said, "That boy never had any serious intent in bustin' fellas out with Barrow and Fults. What the hell for? A gang? Guys at Eastham were a sorrowful lot, and once outta there, they'd be takin' off—gettin' lost. The first job Ray joins up with Barrow and Fults was just a bust—runnin' them outta Texas. They went north, all three of 'em, stopping to knock over a couple small lunch joints and a slew of gas stations. But it was corn money and drinkin' it on the run. Ray stuck with the two because he believed he was a born bank robber, and that's the reason he rode along with Clyde Barrow. He'd never had that experience and Barrow was keen on this kind of doin's. Knockin' over small stuff, small joints, was just to keep gas in the cars and for grub, long as you're runnin' on the road. Ray later on told me about women he was chasin' while the three of them bedded down in hotels or flops around Missouri and Kansas, and up in the south part of Nebraska. He bragged he'd had a gorgeous redhead in Lincoln, but Clyde chased her outta their camp, sayin' she had a mouth as big as her milk-jug tits, and no brains in her head. Ray said he didn't care about brains in a broad. Clyde warned him if he chased and bragged to tramps with twats as big as their mouths, they'd wind up back in Eastham.

"Ray's trouble was he thought of himself as a ladies' man. He wanted to have the same thinkin' as Clyde, but Clyde didn't have any care about any other girl except the one he had, though how much is gospel I'd have no idea.

"Clyde was a prude, Ray said—wasn't after any women and claimed he had all he wanted waitin' for him in West Dallas, and sayin' how eager he was to be there soon as things blew over. What he meant was the job they'd tried in East Dallas that'd got them on the road goin' north—too far from Texas.

"Hamilton wanted the dough they'd be pullin' in from hittin' a few small banks and joints, like he was after doin' more than one job in a day. Makin' a heyday of it since he didn't see himself in any long partnership with Clyde and Fults. I gather Ray was hoardin' what he could so he could live high on the hog soon's he took off, movin' to jobs on his own, or with a partner where Ray wasn't low man on a pole. Ray had ideas about bein' a top man, but he told me Clyde's always the top man, and somehow you knew that's what he was.

"So the story goes that food poisonin' hit Ray in Oklahoma and laid him up shittin' all over while Clyde and Fults pulled a job that brought in nearly six grand. Ray said Fults wasn't keen on divvyin' the score, but Clyde insisted on Ray gettin' his share because, as Clyde put it—and this is accordin' to Ray—the same could be true the other way around if Clyde or Fults took a sick shit and couldn't stick it out.

"Back on the road, the three got as far as Minnesota, but the ice caused problems. They took flophouse rooms while casin' jobs, or on the move, the wheels never seemin' to stop. Ray admired Clyde's knack for handlin' almost any kind of car, though he was partial to Fords with the big V-8 engines. Sometimes he drove with one shoe off the foot he'd lost those toes on."

While Ray was laid up with food poisoning, Clyde and Fults snaked through the city grabbing what they could. They hit one small bank, and a lawman said, "Two men, armed to the teeth and lookin' mean as badgers, but smooth and fast, totin' shotguns beneath their overcoats, and pistols in their pockets. Sweepin' through so quick they were in and out fast as flies you're tryin' to swat, and you weren't even sure what they'd done."

They drove, sleeping in shifts or laying over in cornfields when none of them could stay awake. "Ray said they did one more job together," the ex-con recalled, "and it brought a few hundred they split up. Ray said he'd had enough, was off for Michigan where his father lived. That's how it went, Ray said, Clyde and Fults talkin' all the time about their raidin' Eastham, and Ray said he got sick of hearin' it—damn near as sick as he'd been shittin' out that poison. Finally comin' to a showdown, Ray said he told Clyde he had no desire to get himself shot full of holes freein' a bunch of bums he didn't give a shit about. He said Clyde just looked at him cold—his eyes like ice cubes—and said, 'No hard feelin's, pal.'

"The big coincidence was that later, Clyde—and Bonnie—got Ray outta Eastham in the cockeyed raid, so Ray once again hooked up with Clyde. He says Clyde told him, 'I was so pissed off at you, I scribbled your name on a ten-gauge shell and planned on stickin' the barrel straight up your ass....'

"There's been more than a few who've said Barrow was like a dog that gets hold of your leg and never lets go. Couple or so years later, not long before Ray got sent to the electric chair, I heard that Ray told a guy after gettin' back with Clyde—after Clyde and Bonnie had busted him outta Eastham—that Ray had a fling with Bonnie and was jokin' that Clyde never knew about it. Ray was sayin', 'I got it over on Clyde, and Bonnie done fucked like a monkey on a bed of bananas.'

"Now, it's safe to say that kind of talk was very dangerous, and would certainly have bought Ray that ten-gauge shell emptied up his ass and straight out the top of his head—that is, if the law hadn't already fried him in the chair. You could only put limited stock in any of Ray's talkin', especially his braggin' to do with females. He'd had his share of nickel and dimers, and maybe a looker or two chucked in, but lyin' about Bonnie Parker was signin' your own death warrant. And if Clyde wasn't about to fill Ray full of holes for the liar he was, I believe Bonnie herself, who'd never shot a soul her whole life, would've taken up the shotgun and blown Ray's head clean off his shoulders."

Blanche and her husband, Buck Barrow, "on the run" with Bonnie & Clyde.

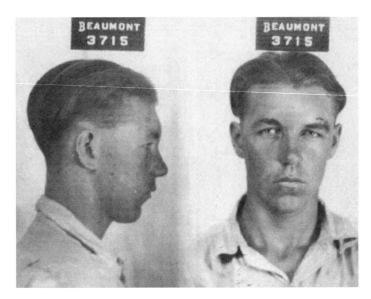

Busted in Beaumont. W.D. Jones, called "boy" by Clyde, joins Bonnie & Clyde, often sleeping in the same bed with both of them.

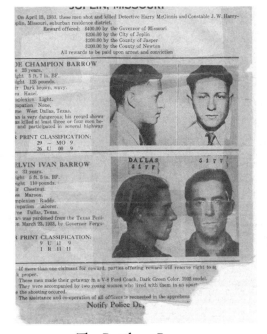

JOPLIN, MISSOURI

On April 13, 1933, these men shot and killed Detective Harry McGinnis and Constable J. W. Harry-
oplin, Missouri, suburban residence district.

Reward offered: $400.00 by the Governor of Missouri
$200.00 by the City of Joplin
$200.00 by the County of Jasper
$200.00 by the County of Newton
All rewards to be paid upon arrest and conviction

DE CHAMPION BARROW
e 23 years.
ight 5 ft. 7 in. BF.
ight 125 pounds.
ir Dark brown, wavy.
es Hazel.
nplexion Light.
upation None,
me West Dallas, Texas.
an is very dangerous; his record shows
as killed at least three or four men be-
and participated in several highway

PRINT CLASSIFICATION:
29 – MO 9
26 U 00 9

ELVIN IVAN BARROW
e 31 years.
ight 5 ft. 5 in. BF.
ight 110 pounds.
r Chestnut.
es Maroon.
nplexion Ruddy.
upation laborer.
ne Dallas, Texas.
an was pardoned from the Texas Peni-
in March 23, 1933, by Governor Fergu-

PRINT CLASSIFICATION:
9 U 11 9
I R 11 11

DALLAS
6177

If more than one claimant for reward, parties offering reward will reserve right to a
k proper.
These men made their getaway in a V-8 Ford Coach, Dark Green Color, 1932 model.
They were accompanied by two young women who lived with them in an apart
e the shooting occured.
The assistance and co-operation of all officers is requested in the apprehens

Notify Police De,

The Brothers Barrow.

W. D. and Bonnie. He said, "I call her Sis, but she's better'n any sis could ever be."

Above: Clyde Barrow, hero to W.D., beside him;
Below: W.D. and Clyde in desperado poses.

Thomas Persell, a Missouri motorcycle cop and Clyde's "kidnapped" captive, enjoying a nap on the floor of the rear seat.

W.D.'s shutter mishap of an unposed Clyde, showing Persell's nickel-plated gun as a hood ornament.

W.D. posing before a small part of Clyde's arsenal.

Buck and Blanche, still acting the newlyweds.

Joplin, Missouri, apartment and garages; two weeks off the road before a major shootout.

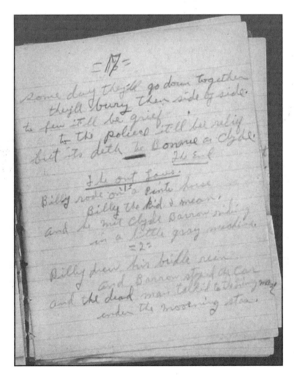

One of Bonnie's notebooks; her writings and poems.

Blanche Barrow: "Everything that happened just happened. You run and keep runnin' until you hit the end of the line."

Red Crown Tavern, Platte City, Missouri: the scene of another gun battle with the law.

Clyde with his two BARs (holding one) and sawed-off shotgun.

Hiding out in Dexfield Park, Iowa, 1933. "Campin' we called it, until the laws started firin' at us."

Blanche being restrained after Dexfield Park shootout.

Buck lies mortally wounded on the ground.

Blanche, arrested, handcuffed, and on her way
to the lockup.

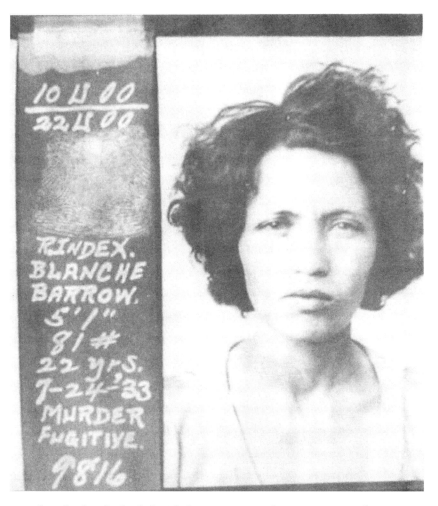

Blanche booked while Clyde, Bonnie and W.D. stay on the run.

Buck, with head bandaged, led away after being captured at Dexfield Park.

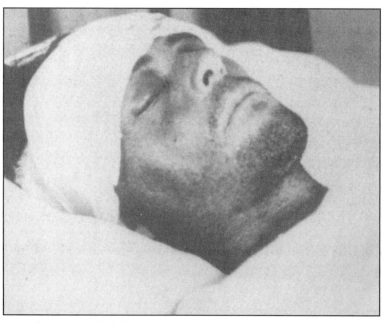

Buck Barrow didn't make it. Death in a Perry, Iowa hospital.

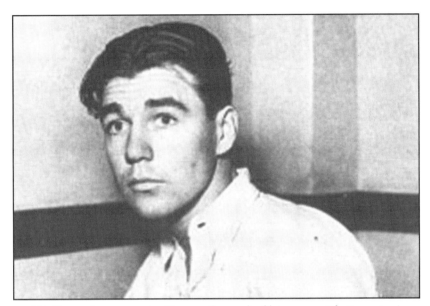

W. D. under arrest in Texas, the end of his run with Bonnie &
Clyde. He would quickly tell a different story to the Dallas police.

On the last secret family
meeting, Bonnie's
frailness was alarming.
She said, "The end
is comin'."

A clandestine family meeting. Top row from left: Billie Jean, Clyde, Cumie, and L. C. Barrow. Bottom row from left: Marie Barrow, Emma Parker, and Bonnie.

Clyde posing solo at family get-together (note hat covering license plate).

*Ambushed by the law, Clyde switched cars after both he and
Bonnie were shot in the legs.*

*Trunk of the stolen coupe was crowded with stolen license
plates, ammunition, clothes, and Bonnie's magazines.*

Bonnie posing at being "armed and ready" with one of the many stolen cars.

With Henry Methvin, after Clyde's raid on Eastham prison farm.

*The Grapevine, Texas scene of the killings by Henry Methvin,
for which Clyde & Bonnie are blamed.*

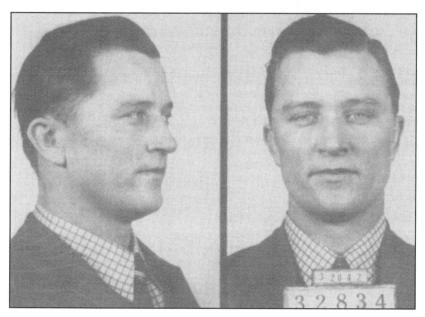

Henry Methvin, Texas and Oklahoma killer.

Eleven

With Ray Hamilton having hightailed it north, Clyde and Ralph headed back through Texas to "corral a team," as Ralph put it, acknowledging Clyde's determination for staging the raid on Eastham. Later, he said, "Clyde was a fanatic about an assault. Havin' spent my time in that rat hole, I could see his wantin' to get back at those bastards, as risky as it was to be a sittin' duck unless you had a helluva lot of surplus at your back."

What was needed was artillery, and Clyde knew where to find it. He talked about the hardware and gun supply in the town of Kaufman. "I've been in there," he told Ralph. "Seen what they've got. It's what we need, and the extras we'll stash."

Ralph said, "His plan was to make a run from Dallas to Tyler, get rid of the car we're drivin', and grab two big ones—heavy, fast cars—get 'em in Tyler that night. A lot of fancy people had big cars sittin', then we'd swing back and grab the guns in Kaufman. At around that same time, Ted Rogers and the other boys holin' up in Lake Dallas are hittin' Celina for weapons—the same we're doin' in Kaufman. Clyde's seen the stock—ammo crates stacked in back. We'll have two four-door cars with big trunks and floors, and a lot of room for company."

While Clyde was planning "the run for guns" and the trip to Eastham, Bonnie had been telling her mother about a job at a cosmetic company "way west of Dallas," and that very morning she was going in for work. "Gettin' a lift with a friend," she said. Hugging her mother, she said she'd get in touch with her later, and then hurried away for the meeting with her "friend" (who had nothing to do with a cosmetic company "way west of Dallas").

"When it gets dark," Clyde told Ralph, "we'll get the cars, you takin' one and me and Bonnie in the other." Though he fancied Ford V-8 sedans, he said they needed more room for guns and ammo and the guys' break from Eastham. All part of a "strategy," he said. "The guns in Kaufman and in Celina were enough to stock a small army. We hit Eastham and keep goin' the rest of the year."

Bonnie was driven to the prison, posing as a cousin to Clyde's old friend, Aubrey. Waiting with the other visitors, she tried to look meek, though giving a smile to the guards.

Seeing Aubrey, she told him of Clyde's plan, where pistols in paper sacks would be stashed, and where cars would be waiting for the getaway. "Clyde's been studyin' weather bulletins," she said. "He's countin' on fog. Says soon as you're marched out in the field, you'll get a fix on where the guns are, and when the ruckus starts, you'll make a break for the cars. He says he'll be givin' you cover, and for you to shoot over the guards' heads. He says you'll hear the horns blowin'." At the end of the visit, she left Eastham with the other visitors.

Late the following afternoon, Bonnie made her way to the Star Service Station, and spent time with Clyde's sister Marie, letting her know Clyde was sending his love to her and the family. Bonnie said, "He wants to see all of us soon. Gotta be in a place where he won't be seen."

"What about you?" Marie asked. "You've been with him so much, do you know if the laws know who you are?"

"They know nothin' about me," Bonnie said. "I've done nothin' to be in trouble over, unless the laws say lovin' a fella who's wanted by 'em is now a criminal offense."

Marie said, "Far as I know, I haven't heard any new laws sayin' you're not allowed to love whoever you please—as long as you personally aren't part of the goin's on."

"It's a plain mystery to me," Bonnie said. "I just shut it out of my thinkin'."

Marie gave a knowing smile. "Clyde's very persuasive, isn't he? What you're sayin' is the best way to be, so just shut it all out."

"You know how I'm feelin'," Bonnie said. "You know I can't see any other way for anythin' to be other than what it is."

"Come on, baby," Clyde said. "We got us a load of shoppin' to do." As Bonnie climbed in alongside Clyde, Ralph was smiling from the rear seat, and biting into a banana. Soon as Clyde was rolling south, Ralph tossed the banana skin out the window, followed by the wrapper from a candy bar. He broke the bar in half and passed a hunk to Bonnie. Munching at it, she said, "What I'm starvin' for is a stack of buckwheat cakes, poured all over with hot maple syrup and meltin' butter."

"Lord, that sounds good," Ralph said. "I'm starvin' myself, and this ain't fillin' me."

"We'll do all our eatin' soon as we get rid of what we're drivin'," Clyde said. "And get us two others before we hit Kaufman."

"Almost dark," Ralph said. "Damn clouds've been dark all afternoon. Supposed to rain?"

Clyde said, "What if it does? I'm not in any rush for rain, but don't want any laws sniffin' behind us."

It took less than thirty minutes in the town of Tyler. First to get another car—a Buick sedan, parked in the driveway of the Tyler Rest Home. Blocks later, they abandoned the car they had been driving, gathered the tools needed, and rode in the Buick until Clyde spotted a Chrysler on a dark street. "There's a beauty!" Ralph said.

Clyde got out, looking up. "It's startin' to rain. That's good. You take this one, and Bonnie can stay with you. Go on ahead now and I'll follow you." As Clyde crossed the street, Ralph turned the Buick north and cruised slowly on the dark street.

Bonnie poked at the windshield. "It is rainin'," she said. "People're gonna go hide in their houses." In a matter of seconds, Clyde was behind the wheel of the Chrysler. He had the car started and closed in on the Buick, the windshield wipers wagging back and forth.

When the two cars reached Kaufman, Ralph slowed to the curb on Main Street, letting Clyde take the lead in the Chrysler. The town was quiet, the roads deserted, shops closed and doors locked. Another block and Clyde turned the corner. He abruptly headed into an alley, his headlights off. Ralph followed slowly, and stopped behind the Chrysler. He rolled down the window as Clyde came to the car. "Let's go," he told Ralph, and said to Bonnie, "You see someone, you lay low, and stay down."

Minutes passed while Ralph jimmied the shop's rear door. Out of the corner of his eye Clyde caught a glint of metal, then saw the shadow of a man at the rear of the Buick. In a second, the flashlight beam hit Ralph and Clyde. "We're spotted!" Clyde said. He drew out his pistol and was about to fire into the air above the shadow, but the flashlight suddenly fell to the ground, the beam jumping. Whoever had been holding the flashlight had dropped it and ran.

Bonnie was still hunched down on the seat, but sat up and said, "I could see him—it was a watchman. Some kind of uniform."

"We won't have time to get in there," Clyde told Ralph. "Better get the hell out. You take the Chrysler—" Ralph jumped when a bell started ringing.

"That's the town bell," Clyde said. "Let's go!"

What followed was a desperate race to get out of Kaufman. They sped north on the main street only to find it blocked by what looked like a posse—a few men standing in the road with shotguns. Clyde turned, tires screeching in the dirt and gravel, and raced away in the opposite direction—gunshots tailing them.

In minutes, more armed men appeared on the street. They parked two pickup trucks nose to nose, blocking the road. Soon as Clyde saw the trucks, he skidded into a turn, floored the gas. Ralph drove an about-face so sharp two wheels slid and the car almost tipped to one side. In moments he caught up to Clyde, and followed close behind, the speedometer bouncing at eighty.

The rain, now heavy, pounded at the dirt road, quickly turning it to mud. A torrent beat at the windshield so hard Bonnie could barely see the road ahead. "It's gonna flood!" she cried. "We're headin' into a swamp!"

Fishtailing, the Buick suddenly slid to the right, Clyde fighting the skid, but a heavy thump jarred and stalled the car. "We're in a hole!" he said. The Chrysler veered into the same mud and slid so abruptly the car half-turned around, stalled with steam shooting from the grill. Ralph threw open the door and got out, cursing that the car wouldn't start again. He slipped, almost fell but grabbed at the rear of the Buick for balance. "Son of a bitch!" he yelled, seeing headlights back on the road. "They're comin' after us!"

"We're stuck," Clyde said. "This fucker's in a hole."

"What're we gonna do? This rain's rotten."

Clyde tried several times to start the car without success. "Gotta get out and find us another car," he said. "Let's go," he said to Bonnie.

They trudged in the rain and mud, their feet sticking, slopping in the muck of the bottomland. Bonnie pulled off her shoes, saying, "I can't walk without losin' my shoes—like I'm in quicksand!"

"No damn solid ground," Clyde said, "but we gotta keep goin'. Those fellas are at the cars. We made us a roadblock, but gotta find another damn car."

Struggling ankle-deep in the mud, Ralph said, "I see a house way over there. See the light the other side of that field?"

They reached the house, Bonnie soaked, shaking, wet with mud splattered to her knees. She stood alongside Clyde, breathing hard. With his gun in hand, he rapped on the door. Waited. He rapped again. Another minute and an older man opened the door.

"Holy lord!" he said, seeing Clyde's gun. He stepped back, one hand at his chest. "Y'all gonna shoot me? What in the name of heaven y'all wanna shoot me for?"

"Not here to hurt anyone, sir," Clyde said. "Just gotta have a car— or a truck or what you've got. We gotta get outta here."

"I sure hate sayin' it, son, but there's no car or truck. I'm out here in a field, so you better go to the road yonder—" Looking at the mud on their legs, and at Bonnie holding her shoes, the man said, "Seein' you're on foot, I reckon best I can do for you is offer you a pair of mules."

"Mules?" Ralph said. "What're we gonna do with mules?"

"They'll get y'all to the road," the man said, "less'n you wander out in those woods."

"Where's the mules?" Clyde asked.

"Two out back. Just own the pair. Two of you get on the bigger one, and they'll hold you up alright."

Bonnie asked, "What do we do with them when we get to the road?"

"You turn 'em loose, ma'am. They'll know their way back. Smarter'n most folks, not meanin' y'all or myself." She asked if they had names, and the man said, "Bigger one's Sonny. He'll take you to the road." With the rain still falling, Clyde straddled the larger wet mule, and then pulled Bonnie up behind him into a slippery side-saddle position. The mule grunted, chugged forward, its hooves pushing deep into the mud. Ralph was on the smaller mule, squinting in the rain as the mule followed close behind. The farmer called after them, "Hope y'all get where you're goin'!"

Ralph grunted, "I think I'm nuts. Never been sittin' on a mule in my life."

"Better than drownin' in mud," Bonnie said.

"Or runnin' into those hicks," Clyde said. Bonnie pressed her cheek against his back, her arms locked around him as the mules plodded ahead in the rain, through the mud and past stumps of broken trees.

Twelve

They made it to the road, aching and angry. Bonnie's eyes were closed, Clyde's wide open, searching for houses and another car. Nothing. Soaked, off the mule's back and shaking from the cold, Bonnie stroked the big mule's muzzle, bidding goodbye to the smaller mule as well.

Staying close to the edge of the road, the three walked for several minutes, finally spotting an old house, no lights showing in the windows. A faded blue coupe sat parked to the side of the house, and Clyde hurried across the road. He forced open the car door, climbed in behind the wheel and in a few moments had the engine running, then backed the car onto the road. Bonnie climbed in, shivering, then Ralph, all three on the front seat. "Are you freezin', honey?" Clyde asked. She nodded, pressing herself against his side. "We're gettin' outta here," he said.

Accelerating, the car skidded in the mud, grabbed traction, and belched forward, heading south.

"Shows no gas," Clyde said. "Lights don't work worth shit."

As she again removed her shoes, Bonnie said maybe the gauges were broken. "Whole car seems broken," she said, "and it's gettin' into morning soon. A couple hours more before it starts gettin' light. Maybe we'll find a fillin' station."

"Not out here," Ralph said. "We're gettin' into Kemp. We'll find somethin' there."

Shortly, Clyde was driving slowly onto the main street of Kemp. "Somethin's wrong," he said. "Somethin' no damn good."

Several men with guns were gathered on the street. They saw the car. "They're lookin' right at us," Ralph said. "They're yellin'! Hear 'em?"

Clyde increased his speed as Ralph turned on the seat, looking back. "They're runnin'," he said. "Wavin' at some other guys—"

"—they're comin' after us," Clyde said, gripping the wheel and flooring the gas pedal. The car raced ahead but the engine seemed to be belching—chugging.

"Jesus Christ…." Ralph said. "What the hell's the matter? These hicks mean business!" He faced front, shaking again. A mile—a mile and a half. The car chugged worse, sputtered, coasted for a distance then died.

"Bastard's out of gas," Clyde said, rolling to a stop against the side of the road. He angrily threw open the door. "Get out! Come on! We gotta get another car. Those sons of bitches'll be on us."

"There are no cars out on any road!" Bonnie cried. "We're in the middle of nowhere." She bent down, and pushed her feet back into her muddy shoes. Clyde put an arm around her. "Come on, honey. We don't wanna be hanged from one of these trees."

"No houses—no cars," Ralph said.

"Keep off the road," Clyde told him.

"I'm freezin'," Bonnie said. "I think I'm sick…."

"We gotta get to the other side of these woods," Clyde said. "We'll get a car."

"They're comin' for us," Ralph said. "They'll find that car and we're stuck."

"There's nothin' anywhere," Bonnie said.

Ralph said, "We're walkin' targets."

"We get way in the woods," Clyde said, "but if they get their dogs we can't do much hidin'."

Ralph started to speak again, but stopped. They could hear the sound of cars on the road where they'd left the car. One car kept driving on the road in the direction Clyde had been heading.

"Keep goin'!" Clyde said, pulling Bonnie. "We gotta run!"

As they hurried, half stumbling, they could hear the sounds of others somewhere in the woods. Then lights—cars had turned against the road's edge, their headlights shining into the woods. The three kept going, as did those in pursuit. Bonnie said, "I hear water. I can smell it. There's water here—a creek!" Almost collapsing, she sat on the ground. Ralph knelt down, breathing hard.

Still standing, Clyde said, "This creek's runnin' through here, so we get on the other side of it. Ain't a good feelin' waitin' for them to get dogs! We'll have a fuckin' hard time, so let's get movin'." Helping Bonnie to her feet, he said, "Come on, baby!" She was shaking.

"You got any more ammo in your pockets?" Ralph asked.

"I got mostly nothin'!" Clyde said. "This is a pickle I don't like."

After wading across the creek, the three hiked a distance deeper into the wooded area. They stopped, Bonnie gasping. She sat on the ground again. "I can't breathe," she said. Ralph had a handkerchief and handed it to Bonnie. Clyde waved for both to be quiet. He was listening, smelling the air. "I hear those fellas comin'."

Ralph said, "I don't hear 'em."

Bonnie listened. "They're behind us," she said.

"Comin' right on our tail," Clyde said. They moved a few yards away and crouched behind a fallen log. Clyde checked the clip of his .45. "I got three shots left," he said.

Ralph said, "What're we gonna do?"

"Shoot what you've got over their heads," Clyde said. "Maybe scare 'em back."

Bonnie laughed a little. "They aren't gonna scare."

"What if she's right?" Ralph said.

Clyde looked at him. "We stay behind this log, layin' low. They're gonna know where we are and be dumpin' all they got on us."

"Oh, God," Bonnie said, "pretty soon the damn sun'll be up."

Settling in tight behind the log, Clyde told Ralph, "You take a shot above 'em soon as they're at the creek. We don't want 'em gettin' on top of us."

Ralph checked his gun again. "Okay—soon as you say."

"Don't hit any of 'em," Clyde warned. "You don't want to nail any hick's brother and get us hanged right here."

A fast few minutes and Ralph raised up from behind the log, aimed into the tree across the creek and squeezed off a round.

The first gunshot from the men thundered into the log. "Stay down!" Clyde said. "Fuckin' shotgun."

More gunfire followed, cutting at the rotten wood above their heads. Clyde returned a shot, Ralph followed with two more. "They're pluggin' right at us," Ralph said. "Gonna blast this fuckin' log away from between us. They're spreadin' out—gettin' ready for the kill." He fired again but went flat on the ground, groaning painfully. "I'm hit!" he said. "Son of a bitch!"

"Where're you hit?" Clyde asked.

"Right arm. I'm bleedin' bad."

More shots zinged above them or plunked hard into the log. Clyde crawled to look at Ralph's arm. He said, "Gone straight through, buddy. Scraped past your side, too. Just pinch those holes shut. I'm gonna make a break and get past these fellas. You both lay low and I'll get some help—"

"—no!" Bonnie said. "What help? We can't even see 'em."

"They aren't gonna nail me," Clyde said. He kissed her as gunfire stormed above them. "They're shootin' for the hell of it. Soon as I'm outta here I'll get us a car, and they won't do nothin' to you 'cause you've done nothin'. Now listen, honey, you tell 'em we've held you kidnapped—a hostage." To Ralph he said, "Tell 'em it was me who kidnapped her. Make up a name. They got more guns than us and if they hit me, you see to it they finish me off—or else you do it if you got a shell." He held Bonnie and said, "You don't even know us 'cause we kidnapped you. You don't even know our names. They don't hear no more shootin' from us, so they're comin' over."

He kissed Bonnie. "Do what I told you—you'll be okay." Without saying more, Clyde crawled away from the log, through the brush and crouched down until the firing stopped. Men were reloading, and Clyde made a run directly towards the shooters. In seconds, he made his way between the men spreading out, turned south and ran parallel to the road.

When the firing stopped, Ralph told Bonnie, "You yell out now, 'cause we've had it here. Get up and holler at 'em not to shoot 'cause you been kidnapped. You tell 'em whatever you think up to bust you clear of me'n' Clyde."

Bonnie nodded, then slowly raised her hands, reaching above the top of the log, hoping they wouldn't shoot her. "Don't shoot no more!" she called out. "Don't shoot! I'm standin' up!" She stood quickly with her open hands raised. "Help me! You got these boys—this one's been hit." Pointing north, she said, "The other one snuck off that way. I don't know who they are but all you men have saved me!"

Two or three started across the creek, their weapons poised. As they approached the log, Bonnie said, "They wouldn't let me loose! Were gonna use me as a hostage and sell me to white slavers!"

One of the men looked down at Ralph who said, "I've been shot!" The man pushed the muzzle of the shotgun against Ralph's neck.

"Shot or not," he said, "you get on your feet, slow with those hands comin' up, and leave that gun where it lay."

"I can't move my arm," Ralph said. "It's shot through."

Another man got hold of Bonnie while a third grabbed Ralph's gun from the ground. "Where's the other fella?" he asked. "There were three of you. Where'd he go?"

"He ran over that way when this one got shot," she said. "I already thought you'd caught him." The men looked around at each other. None knew where the third man had disappeared to.

The man with the shotgun said, "One of you go get Fred and Clem and track that other one. He goes any further like she's sayin' he won't be goin' nowhere."

"He just snuck off and ran that way," Bonnie said, pointing in the opposite direction Clyde had taken. "They've been holdin' me captive, sayin' they'd shoot me if I hollered! It's been terrible! This one that's been shot tried to let me loose but the other one—he's the bad one, wouldn't let me loose. He said he'd shoot my my head off!" She began to cry.

Thirteen

With no way of getting to Ralph or Bonnie until the laws had them locked up, and chameleon that he was, Clyde had slithered past the posse and made his way back to an alley in Kemp, shaking from cold and fatigue. He stole the first vehicle he could find, an older gasoline truck, loaded with fuel and ready to roll.

Fearing they'd soon spot the stolen truck, as soon as he reached the small, half-abandoned community of Peeltown, without delay Clyde ditched the tanker behind a deserted barn, stole a Ford sedan and headed north, pushing the gas pedal almost against the floorboard.

Arriving in Dallas, he made his cautious way to Eagle Ford, and then to his folks' gas station. He found his younger brother asleep on a couch, and shook him awake. L.C. stared at Clyde for moments, then rubbed his eyes and said, "What the hell you doin' here? Damn laws've been around half a dozen times. Where's Bonnie?"

"That's what I'm here to talk about, brother," Clyde said. "She isn't with me 'cause she's in jail. I reckon they got her in that mousetrap in Kemp, but I figure they'll be takin' her and Ralph to Kaufman."

"They got Ralph?"

"Damned near got us all, but I busted loose. I wanted to get Bonnie and Ralph outta there, but the fuckin' hicks beat me to it. I wanna get word to Bonnie and Ralph about gettin' them outta there, but I can't go walkin' into that jail."

"Blanche is out back," L.C. said. "I'll get her. She'll know what to do."

"Where's Mom and Pop?" Clyde asked.

"They've gone across to Dallas. I shouldn't've been sleepin'."

"Well, wake up and go get Blanche."

Clyde sat on the couch and closed his eyes. His head ached. His legs ached. He realized it was the first time he'd sat still in days. Bonnie wasn't with him. They'd taken her in. They'd separated them, like some part of one being pulled loose from the rest, and everything left shaking to get back together.

The back door opened and Blanche hurried in. "Clyde!" she said. "Be careful bein' here, Clyde. A pair of fat-assed deputies've been stickin' their noses in and outta doors and windows." L.C. was behind her. "They got Bonnie and Ralph?" she asked.

"Those bottoms outta Kemp—was a fuckin' swamp. She's tellin' 'em she's been kidnapped," Clyde said. "She was gonna tell 'em she don't even know us—just fellas who nabbed her. They don't know nothin' about me or where I'd taken off to, but I want to get 'em out—bust 'em outta that jail—"

"—don't do it!" Blanche blurted out. "You'll get a heap of trouble for Bonnie. They'll put it all together—you and her. You don't wanna do that, Clyde. Not to mention gettin' yourselves shot! What're they gonna do to her? Why're they holdin' her for?"

"I reckon till they figure it out," he said. "She won't let on."

"She's got no warrants on her," Blanche said. "She's done nothin' so she can walk anywhere, and nobody's been tyin' her to you. They got no cause to hold her, but bustin' her out before they let her go's the worst that could happen."

Clyde sat for a few moments, then nodded, "You're right, Blanche. I'm just knocked out. Leave her sit till they let her loose. But damnit, I want her to know what's best, and I want her to know I'm out here lovin' her and doin' what I can to see she's gonna be free. She's probably in Kaufman, so you go see her right away, and tell her how much I love her."

Blanche said, "I'll tell her how you're frettin', but she don't need me tellin' her how much you love her, but I'll tell her you'll be sayin' it to her soon enough."

As soon as he switched plates on the Peeltown Ford, Clyde sped north to the Lake Dallas hideout, eager to hear how the action went in Celina. He hid the car a distance from the abandoned shack, and went looking for Jack and the others. Finding Ted Rogers, then Johnny, he asked, "Where's Jack? Where's the other guys?"

Jack and Johnny, a pair of young local bad boys, were eager to go into manhood, gun-barrel first. They were usable, Clyde knew. They'd do whatever he said, and try to squeeze as much as they could out of it, whatever it was. They were as equally resentful of one another as they were of cops and posses. All anyone needed, they reasoned, was a gun.

"They should've been back by now," Ted said. "Truth is, I don't know where they've been, sure as hell not to Celina. Johnny and me are just waitin', doin' nothin' till somethin's ready."

"What happened in Celina?" Clyde asked.

Ted was reluctant to say it, but then told Clyde they'd failed to carry out the plan of getting any guns. "They took off, and me'n' Johnny—just the two of us, we figured we couldn't do it alone."

Impatient and angry, Clyde said they had to do it now—Ted and Johnny joining him. "The three of us," he said. He had to have guns now. Without the weapons, it was suicide. "We'll have to hit Celina tonight."

Ted looked at Johnny, then back at Clyde. "Tonight?" he asked.

"Tonight!" Clyde said. "We do it tonight!"

An ex-Dallas, long-retired lawman remembers what he learned of the determination, the "fierceness," as he called it, of the head of "that small gang," and how "nothin' was gonna get in the path of that fellow's notions." Twenty-two years old in 1932, the ex-lawman says, "I wanted to wear the badge proud, but I didn't get caught up in that mess directly. Nobody knew who it was back then, but later learnin' the one in the lead was Clyde Barrow. What there was of it was all over and a long time passin' before we even knew that, though the town's deputy sheriff was in the thick of it. Had the keys to his automobile swiped from under him, so he couldn't do any chasin'. They came right into town to rob for guns. Knew what they were after and where they were goin', which was right at those guns at the hardware store. I s'pose whatever else they grabbed, as well.

"It was pretty late, I understand, and we had a watchman on the street. He was asked by one of the three for some directions, and soon as he opened his mouth to give 'em the directions, he got whacked on the head. Got his billfold, a few dollars, and his pistol taken. Even took his flashlight.

"It was late, sometime after midnight, and the mayor was just co-min' out of a get-together, had a couple guests with him, and these three boys took all of them, includin' the watchman, at gunpoint. Went across the road a stone's throw from the railroad yard, and robbed the mayor of whatever was in his pockets and his billfold, and his watch, and robbed his companions. Then the boys got them all into a railroad boxcar, the watchman, too, just like they were sheep. Slid that big door shut and throwin' the lock on tight.

"The gang had busted into the drugstore, took a pile of medicines and first-aid stuff—scissors and tape and the like—then raided the hardware store. They gathered up about every pistol, shotgun, and rifle in sight, and what must've been a wheelbarrow of ammunition. Even stole a few flashlights and some tools, and from what I under-stood, soon as they were back on the street they swiped the keys out of the sheriff's car to keep him from comin' after them. They rolled right outta town in a car that was stolen.

"They didn't shoot anybody, worse they did was bang a knot on the watchman's head, but they sure did some lootin'. A long time later was it figured that the town'd been hit by the Barrow gang, though it was only Clyde Barrow that they got a fix on. A little guy, but had the determination of a bulldog. Never figured who the oth-er two were. Catchin' them? Catchin' Barrow?" The retired lawman laughed. "No sir. No such luck. Like he was invisible. Half the town here and the county was expectin' him comin' back for an encore."

Back in the woods surrounding the Lake Dallas hideout, Clyde,

Rogers, and Johnny spent half a day manufacturing hiding places for the loot they'd brought from Celina.

They also tried out a few of the new weapons, firing them by the lakeside. After a few rounds, Clyde said, "Someone's gonna hear these shots. No more shootin'. Ain't no huntin' in here."

For the next two hours, the three men split open automobile inner tubes to wrap the guns before concealing them beneath stacks of branches and leaves. They carefully lined the ammo inside an old truck tire which they half-buried in a deserted shack behind the house. Believing they had successfully camouflaged the loot, Clyde planned to sit back, share a couple beers, and talk about busting into Eastham. He now had the firepower to do it. But instead of launching into plans for the raid, his ears perked up and he half stood. "I hear a car," he said. Then more than one car. "Get outta here!" he ordered. "It's the fuckin' laws!" All three ran for the woods.

Several deputies were on foot, their weapons drawn. Others searched the grounds around the house, quickly discovering the hidden weapons.

"Son of a bitch!" Clyde muttered.

Another car was approaching. Lawmen were at the front and rear of the house, unaware of the three who were hiding in the woods. Rogers said, "That's Jack comin'—that's the—" Clyde whispered for him to shut up. Three deputies surrounded the car. Jack and Fuzz, the last members of the gang, were handcuffed. Two other lawmen discovered the Ford that Clyde had left a distance from the house.

Clyde said to Rogers, "Come on—let's get outta here before they know there's more of us," and took after Johnny who'd hid deeper into the woods.

Fourteen

Broke and the Lake Dallas hideout raided, Clyde told Ted and Johnny they'd have to plan some fast action as they were almost hitting bottom. He told Ted, "You keep your shirt coverin' the butt of that rod in your pants. First car we see we gotta get it. Let's go."

The three stayed off the road while following it until they reached a roadside diner. "Gimme that gun," Clyde said. He took it from Ted and pushed it into the waist of his pants, then handed Ted some crumpled bills. "Go on inside and get us somethin' to eat. Some sandwiches or somethin', and soda pops. Me'n' Johnny'll be out here around the side of the joint."

Clyde and Johnny lit up the last two cigarettes from Johnny's pack, with one left over that Clyde stuck into his shirt pocket as he eyed the three cars parked in the shade. Johnny said, "You wanna hop one of these rides right here?"

Shaking his head, Clyde said, "No. They've been lookin' at Ted in there. That's why we're out here."

When Ted joined them with a sack of sandwiches and two soda pops, he said, "Wasn't enough dough for three soda pops. I drank some water so you guys split the soda pops."

They walked further, avoiding the road. When they came across several houses, Clyde handed the soda pop bottle to Ted and said, "We're gonna get that Ford." He whispered, "Don't say a fuckin' thing or make noise. We'll push it down the road a ways; you jump your asses in soon as it kicks over."

Sticking to the narrow dirt roads, Clyde pressed on the gas, the Ford bucking over holes. He said, "We're gonna head around Fort

Worth to Hillsboro. This old guy named Bucher runs a store there. They had a kid I knew, but I don't think they're gonna 'member me. Been a long time. We'll be goin' in to look around. I don't know if they've moved stuff around, these old fuckin' places don't do much movin' of stuff, 'specially a big standin' safe. You'll see what they got behind the counter. You guys nose around. He's got all sorts of shit from huntin' knives to guitars. We'll come back later on and clean that safe out."

The Hillsboro store was on a country road, a part of the Bucher house. While the three were inside the store, Johnny was asking the old man about a particular hunting, saying he'd have to get some boys together and he'd come back later. Clyde was buying a package of cigarettes when Bucher's wife, an older heavyset woman, looked at Clyde and said, "Heavens! I haven't seen you since you were a yardstick shorter! You're the boy that used to traipse around here. You and your brother."

"That's right, ma'am," Clyde said, backing for the door. "Good seeing you, ma'am." He stepped outside quickly, Ted behind him. "Son of a bitch!" Clyde said.

"She remembers you?" Ted said.

The three climbed into the Ford. "They don't know you guys," Clyde said. "It's an easy job. You saw that safe?"

Johnny said, "It was wide open, the old guy puttin' stuff in it. Had a gun in it."

"Easy pickin's," Ted said.

"Used to keep it locked at night," Clyde said, "open for cash or other crap. We're gonna go off the road until it's dark, then you guys go back. You tell him you want to get a guitar string, and give him this bill so he'll open the safe for change." Clyde handed Ted the revolver. "Just get it and get the money and get your butts out here. I'll give you five minutes 'cause I'm waitin' far enough that neither those old folks'll be gettin' another look at me. I'll come along and grab you, so get outta there 'cause I'll be takin' off."

Ted tucked the gun behind his belt. "They get a look at this, it ain't gonna take five minutes."

"Now listen to me," Clyde said. "No fuckin' shootin'. You do any shootin', your ass is finished. I hear shootin' and I'm takin' off. You'll be fryin'."

A short way from the store, Ted and Johnny climbed out of the car, Johnny tying a handkerchief around his neck. Looking at him, Clyde said, "This is a store, man, it's no stagecoach."

"They still gonna be lookin' at us," Johnny said.

"A helluva lot faster than you goin' in wantin' a guitar string," Clyde said. "Don't do any stupid shit or you'll both be standin' here waitin' for the laws."

Clyde quickly turned around, drove a distance from the Bucher property, turned around again and pulled to the side of the road. He figured thirty seconds had already passed, and lit a cigarette. He puffed, waiting for almost four minutes. Then he heard a single gunshot. He threw the car into gear and raced ahead, then hit his brakes as Ted and Johnny came running onto the road. Both climbed into the car, which bolted ahead before the doors were shut.

"Fuckin' gunshot I heard," Clyde said. "What the hell was it?"

"Went off—shit!" Ted said. "Just in my fuckin' hand it went off!"

"What the fuck happened?" Clyde demanded.

"Old man was behind the counter and he hollered somethin' for his wife to come down and get somethin' out of the safe—then the goddamn gun went off."

Clyde said, "I heard it, asshole! I asked you what happened?"

"He fuckin' shot the old man," Johnny said.

"Grazed him!" Ted said.

Johnny laughed. "You didn't fuckin' graze him. Shot plumb through him 'cause it busted some shit on a shelf. The old guy went down on the floor and that old lady was comin' down into the store hollerin', and lookin' right at Ted who's got that fuckin' gun in his hand—just standin' there—"

"—because it was an accident!" Ted yelled. "I got stunned—I thought, 'Holy shit!'"

"It's shit time alright," Clyde said, and then slowly, evenly, asked, "Did you kill him?"

Ted said, "I said it was an accident!"

"Was he dead?" Clyde said.

Johnny gave another laugh. "He was dead as a plain duck."

"Shut up!" Ted yelled.

"You shut up! You got both our asses hangin' on your fuckin' murder!"

"Both of you shut up," Clyde said. "I don't want to hear any bitchin' like a pair of cunts. I oughta kick your goddamn asses."

"You can kick his ass," Johnny said. "He's done kicked mine with his fuckin' murder rap, and I didn't do any shootin'." Leaning forward from the backseat, he said, "Raidin' up Celina like we did, it was a good time, I tell you, Clyde. I'll bust in anywhere and steal anythin', but fuck if I'll buy myself a shootin'. I don't relish goin' to any goddamn electric chair."

"You think I do?" Ted grunted.

Clyde suddenly asked, "You get the money or what?"

"I grabbed what I could," Johnny said. "Ted's standin' there and that old woman's screamin', some kind of shit comin' outta that old dead man's mouth. There was watches and stuff like silver-lookin' shit in that safe, and rings, but you said five minutes, so I grabbed what bills there were."

Ted said, "I'm sorry as hell, Clyde. I swear this fuckin' gun went off like I was barely touchin' the trigger."

"Shut up about it," Clyde said. "Learn to keep your goddamn finger off a trigger unless you're intendin' to squeeze it. I reckon the old lady got a good look at both of you?"

"I put my hand on my face," Johnny said, "soon as she was bustin' around. She was lookin' at Ted and that gun, and the old man, then she got down on the floor hollerin' and I told stupid here, 'Let's go,' 'cause he wasn't even movin', like somebody'd turned his ass to stone." He reached over the front seat, handing Clyde the wad of bills. "Feels like it's back to the woods, spoonin' up beans and swattin' skeeters."

"Better than Eastham," Clyde said.

Ted grunted. "And better'n the chair," he said. "I'm gettin' sick."

Johnny sat back. "I hear the hot seat's like gettin' thumped square on the head with a big sledgehammer. You don't feel no shakin' and jumpin' as the juice goes through you, even if you start smokin' up the joint you don't feel nothin', 'cause there's nothin' left to feel."

SUICIDE SAL

by Bonnie Parker, April, 1932

We each of us have a good "alibi"
For being down here in the "joint;"
But few of them really are justified
If you get right down to the point.
You've heard of a woman's glory
Being spent on a "downright cur,"
Still you can't always judge the story
As true, being told by her.
As long as I've stayed on this "island,"
And heard "confidence tales" from each "gal,"
Only one seemed interesting and truthful —
The story of "Suicide Sal."
Now "Sal" was a gal of rare beauty,
Though her features were coarse and tough;
She never once faltered from duty
To play on the "up and up."
"Sal" told me this take on the evening
Before she was turned out "free,"
And I'll do my best to relate it
Just as she told it to me:

I was born on a ranch in Wyoming;
Not treated like Helen of Troy;
I was taught that "rods are rulers"
And "ranked" as a greasy cowboy.
Then I left my old home for the city
To play in its mad dizzy whirl,
Not knowing how little pity
It holds for a country girl.

There I fell for the line of a "henchman,"
A "professional killer" from "Chi;"
I couldn't help loving him madly;
For him even now I would die.

One year we were desperately happy;
Our "ill gotten gains" we spent free;
I was taught the ways of the "underworld;"
Jack was just like a "god" to me.
I got on the "F.B.A." payroll
To get the "inside lay" of the "job;"
The bank was "turning big money!"
It looked like a "cinch" for the "mob."
Eighty grand without even a "rumble"-
Jack was the last with the "loot" in the door,
When the "teller" dead-aimed a revolver
From where they forced him to the floor.
I knew I had only a moment -
He would surely get Jack as he ran;
So I staged a "big fade out" beside him
And knocked the forty-five out of his hand.

They "rapped me down big" at the station,
And informed me that I'd get the blame
For the "dramatic stunt" pulled on the "teller"
Looked to them too much like a "game."
The "police" called it a "frame-up,"
Said it was an "inside job,"
But I steadily denied any knowledge
Or dealings with "underworld mobs,"
The "gang" hired a couple of lawyers,
The best "fixers" in any man's town,
But it takes more than lawyers and money

When Uncle Sam starts "shaking you down,"
I was charged as a "scion of gangland"
And tried for my wages of sin;
The "dirty dozen" found me guilty -
From five to fifty years in the pen.

I took the "rap" like good people,
And never one "squawk" did I make.
Jack "dropped himself" on the promise
That we make a "sensational break."
Well, to shorten a sad lengthy story,
Five years have gone over my head
Without even so much as a letter -
At first I thought he was dead.
But not long ago I discovered
From a gal in the joint named Lyle,
That Jack and the "moll" had "got over"
And were living in true "gangster style."
If he had returned to me sometime,
Though he hadn't a cent to give,
I'd forget all this hell that he's caused me,
And love him as long as I live.

But there's no chance of his ever coming,
For he and his moll have no fears
But that I will die in prison,
Or "flatten" this fifty years.
Tomorrow I'll be on the "outside"
And I'll "drop myself" on it today:
I'll "bump 'em" if they give me the "hotsquat"
On this island out here in the bay
The iron doors swung wide next morning
For a gruesome woman of waste,

Who at last had a chance to "fix it."
Murder showed in her cynical face.
Not long ago I read in the paper
That a gal on the East Side got "hot,"
And when the smoke finally retreated,
Two of gangdom were found "on the spot."
It related the colorful story
Of a "jilted gangster gal."
Two days later, a "sub-gun" ended
The story of "Suicide Sal."

Fifteen

A grand jury had been brought together in Kaufman where Bonnie stuck to her story about two men taking her against her will. She claimed she didn't know either man, though Ralph Fults, she indicated, had looked familiar to her. She described the second kidnapper as over six feet tall, "a fat man with somethin' wrong with his mouth." She swore, "I was taken against my will," and the jury released her to return to Dallas.

"I said to my momma," Bonnie told Clyde, "just what she wanted to hear. I said, 'It's a cold day in hell when I'm seein' Clyde Barrow again.'" At that she threw her arms around his neck, kissed him and said, "Let's go, daddy! Let's go wherever you're drivin' to. I wish we were flyin' on a magic carpet."

"We're not goin' far," said Clyde. "But far enough where they aren't snoopin' around like a bunch of dogs." He squeezed her hand. "Was it hard on you? Did you get all upset bein' in there so long?"

"I've been writin' poetry and thinkin' of stories. No," she said, "it wasn't so bad and they treated me fine 'cause they knew I was bein' held unfairly. Momma kept askin' me, 'What's the matter with you, Bonnie Elizabeth? Writin' poems you're callin' "Suicide Sal," and all the words you've got in there—they're the kind people use on the wrong side of the law!' And then she says, 'For the love of God, you aren't gonna kill yourself, are you?' I said, 'Momma, the day the devil in hell's gonna be givin' bibles to sinners, that's when you'll find me layin' dead by my own hand.' She was just silly, I told her. I said, 'The day just isn't gonna come when I'm gettin' myself in a jam over any man, livin' or dead.'" Then Bonnie said, "Not countin' you, daddy."

Clyde pulled the car to the side of the narrow road, shut the engine off, and kissed Bonnie again. He said, "Honey, I've missed you more'n anythin' I've ever missed in my life, and you know damn well why I took off to get help, thinkin' I'd bust you outta there, but that would've been a mistake against you, honey. I knew they'd cut you loose, believin' what you'd tell 'em."

Hugging him again, Bonnie said, "I told Momma all that to ease her thinkin' and knowin' she'd be pleased to be hearin' all that because she's thinkin' I've gone crazy writin' everythin' like I am. Why, daddy, I had a lady in that hoosegow tellin' me to write to magazines and send them my poetry. She was sayin' to me, 'Young lady, you are a real poet! My goodness,' she was sayin'. Should I mail my poem to a magazine?"

Clyde said, "I like that, honey. Just don't give 'em any return address."

Bonnie laughed, and said, "I can call 'em 'Written on the Run.' I can make it up like a serial in the picture shows. Couldn't I do that, daddy?"

Laughing a little and starting the car again, Clyde said, "Sugar, you can do any damn thing it pleases you to do, and I'll be standin' right behind you."

Ray Hamilton told his sister he felt like a "dog in a box with the lid nailed down." He said, "Might as well be in a goddamn coffin." He'd had to get out of Michigan. He said he could "smell laws" everywhere he went. From his younger sister he learned he was wanted for the Bucher murder. He cried, "What the hell! I don't know what they're talkin' about!"

Hearing that both he and Clyde were being hunted for the Hillsboro robbery and killing at Ray said, "Goddamnit to hell! I wasn't even there! I wasn't even in Texas!"

His sister said, "You coulda come back and gone again. How would I know what you do?"

"Fuck you," he told her. "It had to be Clyde—he must've been in on it with someone they got me confused with."

Ray's sister said, "I heard it all from L.C. at the gas station. He learned Clyde knew about it but said he didn't do any of it either. Said he couldn't understand them identifyin' him. L.C. also said he knows you weren't around to shoot that old man."

"Doesn't sound like Clyde doin' somethin' like that, but why me, goddamnit? Who the hell says I did it?"

"What I hear's the old man's wife's sayin' it. They got a wanted sign with you and Clyde on it. The old lady said it was you and Clyde, so you better get outta here 'cause the laws're lookin' all over for you and for Clyde, who's done run off somewhere. Billie Jean said Bonnie's gone to work up Wichita Falls way, but I seen her drivin' off in a blue car with Clyde, who had his hat all down on his head so you couldn't see him good."

Ray got a ride with his brother, Floyd, who told him, "I know where Clyde and Bonnie are if you're goin' lookin' for 'em, but we'll get out of here 'cause the fuckin' laws'll be back like they're usin' a clock. You can set your goddamn watch by 'em."

Riding the same back roads as Clyde, though only half as fast, Floyd snuck his brother out of West Dallas. They stopped in Bellevue for coffee and a sandwich, but Ray stayed in the truck while Floyd bought the sandwiches and returned to the truck. They ate as Floyd drove to Wichita Falls. He soon slowed down on a dirt parkway to several green-painted tourist cabins. Floyd said, "See that one with the newspapers stuck over the windows? That's where they are. He's probably got a car around back where it's dark as a nigger's ass. I gotta shag outta here, but if y'all got action planned, you gonna let me know?"

Ray looked at his brother. "I don't know what Clyde's got planned. You longin' to get your picture on a wall as well?"

"Fuck no!" Floyd said. "Just thinkin' I can help you guys out and get a little extra scratch. Fuckin' holes goin' in the seat of my pants."

"I don't know what we're gonna do," Ray said. "Maybe just sit around and jaw over gettin' our butts framed by the fuckin' laws." He climbed out of the car, saying, "But I'll get a word to you, brother. Take care of sis."

Standing at the cabin door, Ray watched the truck turn back onto the road again, then he gave a knock that only Clyde, Bonnie, Ralph Fults, and Ray knew.

For the following two days, Clyde played his saxophone or played poker with Ray, who otherwise shuffled cards and drink whiskey. Clyde said, "By Friday the cash at the Grand Prairie's gonna be ripe enough for pickin'."

Ray disagreed. He wanted to go sooner. He was anxious and antsy, his pants itching. His face was breaking out in a rash. Sitting on the creaky bed, the pillows behind her, Bonnie kept writing on a school tablet, her pen point scratching at the paper. She looked at Ray and said, "Your face is all gettin' red and puffed up. Sure hope you didn't catch no contagious fevers while you been runnin' around."

Ray said, "I didn't do no runnin' around! I just wanna get goin'."

"Sit down and shut up," Clyde said. "We're goin' when it's time."

Ray sat down on a three-legged footstool, watching Clyde carefully clean the .45 automatic. "You get worryin' too much," Bonnie said, "and you're gonna bust out in hives."

"What're you writin' so much for?" Ray said. "You writin' a book? You keep scribblin' on that paper."

"I'm not scribblin'," she said. "If it's any of your business, I'm writin' a letter to a magazine company in New York City."

"You're writin' some magazine company?" Ray said. "While the laws're cookin' us on murders we never done?" She just looked at him for a moment, shrugged, and then continued writing. "Any more booze left in that bottle?" Ray asked Clyde.

"No," he said.

"You swallowed it all last night," Bonnie said, "or was it this mornin'? You swallowed the beers and swallowed the whiskey I bought."

Looking at Clyde, Ray asked, "How long we gonna stay cooped up like this?"

"Until it's time to go," Clyde said, then almost in a sing-song tone: "We grab a car and get down to Grand Prairie, then grab another one for Bonnie to wait in while we pull the job—then we dump the other car and head here."

"Hightail it back here...." Ray said. "This place shuts in on me. I'm all for gettin' on the road. Get outta Texas. It don't bother me none what the laws're pullin'. I'm thinkin' to hell with 'em. Right? What we need is hittin' that bank."

"Interurban first," Clyde said. "It was your idea. Then the Neuhoff job."

Ray clapped his hands together. "We'll do it! Get both. Then the bank. I'm itchin' for the bank! You takin' the shotgun?" Clyde pressed a loaded clip into the butt of the .45. He cocked it, blew on the muzzle and looked at Ray. "You got your .38. We go in fast, pal. No shittin' and no shootin' unless someone else starts somethin'."

"I'm not doin' any shittin'," Ray said.

"We drop Bonnie at my folks," Clyde said. "She don't want her mom seein' her with me."

"I'm gonna be listenin' to the radio," she said.

Clyde nodded. "Seein' if we make it."

Sixteen

Clyde told Ray, "Ross Dyer's okay. We need him on the wheel."

Shaking his head, Ray said, "He's a fuckin' nervous guy. He don't want nothing big. I tried to talk him in on a job but he's after small shit—peanut shit."

"He can drive, can't he? We need one of these guys at the wheel."

Ray got Dyer and told him what was in store. Ross told Ray, "I just wanna get drunk and get some pussy, man. That don't take any arm and leg, and buyin' myself a fuckin' coffin, man."

"Oh, bullshit!" Ray said. "You fuckin' owe me, Ross. We need a third man and you're here. I thought you were solid—what're you pullin'? You sayin' you're a squirt? Get your fuckin' shoes on and let's go. You want some bucks, don't you?"

Ross stayed behind the wheel while Clyde and Ray entered Neuhoff Brothers Packing Company. A bookkeeper was counting out the payroll as the two came into the office where the company owners were working. With pistols drawn, Clyde and Ray cornered the Neuhoff brothers, Clyde saying, "This is a stickup, so y'all take it nice and easy and we'll be outta here in a minute." Ray produced a grocery bag and scooped the cash payroll off the table. An older safe proved empty except change used to pay for postage.

Backing out of the office, Clyde warned, "You stay where you are and nobody gets hurt." They made their way to the loading dock, jumped down and climbed into the idling car. Ross was sweating as he drove quickly away from the plant.

Two miles away, they turned onto a side road where the three abandoned the car, got into a second one they had stolen that morn-

167

ing and left parked off the road.

Behind the wheel again, Clyde maneuvered the side roads back towards West Dallas. Ross said, "I'm glad we're gettin' outta that car. Some guy kept lookin' at it like what the hell was I doin' there. Made me fuckin' nervous. You guys didn't take no time at all."

When they reached Eagle Ford road, Clyde stopped and Ray climbed out onto the backseat next to Ross. Clyde then drove to the Barrow service station, honked once, and Bonnie hurried towards the car. Getting in flushed and excited, she asked, "Where are we going, daddy?"

"First get rid of the plates on this car," he said, "then you pick the best place to buy a good catfish dinner, and tell 'em to burn it black as hell."

Ray said, "Someplace where nobody's gonna be knowin' us."

That night after a fish sandwich and three beers, Ross fell asleep in the car where they'd parked behind the Wichita Falls cabin. Inside the cabin, Clyde played his saxophone, a slow version of "I'm Forever Blowing Bubbles," while Bonnie rocked slowly back and forth and Ray fell asleep on the floor. Bonnie finally said, "Come on, daddy, why don't you tell Ray to go sleep on the chair?" Clyde said to hell with Ray, let him sleep where he was.

Days later, while Bonnie went to downtown Dallas with her mother, Clyde, Ray, and Ross drove south, stole another car in Corsicana and robbed a gas station. After changing plates, they drove north, bypassing Dallas and headed for the Oklahoma border. The plan they'd discussed was to lay low in McAlester where Ross said he had a pal, then all four hit a bank south of Oklahoma City, and beat it south back to Texas.

Hours after nightfall, Ray obtained two bottles of rye and a half-dozen pickled eggs in a juke joint before crossing the Red River into Oklahoma. A few miles north of Atoka as they approached Stringtown, Ross said, "Hey! There's a dance goin' on! They got a band out there and look at them dancin'. Look at those skirts twirlin' around!

Let's go see it!"

"Yeah!" Ray said, tucking the opened bottle of rye between his legs as Clyde drove off the highway and onto the dirt road. He brought the car to a stop on the festival grounds and close to the raised, outside platform holding a small band and the dancing couples.

"There's girls all around here!" Ross said, opening the car door. "I'm gonna stretch my legs, maybe see me a filly while you boys take it easy."

"You take it easy," Clyde said, as Ray raised the bottle for a couple quick swigs. He handed the bottle to Clyde who shook his head. "I don't want any of that crap," he said.

Ray said, "You think ol' Ross'll get himself a hunk of ass?"

"It's a dance," Clyde said. "It's no whorehouse." Then, as though tapped on the shoulder, he turned his head and looked out the window. Two lawmen were quickly heading toward the car. "Put that fuckin' bottle down!" he said.

"I see 'em," Ray said, stashing the bottle. "I saw 'em a minute ago." He reached to the floor of the car and brought up his pistol.

"You fellas there!" the older lawman said, his hand dropping for the holster at his side. "You get your butts outta that car and keep your hands above your head—"

The lawman didn't finish what he was saying or manage to get his gun free of the holster before Ray leveled the pistol a foot from Clyde's shoulder and pulled the trigger. Nothing happened. He pulled it again and the gunshot shook the air. The lawman went down clutching his chest. All hell broke loose on the dance stand— band scattering and people running or dropping to the floor.

The hammer to Ray's pistol jammed again and he cried, "The other law's gonna shoot—" and Clyde fired once, then threw the car into reverse, jammed down on the gas and backed out fast, almost hitting other parked cars. A bullet went through the windshield and Ray said, "That fucker you got's firin'!"

Clyde shifted into low and raced across the dirt towards the highway. He couldn't see the ditch at the side of the dirt road and went careening into it nose-first. The car nearly tipped over, but throwing open the door, Clyde climbed out and ran towards the highway. He could hear Ray running behind him, yelling, "Where the hell's Ross?"

"Fuck him!" Clyde said. "He's on his own!" They ran across the highway and in moments out of sight from the fairgrounds.

Hurrying across the field, the lights and confusion in the distance, Ray breathing hard, Clyde said, "We gotta get another car right now! Too bad you had to shoot first, 'cause these fuckin' Okies'll hang us to a tree."

Ray said, "Son of a bitch was goin' for his gun!"

"He spied you drinkin' is what he did," Clyde said.

Ray said, "What about Ross? I saw him runnin' when we hit the ditch."

"Who knows. He'll get in touch. Hey, there's houses over there."

In minutes they were on a narrow street, looking at cars. The first car wouldn't start. "Come on," Clyde said. The second car started, and Clyde pushed for speed. They reached the main road south and turned onto a dirt road. The car died. "We're out of gas!" Clyde said.

They walked. It was past midnight when they reached a crossroads, then took a lane leading to an old house. Clyde knocked on the door. When a man opened it, Clyde said, "Sorry as heck to disturb you, but we've got a woman in labor and the car's outta gas on the highway. Gotta get her to a doctor...."

Nodding, the man said, "My son'll take you." He called out, "Haskell? Get these fellas to their car. Take the truck. They got a lady in labor."

Haskell threw on a short jacket and stepped outside. "Bad time to run out of gas," he said, leading Clyde and Ray around to the rear of the house. "It's a stripped-down mail truck," the boy said as the three got into the truck. "Takes a couple minutes to kick over."

As they headed for the crossroads, Clyde said, "Take the back road here—goin' south."

"It's the wrong way to the highway," Haskell said. Clyde said they needed to get a doctor and take him to the car. Haskell shook his head. "There's no doctor down this ol' road—" but stopped talking and looked down at the barrel of Clyde's gun pushing at his ribs.

Clyde said, "It doesn't matter about the doctor, Haskell. We got nobody on the highway havin' a baby. Just needed to get on the road."

"You stealin' our truck?" Haskell asked. "What're you gonna do with me?"

Ray laughed. Clyde said, "Nothin's gonna happen to you, Haskell. Just pull over. You get in the middle, and I'll drive your truck."

"You're not goin' to shoot me, are you?"

"I got no reason to shoot you," Clyde said. "Just do as I tell you."

Haskell pulled over, got out of the truck and came around to the other passenger side. Ray got out and let the boy sit in the middle. Ray pulled out his gun and held it on his leg, pointing at Haskell's thigh.

The truck jerked and bucked as Clyde sped ahead, the dirt road narrowing, a tire exploded with a bang. It took a short while to change the tire, all three men slipping on the muddy road, and where the dirt trail ended, Clyde drove ahead to cross a shallow stream. Halfway to the other side, the left front end of the truck dropped with a jolt.

All three climbed out. The front left wheel had come off the axle. "Come on!" Clyde said, angrily. "We're almost on the highway. Let's go—this truck's dead."

"This road goes south," Haskell offered. "I see a car comin'...."

"We'll get a car," Clyde said to Ray. "Go on out and flag 'em down." To Haskell, he said, "Go on over to the side of the road, boy—that's in case we got some trouble." Haskell hurried off the highway as Ray went in the middle of the road and began waving.

Standing at the edge of the road, Clyde watched as the car slowed down, illuminating Ray in the bright headlights. Only the butt of the pistol showed sticking from Ray's back pocket. The car had stopped as Ray approached the man behind the wheel who rolled down his window. Leaning down, Ray said, "A wheel came off our car on that side road over yonder—" He reached into the car, surprising the driver, and snatched the keys from the ignition.

"What the hell!" the driver said as Clyde walked to the passenger side of the car where another man was locking the door and leaning forward to hear what Ray was saying. The man's mouth dropped open when he saw Ray pointing his gun at the driver.

Clyde rapped on the window with the barrel of his own gun, and when the man saw the hammer being pulled back for Clyde to shoot through the glass, he unlocked the door and raised his hands. "What's this? What's goin' on here?" the driver demanded. "What the hell you doin'? What the hell is this?"

"Both you gentlemen get outta the car," Clyde said. "Go to the side of the highway where you'll be safe."

Ray ushered the driver out of the car, then climbed behind the steering wheel. Clyde got into the car and waited until the two men joined Haskell at the side of the road, then he told Ray, "Let's go."

Seventeen

New Mexico was Bonnie's idea. With law crowding in on all sides for Clyde and Ray, she said, "We can go visit my aunt in Carlsbad. It's in New Mexico. We can relax and eat chicken and my momma told me Aunt Millie's got an ice cream-makin' machine. And we can go see the famous caverns."

"So what's the Carlsbad Cavern?" Ray said. "A big hole in the ground—like a fuckin' grave."

Bonnie laughed. "It's a big underground cave—a cavern. It's a lot of fun. I was gonna see it when I was little, so maybe we'll go and see it—and see the desert."

Quiet for moments, Clyde then said to Ray, "After you shootin' the shit outta that laws and gettin' our ass about done in, I'm ready to get out of Texas and Oklahoma—take it easy for a while eatin' chili'n' enchiladas. Nobody's lookin' for us in New Mexico."

Bonnie stayed in the cabin, writing a note to her mother while Clyde and Ray went to exchange cars. They deserted the one they were driving, and headed back to the cabin. Outside in the shade where the branches blocked the morning sun, Clyde loaded the car—guitar, his saxophone, two boxes of Bonnie's junk and magazines, which they stashed on top of the extra ammunition. He put the first-aid tin box in the trunk, then selected an out-of-state plate for the car. Behind the steering wheel, he adjusted the shotgun to his left side, made sure Bonnie was comfortable, and shifted into low. She settled back into the seat, smiling to herself as Clyde slipped the clutch and drove out of the woods.

From the backseat, Ray said, "We gonna get more cash?"

"We got a full tank of gas. I don't want anyone runnin' behind us. We'll get what we need when we get where we're goin'."

Later, the three stopped at a roadside diner west of Abilene. They ate tamales, and when Bonnie finished she took advantage of the ladies' room to tidy up. Ray and Clyde remained at the counter drinking beer.

Leaning closer to Clyde, Ray said, "Those old stiffs are lookin' at us. Over there." He nodded in the direction of an elderly man and woman eating grilled cheese sandwiches. "They're gawkin' like they know somethin's fishy."

Clyde said, "Soon as Bonnie's done in the can we're gettin' outta here."

"What're we gonna do in this here dirt town we're headin' to?" Ray asked. "Plant cotton?"

Clyde looked at him. "You're fuckin' dumb, you know that? You ever look in a fuckin' mirror and say, 'You're dumb'?"

"So what've they got where we're goin' except a hole in the ground? They got a fuckin' cathouse down there, for Jesus' sake?"

Clyde stiffened. "If they do, it won't be for the sake of Jesus. I don't know what they got down there. I never been there and I don't give a shit if they got a cathouse or not."

"No," Ray said, "you don't need a fuckin' cathouse—"

"I want to sleep," Clyde said. "I want to eat and walk around in the fuckin' sun without some bastard stickin' a gun at me."

"Okay, okay," Ray said. "You don't have to get salty." He glanced toward the rest room. "What's she doin' in there?"

"Whatever she's doin'," Clyde said, "she's mindin' her own business."

"She should come on so we can get outta here," Ray said. "Those two old farts're drillin' holes in me with their damn bug-eyes. They're not lookin' at you."

"So stop starin' at 'em. They're thinkin' the same about you— somethin' fishy about you gawkin' at them." Clyde glanced over at the elderly couple. He nodded, and smiled. Ray got up and headed for the door, saying he'd wait in the car.

The couple returned the greeting to Clyde. He looked up as Bonnie came out of the restroom, wearing a bright new red shade of lipstick, and a light rub of rouge on her cheeks.

Clyde said, "Honey, you look beautiful as the first day I saw you." Bonnie sat beside him. He said, "You knew I loved you then, didn't you? I didn't know it and you knew it. I didn't even know you. I loved someone I didn't even know. That's never done any changin'," he said. "I never knew what it was to love somebody and they love you back."

"Two people becomin' like one," she said. "That's what we are. I don't think words without hearin' you speakin' inside me." She smiled. "And I hear 'em in my heart, daddy—in the heart I've given to you."

The sun was setting blood red by the time the back roads delivered the three to Carlsbad. "My face is sunburned," Bonnie said. "I hope my aunt's as nice a lady as Momma's said she is. I just don't remember her. I was too little."

Millie Stamps, Bonnie's aunt, had no idea her sister's daughter was planning on a visit to Carlsbad. Pleased, but surprised to see Bonnie, the woman said, "You're so grown up, and all I've got's a memory of the little girl your momma brought to say hello. My goodness," she said, "I wouldn't've recognized you in a hundred years! You're so pretty you look like you're someone in the picture show! It's years since I've even see you, isn't it? I'm so surprised!" She was more surprised by the two young men accompanying Bonnie.

To keep things proper, Bonnie introduced Clyde as Jack Smith, saying, "Jack and I just got married, and this here's Jack's cousin, Jimmy White. He was best man at our weddin'."

"My goodness," Millie said. "I had no idea! Your mother never let me know—"

"—we eloped!" Bonnie said, smiling. "Momma doesn't know

it, so it'll be a big surprise when we're back in Dallas and I break the news." Blushing, Bonnie said, "We're on our honeymoon time, Aunt Millie, and I'm hopin' you might know a quiet cabin or room nearby? We've all been thinkin' of seein' the cavern."

"I'm sittin' on a spread here," Millie said, "and about as quiet as it gets. You and Jack're welcome to stay if you don't have any objections. Jimmy can have the little room in back—just off the porch."

Ray and Clyde went out to the car while Bonnie and her aunt chatted over coffee and graham crackers, talking about the time Bonnie's mom and Millie made homemade ice cream.

Outside, Ray said, "I'm sleepin' in a shed while you're in a honeymoon suite."

"You don't want the couch," Clyde said, "you can sleep in the car?"

"Yeah, I'll sleep in the fuckin' car," Ray said. "Did'ya know Bonnie was gonna tell that old gal about y'all gettin' married?"

"You thinkin' there's anythin' wrong with it?" Clyde said.

"Hell, no," Ray said, smirking. "Ain't nothin' gets me happier than holy matrimony—"

"—just remember your name's Jimmy White," Clyde said. "That old lady'll be goin' to bed, and I want this shotgun in the 'honeymoon suite.' Leave all the rest of the shit in the car."

As soon as he lay on the bed and closed his eyes, Clyde was already falling asleep. He didn't even sense Bonnie crawling into bed and cuddling against him. When he did open his eyes he was startled for a moment, realizing he'd dropped off without anyone standing guard. Bonnie stroked his shoulder and said, "It's okay, daddy, not a soul knows we're here and nobody's gonna know, so go back to sleep."

"I can't," he said, turning towards her.

The next morning, Clyde was up early, shining his shoes while Bonnie and her aunt were in the kitchen making plans to whip up some ice cream. When Bonnie came into the bedroom she complimented Clyde on his shoeshine, and said, "Later we'll go buy some clothes and see the cavern." She smiled. "Me'n' my aunt are gonna make some homemade ice cream. Get Jimmy to go to the market for some ice. Aunt Millie says the store's right there in the town on the highway."

"I'll get him," Clyde said. "He's outside smokin' and bitchin'." Looking at her, he whispered, "I'm sure not sorry we're here, but I'm sorry he's with us."

Bonnie kissed him. "Have him get ice so we can make the ice cream." Whispering, she said, "Last night's gonna be one of the happiest night's of my life. Do you believe I love you more'n anythin' in the world?"

"Honey," Clyde said, "you are my world."

While Ray drove into town for the ice, Bonnie followed her aunt around the vegetable garden. "It just grows and keeps producin'," the woman said. "My neighbor helps me gather it for a vegetable stand down by the market. We get many customers from the folks around here, and there's always people comin' by, travelin' through like y'all."

Clyde took a quick hot bath, shaved in the tub, and Bonnie came in to wash his back. While she went back to visiting with her aunt, Clyde changed his trousers and shirt, then lay back on the bed, the shotgun on the chair by the door. When the older lady knocked on the bedroom door, Clyde got off the bed and opened the door. "Yes, ma'am," he said. "I was admirin' how good this bed feels. I went to sleep so fast last night I didn't even know where I was layin'."

She was staring at the shotgun. Clyde said quickly, "Somethin' my daddy gave me. I don't like to leave it layin' in the car."

"You always drivin' with a shotgun in the car?" she asked.

"Well, yes, ma'am, my cousin and I go huntin' pretty regular. Never know when the wantin' is gonna be the right time."

"What do you hunt with a shotgun?" she asked, and added, "one that looks like somebody's cut the shootin' barrel down shorter?"

"Just close range," Clyde said. "Rabbits and such." He shrugged, smiling.

A few minutes later, Bonnie came into the house. Clyde asked, "Where's the old lady gone?"

"She was outside," Bonnie said. "Said she had to take somethin' over to her neighbor."

"She was talkin' about the shotgun," he said.

Bonnie said, "Earlier I saw her lookin' in the car window before Ray drove off."

"She say anythin' to you?"

"No," she said. "But she was gettin' shaky."

A half hour passed. They heard the car as Ray pulled in front of the house and parked. He got out with two bags of ice and several bottles of beer. Clyde could hear him saying something to the old lady before he brought the ice and beers into the house. Bonnie said, "My husband's in the bedroom."

"Very funny," Ray said and walked down the hallway. In the bedroom he asked Clyde, "What's goin' on?"

"Ice cream," Clyde said. They both heard the kitchen door open, then shut, and the woman speaking to Bonnie. "She got nosey seein' the shotgun."

Ray said, "She asked me if we're goin' huntin'. I said, 'Huntin' what?' She didn't say nothin' else."

Clyde put his finger to his lips as the woman approached the bedroom. "I saw the ice in the sink," she said. "If you come in the kitchen we can start workin' on the ice cream." Ray nodded and joined the woman in the kitchen where Bonnie was opening beer bottles.

About thirty minutes later there was a knock on the front door. "I'll see who it is!" Bonnie went from the kitchen to the front room. She opened the door. She didn't say anything. A uniformed deputy was at the door. He asked about the car. "Oh, it belongs to one of the boys," she said in a calm, pleasant voice—actually a signal that the law had arrived. "They're dressin'," she said. "They'll be right out."

Clyde picked up the shotgun and snuck into the front room. Through the window he saw the laws snooping through the car windows, then walking to the rear of the car and trying to open the trunk. Ray came out of the kitchen. Clyde said, "Laws." He took a deep breath, pushed open the screen door and walked outside with the shotgun leveled. Startled, the deputy reached for his own gun, but Clyde sent a loud load of buckshot into the ground inches from the man's boots.

With his hands raised the deputy said, "I'm not movin'. You got me cold, alright."

Clyde could hear Bonnie trying to quiet her aunt as Ray came out of the house. He snatched the deputy's pistol from the belted holster. "A Colt .45," Ray said. "Frontier special."

"What're you going to do?" the deputy asked. "I already got a call in on your vehicle. They'll be all over here in minutes."

"You're lyin'," Clyde said. "Nobody's burnin' their balls over a hot car. Frisk him," Clyde told Ray.

"I have no other weapons," Ray said.

Aunt Millie was at the door, crying, "Oh, my God—what's hap-penin'? That's Deputy Sheriff Johns!" she said. "What happened here?"

"Nothin' to worry about, ma'am," Clyde said. "Go on back in and fix your ice cream. It's all under control out here, isn't that right, Deputy?"

The deputy nodded. "We're all under control, Miss Stamps. Just havin' us a discussion."

Clyde said to Bonnie, "Take your aunt back into the house, and you come out with what's left behind."

"I left my shavin' bag on the porch," Ray said.

"Give here the keys to the car and the deputy's gun," Clyde said. "Go get your stuff on the porch and tell that old lady to stay in her house there till we're gone."

"What about him?" Ray asked.

"Deputy Johns's goin' for a ride with us," Clyde said. "Walk around the other side of the car, Deputy, put your hands down and turn your back to me." Clyde unlocked the driver's door, pulled it open and said, "Come back this side where I am, and you get in the car and over to the middle of the seat. Keep your hands together like you're prayin' right there by your chin." Ray came back outside and Clyde said, "Go get Sis and whatever crap's left, and hurry up. We're takin' off."

"What about the old woman?" Ray asked.

Clyde said, "Tell her if she starts yakkin', this here laws is gonna get a grave earlier than I bet he's countin' on."

Ray ran back into the house and the deputy asked, "What're you goin' to do?"

"When they get out here, they're gettin' in next to you," Clyde said as he adjusted the shotgun against the driver's door. With the Colt in his left hand, he got into the car behind the wheel. "Cozy, eh? We're all gonna be in the front 'cause there's no backseat as you saw snoopin' around, and I've got your Colt pointin' at your gut."

Eighteen

Clyde raced east on empty back roads, speeding over bumps and holes, the car bouncing like a plane fighting to get off a runway. Deputy Johns, pinned between Clyde and Ray, with Bonnie on Ray's lap, stared ahead through the windshield as Clyde drove with the force of a hurricane. Bonnie frowned as she asked Johns, "Why'd you follow us and get all this trouble goin' when we were havin' a vacation?"

The deputy said, "My job, ma'am."

"To hell with your job!" Ray said.

"Look," Johns said, "I was asked to check y'all out. Soon as I got to where you were—to your aunt's house—I checked the car, the plates. I had to see the registration." Glancing at Clyde, he said, "I got my answer damn quick."

Clyde said, "I knew you were lyin' about laws racin' around. Sure wanted to stay there," Clyde said. "Woulda been damn nice."

"I'm sorry I busted up your vacation," Johns said. "It wouldn't happen if you weren't in a stolen car. All I got to say now's where the devil are you takin' me?"

"Would you like it better if I'd shot you?" Clyde said.

The deputy started to say something but Bonnie cut him off. "We're gettin' blamed for all the thing's goin' on, sayin' we've done this and we've done that, and I know different."

"Of course," Johns said. "They're goin' to throw a lot of crap at you. Try to catch you and make it stick. Makes them look good."

"Sure that's what it is!" she said. "You're sayin' they don't care who's done somethin' long as they've got a body to answer for it."

181

Clyde said, "They don't care whose body it is long as they can hang it."

"That's about it," Johns said. "Say, if you dump me off and I'm still breathin', they'll pretty much call the shots and grab some trigger-happy sap for shootin' a deputy sheriff."

Laughing a little, Clyde said, "We're not gonna shoot you, Deputy. What reason we got to shoot you about?"

"Being an eyewitness—" Johns started to say.

"—but we've done nothin' to you!" Bonnie said.

"Well, you've kidnapped me," Johns said. "You know the new Lindbergh law."

"Is that what we've done?" she said. "Kidnapped you?"

Clyde put his shoeless foot on the brake, slowing a little, and said, "Then that law's enough a good reason to shoot you right now."

Bonnie said, "We're thinkin' you're not complainin' since you're enjoyin' our company."

"Frankly," Johns said, made nervous by Clyde slowing down, "I'm enjoyin' your company, ma'am. You're quite a pair, you two, and with your pal pointin' my gun at me. I just keep thinkin', wonderin' where we're goin'…."

Clyde picked up his speed again. "You won't be goin' to a graveyard," Bonnie said, "in case that's what you're thinkin'."

Johns nodded. "That's what I've been thinkin', ma'am."

"I'm not enjoyin' bein' called ma'am," she said. "My name's Bonnie. That's my name."

"Just being respectful," the deputy said. "I know your Aunt Millie, and she called you by name."

Ray said, "That lady got down on her knees in the kitchen and begged us not to kill you. She said she was askin' God to save you."

"And she asked the Lord to save us all," Bonnie said. "Are you still scared?"

"Sure he's scared," Ray said. "He's sittin' here shakin'."

"To be honest," Johns said, "I'm a little scared, in fact, not knowin' what you're doin' with me."

"We're socializin'," Bonnie said. "We see our folks hardly at all, so we don't get much socializin'. People have to have some social interactin' with their family."

"I can understand that," the deputy said.

Clyde said, "Even when the laws want me in the electric chair."

"New Mexico doesn't want you in an electric chair—"

"You said about a Lindbergh law and you've been kidnapped," Clyde said. "Accordin' to that law, if anybody's gonna press it, I might as well park you in the woods and take a load off the car."

"I'm for that," Ray said. "This jabberer's puttin' me to sleep."

"I take that back about bein' kidnapped," Johns said. "I'm here 'cause I'm enjoyin' your company, like Bonnie's sayin'. I'll write you a note sayin' so."

Clyde said, "That'll go over 'bout as big as a dog gettin' through a keyhole."

Johns stiffened. "I don't see it makes a difference what I say. You'll do what you're gonna do. I was only reachin' for my weapon, since he had a shotgun on me."

"Don't fret," Bonnie said. "We aren't gonna to harm you. You didn't really try to shoot anybody, and Clyde's partial to someone who doesn't try to shoot him. We're enjoyin' your company and want you to think of us as bein' friendly travelin' companions."

Johns said, "I'd enjoy our travelin' more if we weren't goin' so fast."

"You're alright," Clyde said. "Give him some of those chocolate cookies, honey. He's lookin' less nervous."

The deputy wasn't less nervous. He'd never driven with someone who propelled over narrow dirt roads at the speed Clyde traveled, the speedometer shaking in the danger zone. Clyde, driving with his right shoe off, had the gas pedal almost to the floor, and the moments the road straightened he broke ahead like a horse at a starting gate. He barreled through a wet ditch, his windshield so splattered with mud his view of the road was blocked. Instead of slowing down, Clyde opened his door and half-leaned from the car to get a view of the road, keeping at the same breakneck speed, turning and twisting on the narrow trails. They stopped by an irrigation ditch and Ray washed the windshield before they sped ahead. By now, the deputy had been enlisted to consult the Texas map and offered suggestions on the roads infrequently traveled. After a few minutes Clyde asked Johns, "Why'd you come bargin' to her aunt's anyway? What brought you sneakin' out there?"

Johns cleared his throat, chasing down the last of the cookie with a gulp of Coca-Cola. "Well," he said, "I owe you that. Some ol' boy called us, sayin' he was callin' for Bonnie's aunt. Said she was scared out of her wits seein' one of your guns—a sawed-off shotgun. She didn't know what to do. Seein' I'm acquainted with the lady, I said I'd talk to her. I got there and figured the car was stolen so I wanted to talk to you, but none of you were in a mood for talkin'."

Bonnie said, "But we're havin' our talk now, aren't we? Are you uncomfortable, Deputy?"

"Uncomfortable?" he said. "I don't know as I'd put it that way, Bonnie. I'd say I'm concerned and thinkin' how long you're havin' me on this ride."

"Nobody's gonna harm you," Clyde said. "You haven't given any good cause to get yourself shot. I've got no plans of hurtin' you."

"I appreciate that," Johns said. "And I'm enjoyin' your company, but I've never been in a situation like the sort we're havin'."

Clyde said, "What do you mean 'situation'?"

"I've never been kidnapped before—"

"—kidnapped?" Bonnie said. "You're not bein' kidnapped. That's what you're still believin'?"

"It crosses my mind," he said. "I don't know what else it is—what you'd call it."

"Bein' a companion!" she said. "We're all company and enjoyin' the occasion. Aren't we?"

"Sure," Clyde said.

"Then so am I," Johns said, sighing a little. "That's a mighty friendly way of puttin' it."

"Don't let it be a big load off your mind," Clyde said. "It'll depend on your cooperatin' with us."

Silence except for the straining engine, and within minutes, Bonnie's eyes had shut, her head nodding slowly. Clyde reached across the deputy and nudged her shoulder. "Wake up, honey, we gotta get gas. We're damn near in the middle of a cattle pen, but I saw a pump."

"It's up ahead," Ray said. "Looks like a shack that's got a gas pump."

Bonnie raised her head. "Out here in nowhere, and they got a gas pump."

"They got their own gas," Johns said. "For the ranchers that live around here."

"It's all cattle," Clyde said, then to Ray, "Get Bonnie off your lap and go get us some gas." He handed Ray some money and said, "Let's have the deputy's fancy Colt."

Handing the gun to Clyde, Ray said, "Smells like these cattle're shittin' everywhere." He squeezed out beneath Bonnie, bracing herself with one hand on Johns' shoulder.

Clyde said, "Check that right rear tire, and clean off the windshield again."

Ray gave a salute. "Yes, sir! Right now, sir!"

"Sometimes Ray and Clyde don't get along," Bonnie said to the deputy.

"Why's that?" Johns asked.

Clyde said, "He likes to think he's a hotshot—thinks he's Baby Face Nelson. He's good on the spot but gettin' there and after it's done he's a pain in the ass."

"You're some driver," Johns said. "I've never seen anyone take these roads like you're doin'. I thought we were gonna get killed half a dozen times."

"Doesn't bother Clyde," Bonnie said.

"Don't you ever get tuckered out?" Johns asked.

"Not drivin'," Clyde said.

Bonnie said, "We can go through four or five states in a day every day, and Clyde never stops drivin'—except to get different cars. Sometimes three cars in a day." She looked at Johns. "Guess I shouldn't be talkin' like I am. You might be the man who's gonna arrest me."

"What would I be arrestin' you for?" he said.

"You'd be knowin' that better than I would," she said.

When Ray got back in the car, shifting for Bonnie to squeeze onto his lap, he said, "I gotta get some fuckin' sleep. I feel like I'm walkin' drunk or ridin' a fuckin' rolleycoaster."

"Rollercoaster," Bonnie said. "None of us have eaten all day," she told Johns. "Didn't you get any breakfast?"

"Coffee and a roll," Johns said. "Some of your chocolate cookies. I don't like eatin' much for breakfast. Gets night like this a body does get hungry."

"I could eat one of these goddamn steers," Ray mumbled as Clyde passed the gun back to him. The deputy did not glance down at the Colt as it crossed his stomach. Ray said, "How you doin', Deputy? You holdin' up?"

Johns laughed a little. "Just wonderin' how far we're gonna be gettin'."

"Wherever it is, somebody wake me when we get there," Ray replied.

Clyde turned the key, checked the fuel gauge, and made a wide turn. They drove across a field, maneuvering past the cattle, and onto to a dirt road heading east. Clyde asked Johns, "This the road that takes us to the south turnoff?"

"Yes," the deputy said.

Ray said, "Our kidnapped law's wonderin' how far we're goin'?"

"He said he's not kidnapped," Clyde said, then to Johns, "Isn't that right? You're nobody kidnapped?"

"I reckon you're right," Deputy Johns said. "I'm company—a companion."

"That's right!" Bonnie said. "Do you want some more Coca-Cola?"

Clyde said, "But he's in his rights sayin' he's kidnapped, and gettin' that Lindbergh law stuck on us. But it won't make any difference, because if they grab Ray he's sure to fry—but it's just once they can give it to him. The same for me only nobody's gonna get me."

"What about you?" Johns asked Bonnie.

"Nobody's gonna get her either," Clyde said. "She hasn't smoked no one or stuck up any bank or nothin' else. She ain't accused of nothin' except stickin' with me."

It was clear from all the deputy heard that Bonnie had not actively participated in any crime, other than being an accomplice. On the other hand, Ray Hamilton was the wild card. Johns guessed that Ray had never trusted anyone in his life. He could shoot the deputy for the plain convenience of it, to make more room on the seat of the car. He guessed that Clyde enjoyed the "cat and mouse" encounter. Clyde, the lynchpin, probably wouldn't kill Johns unless he made a move against him, which of course was the furthest thought from the deputy's thinking.

Clyde at the helm, they raced southeast on dark trails to avoid being spotted on an open road. Bonnie had dropped off in sleep, her head tipped and resting against the sheriff's right shoulder. Johns sighed. He hoped he wouldn't be shot and get his body dumped on the side of some pitch-black desolate back road to be picked over by crows and coyotes.

Nineteen

It was five thirty in the morning, a few miles from San Antonio. Clyde drifted to the side of the road, got out of the car, lit a cigar and said to Deputy Johns, "Well, come on and get out."

"What're you aimin' to do?" Johns asked.

"This is where you're gettin' out," Clyde said, reaching into his pocket. "Aren't you tired of us all bein' cramped in the front of this heap?"

Johns was staring at Clyde. "I won't be shootin' you." Clyde said, "I'm gonna give you some money so you can get back where you're goin'."

Relieved, Johns sighed and shook his head, sort of waved a little. "No, thanks, I got some money, not much…"

"Now you got more," Clyde said, pushing some folded bills into Johns' shirt pocket. "You've got a watch, so you look at it and give me an hour before you head off alertin' laws. Give us a little break."

"We've given you one!" Bonnie called from the car.

Johns nodded. He shook hands with Clyde, and then said, "What about my gun? Can I have my gun back?"

"Well," Clyde said, "it's a pretty good gun, and I'll have to keep it." He got back into the car and drove away quickly.

The sun was sinking in the west as Clyde stole a Ford V-8 sedan in Victoria, then quickly maneuvered out of the town. Bonnie, half-asleep, lay stretched on the passenger seat with her feet on Clyde's lap.

Ray, manning the Ford coupe, followed Clyde as they drove northeast to Wharton and the bridge across the Colorado River. Clyde turned off the highway and onto a side road, but as soon as he crossed some railroad tracks he realized the dirt road was going west. "Gettin' in a hole," he said and stopped. Bonnie sat up and lit a cigarette. A moment later, Ray pulled alongside the sedan. Clyde said, "We gotta go back—get off this dirt road and cross the bridge."

Ray waved for Clyde to turn around. In moments both were back on the highway to Wharton. Up ahead was the bridge, but also another car that came abruptly off a side road and onto the bridge.

Immediately the car made a turn at the other end of the bridge and was coming back, head on, towards Clyde's car. "This is no good," Clyde said. "Son of a bitch is showin' a gun—get your head down!" Clyde kept going, increasing speed, and as the oncoming car approached within a few feet of the sedan, the driver fired straight through Clyde's windshield.

Bonnie cried and said, "You hit?" He shook his head. She turned to the rear window. "He's stopped. They're gonna block the bridge. Some other guy's got a gun and Ray's comin' on the bridge!"

Seeing the second cop aiming at him, Ray ducked behind the wheel, slumping as low as he could. He heard the shot, felt the bullet as it hit the car door, but didn't know whether he'd been hit or not. He accelerated as more bullets struck the car, shattering the rear window as Ray chased after Clyde.

A few miles north, Clyde and Ray pulled off the road onto a dirt trail behind a cluster of deserted buildings. "Shit," Ray said. "We almost got our asses blown off!" He helped Clyde and Bonnie empty the coupe, saying, "You got some ventilation in your window." Quickly, the three climbed into the sedan, Clyde driving with Ray sprawling on the rear seat. "Fucker thought he'd shot my ass," Ray said.

Clyde said, "Slug didn't go through the door. Stuck in the middle."

"Better there," Ray said, "than in my ass. They must be crawlin' everywhere for us."

"And shootin' on sight," Bonnie said.

"I'm not nuts about gettin' shot without even knowin' who's doin' the shootin'. If you two don't mind, I'd like to set my ass where nobody's drawin' a bead. I've had enough of this committin' suicide shit."

Bonnie laughed.

Twenty

It was all kind of in the family. Clyde's younger brother, L.C., admired Clyde but was growing quickly aware of some insurmountable, impenetrable lump between them, keeping the closeness Clyde often shared with Buck at a distance. L.C. had told his sister Nell, "With Buck gone off in prison, and Clyde runnin', seems we can't hold together like it used to be."

Nell said, "There's nothin' like it used to be."

Not a blood cousin with the others was William "Deacon" of the Jones family, cronies with Cumie and Henry Barrow. W.D., as they called him, unlike L.C., admired Clyde the same as he'd hail to the desperate heroes in the funny books he stole from Dallas markets. Sixteen years old and running around with L.C., W.D. often tracked Clyde as an envious dog seeking the ideal master.

Present at the Christmas Eve family get-together, L.C. having notified the family members, W.D. found himself side by side with Clyde, and said to him, "I'd sure like to drive with you, Bud. I can drive good, you know, and I don't never get nervous of what I'm doin.'"

Clyde nodded absently. "What do you get nervous about, boy? You lookin' to drive my car?"

"Or any car you happen to be sittin' in," W.D. said, smiling. "I could go along, helpin' you and Bonnie."

"Helpin' us do what?"

"Whatever you're doin.' What you're doin' at the time, you know?"

"No, I don't know," Clyde said.

"I do a lot of stuff," W.D. said. He looked around and, in a hushed tone, said, "I can shoot, too. I've done robbed already, you know."

"I don't know nothin' about what you've done," Clyde said, "but I'll tell you, boy, shootin's damned easier than robbin'. The idea is robbin' without any shootin'. You get what I'm sayin'?"

"I understand that," W.D. said. "I can rob as good as I can shoot."

"I don't need anybody to do shootin'. Any shootin' to be done I already know what's gotta be shot at. You can steal a car?"

W.D. straightened himself up. "I sure can, Bud. You point one out and I'll get it runnin' fast as any key'll do it."

Clyde said, "Swipin' cars and robbin' gas stations and such, you gotta be on your toes. Sounds like chicken feed—like you go in and pick it up. You don't. You go in fast and you get out fast and you don't do any shootin' unless it looks like laws or someone's got a drop on you. Even then, somebody like you, well, you don't know shit from a head of cabbage."

Insisting, W.D. said, "Yes, I do so, and I learn fast. You and Sis are outlaws—"

"She's not an 'outlaw'," Clyde said. She's never pointed any gun at anybody in her life."

"Okay, I don't mean it. I mean is I got the guts to do a lot and I can learn a whole bunch more. My momma, Tookie, bein' close with your momma, well, they say I'm smart as a whip. That's what your own momma said."

"You're a squirt-nose kid," Clyde said. "I've been seein' you as a kid since you've grown as tall as you are, but you never seemed so smart to me. You take a magazine course on gettin' smart—on just bein' an outlaw? What you want to learn, boy, is you smoke someone you sure as shit'll be sittin' in the hot seat, so learn to put your brain where your finger is, and don't go stickin' it up your nose."

"I know all that," W.D. said. "No one's got you in any hot seat."

"No," Clyde said, "but they got my name on the list and underlined in red ink, though they're never gonna strap me into that son of a bitch. Nobody's gonna get me against a wall 'cause I think on my feet and I won't be goin' down. You think you can think on your feet?"

W.D. took a breath. Again, he said, "I can learn fast. I can learn if I was helpin' you doin' the stuff, like maybe stuff you don't want to do."

Clyde stared at him. "What the hell would you be doin' that I don't want to do?"

"I don't know—whatever you'd me to do that you don't want to do."

"Look," Clyde said, "you're wantin' me to be draggin' you off, and you don't know what you're gettin' yourself into. Draw a line, boy, and don't cross over it."

"I'm gonna cross it, Bud. I want to go along with you and Sis."

"Jesus Christ!" Clyde said and drank the rest of the cola. He sighed and said, "Me and Sis are takin' outta here, and you wantin' to ride with us, you go on walkin' down the road and we'll get you in the car."

Grinning, W.D. said, "Why not right here?"

"I don't want your momma or mine seein' you settin' out with us. And don't be sayin' to L.C. you're takin' a ride with Bonnie and me. You understand me, boy?" He took W.D.'s arm and said, "Write this in your head and wake up readin' it. Anyone gettin' into a car with us is no different than turnin' yourself into a tin duck at a shootin' gallery. You know what I'm sayin'?"

W.D. said, "Sure, I know what you're sayin'. But you aren't any tin duck, and I ain't gonna be any duck for anybody."

That night, when Clyde and Bonnie reached Temple, Texas, W.D. was hunched down on the backseat, smiling as the lights of the road ran popping like a string of electric lights. When the car pulled off the road towards a row of cabins, Clyde and W.D. stayed in the car. Bonnie went into the motor court office and got a cabin for the night.

Backing up to the cabin, they passed a swing and Bonnie told W.D., "Soon as we're in the cabin, you come over here and get that cushion. That's what you'll sleep on."

"But you'll be awake for a spell," Clyde said, "until I wake up, and we're gonna take turns sittin' at the window to see who's comin' and who's not comin'."

"How am I gonna see who's not comin'?" W.D. asked.

"That's what you'll be ponderin' as you're sittin' there," Bonnie said.

A few minutes later while Bonnie was in the metal-walled shower stall, steam filling the room, Clyde was on the bed, the shotgun and a revolver in easy reach. W.D. said, "Won't I be needin' a gun for lookin' out?"

"No," Clyde said. "You wake me if anyone's creepin' 'round out there."

After her shower, Bonnie turned off the light and climbed into bed alongside Clyde. She said, "I used a towel but we'll take both with us." She turned over in the dark to the silhouette of W.D. at the window, and said, "Tomorrow's Christmas, boy, and maybe Santa Claus'll bring you a present."

Early the next morning, as soon as Clyde dressed, he pushed W.D. awake. "We're goin', boy, so take your piss or whatever you gotta do, and bring this cushion with you."

W.D. bolted up. He went into the toilet and soon as the makeshift door was shut, Clyde removed a pillow case into which he tucked the .45 Colt pistol. He handed it to Bonnie who had gathered the towels, napkins, personal wipes, and the pillow without the case, and took the gun-heavy case. She was ready to go. When W.D. came out of the bathroom, he said, "There's no towels in here."

Bonnie said, "Wipe your hands on the sheet, then fold it and take it with you to the car."

Gray and cold outside. Clyde had the engine running as they waited for Bonnie. She came out wearing her coat and hat, and handed all she was carrying to W.D., including the pillow case containing the deputy's gun. Getting into the front, she leaned to Clyde and kissed him. "Merry Christmas, daddy."

As Clyde drove away from the cabins and onto the road, an ex-cited W.D. said, "There's a gun in this stuff!"

Bonnie said, "I already told you Merry Christmas. That's your present."

"Wow!" W.D. said. "Kinda pearl handles with cows' heads—"

"—cattle heads," Clyde said.

"It's loaded," W.D. said.

"Not much good if it weren't," Clyde said. "You're gonna be on lookout while I got some business, so you keep your finger off that trigger unless it looks like you gotta stick it there, and that's only if one of those are pointin' at you. Don't point that at the back of these seats, and don't push that barrel down your pants or you'll be blowin' your balls off."

The orange sign outside the grocery store read OPEN CHRIST-MAS DAY. Clyde entered the market, picked out half a dozen doughnuts, and waited until an old woman customer left the store. He reached the register and drew his pistol. Clyde said, "It's a stick-up...." The proprietor, confused, stared at him for a moment, then without an argument, opened the cash register and handed Clyde the bills, then the bag of doughnuts. Nodding, the man said, "Merry Christmas, and I hope you're not gonna shoot me on our Savior's birthday?"

"I won't be shootin' you," Clyde said, backing towards the door. "Thanks for the doughnuts."

W.D., waiting outside, quickly followed Clyde into the car. Steam and smoke from the exhaust was clouding the cold air. Clyde sped away from the market, leaving the proprietor watching from behind the window.

Clyde ate one of the doughnuts. Bonnie and W.D. munched more as they cruised the streets north of the town, looking for an-other car. Spotting a new Ford model A roadster parked facing the wrong way on Thirteenth Street, Clyde told Bonnie, "Me and the kid are gettin' out and we'll push that car away from the house. You go on a couple blocks, and I'll pick you up."

W.D. and Clyde both pushed the Ford a short way from the curb. W.D. said, "I'll start it."

"Hurry up," Clyde said, and stood impatiently for seconds, then turned as two men—one younger and one older—charged from the house, yelling for Clyde and W.D. to get away from the car.

Clyde drew out his pistol. "Go on back!" he hollered to the men, making sure they saw the gun. "Go on back in your house!"

The two men stopped, then slowly backed away, but stayed in front of the house while W.D. tried but failed to start the car. "Move over!" Clyde said, pushing him to the passenger seat, and got behind the wheel himself.

W.D. said, "There's a woman on the porch! She's lookin' right at us but those guys haven't moved." The engine started immediately and W.D. suddenly cried, "Here comes some guy runnin' right at us!"

In a moment, a third man, younger and athletic-looking, ran to the driver's side, jumped on the running board, and grabbed at Clyde to pull him out of the car. "I'm gonna shoot you!" Clyde yelled at him. "Get the fuck off or I'll shoot you!"

As they struggled, Clyde's gun fired but the bullet went wild, hitting the left front fender. Accelerating the engine, Clyde went for the clutch, still trying to fight off the man's grip. As Clyde pulled down on the gearshift, W.D.'s hand, gripping his Christmas gun, pushed past Clyde and fired point-blank at the man on the running board. The bullet entered the man's neck and threw him backwards into the street. "Damn fool!" Clyde shouted at the shot man, then floored the gas. At the corner he yelled at W.D., "You just killed that fuckin' guy! You're stupid, boy!"

W.D. said, "Might justa wounded him!"

"Like shit!" Clyde said. "You got him dead as hell right in the neck." He turned on the next street, pulled behind the car where Bonnie was waiting, and told W.D. to get out and get in the other car. "Laws'll be huntin' this one and we got no time!" Quickly, they climbed back into the V-8 they'd driven, Clyde at the wheel, and they sped away from the dead man's car. Clyde said, "Son of a bitch just shot that guy."

Bonnie turned to W.D., who was looking at his gun. "You killed him?" she asked.

"I reckon," he said. "Bud says he's dead—I guess he's dead. He was tryin' to stop us."

"Wasn't anybody I'd've shot," Clyde said. "Fucker was damn near off the car when you pulled that trigger."

"Well," W.D. said, throwing the spent shell out the window, "here I'm sittin' bein' an outlaw."

"You can bet your fuckin' ass on that," Clyde said. He pulled to the side of the road. "Get those wire cutters off the floor at your feet and go climb that telephone pole. Cut the wires right now and make it fast!"

"Like an Indian," W.D. said, jumping out of the car.

"Yeah," Clyde said to Bonnie, "like a dumb fuckin' Indian."

While W.D. shimmied up the pole and was cutting the phone lines, Clyde urging him to hurry up, Bonnie asked, "You sure he killed whoever it was?"

Clyde nodded. "Got him square in the neck, from close as you're sittin'. Damn guy went off the runnin' board like a sack of cement."

Having cut the wires, W.D. climbed down and into the car. Looking at W.D. through the mirror, Clyde said, "You got your wish, boy. Might as well see it, boy. You won't be goin' anywhere else now, seein' you've killed somebody."

W.D. nodded, then asked Bonnie, "Sis, we got any of them doughnuts left?"

Twenty-One

Ray Hamilton was back behind bars, picked up on a bank job with another partner the law was hunting. The stickup scored $3,000, but Ray wouldn't be blowing the money so quickly since he'd been transferred to Hillsboro to be tried on first-degree charges for the murder of old man Bucher.

"Ray didn't do the shootin'," Bonnie told W.D. "Someone else pulled the trigger, and told Clyde it was an accident. Ray says he wasn't in Texas when it happened, but the laws're gonna try him and fry him. That is, unless Clyde can get him busted out. That's why he had Ray's sis Lilly take that old radio to Ray, 'cause there's two hacksaw blades behind the tubes."

W.D. said, "Ray's gonna saw his way out of jail?"

"He's done it before," Clyde said from the front seat as the car bumped over Eagle Ford. "He knows what he's doin', least he thinks he does. Problem's he's bank happy. You can't be fuckin' happy when you're stickin' up a bank."

"We don't know if Lilly got the radio to him," Bonnie told W.D. "That's why we're goin' to Ray's sister Maggie's."

"Yeah," W.D. said. "I know her. Everyone knows Lilly. They all know the McBrides, but these laws're lookin' for Bud, and you aren't worryin' bein' seen around here?"

"They're lookin' for you, too," Clyde said. "Only they don't have a name stuck on you yet, so aren't you worryin'? They haven't got a name but they've got a face. They get you, they'll put you in Ray's lap and start pullin' that switch."

"I'm not worryin' about any switch," W.D. said. "Long as I'm bein'

197

with you and Sis, I'm not gonna be worryin' 'cause you got some juju that gets you goin' past 'em while they're lookin' straight at you. You both got it, too. Sis, it's like you're holy or somethin', castin' spells so nobody's seein' you. Makes me feel like my bein' with you's like nobody's gonna see me either. That's why I'm not wastin' time thinkin' about gettin' stuck sittin' with Ray when they're pullin' a switch..." Bonnie laughed, but then W.D. said, "It's had me worryin' over shootin' that fella jumpin' on the car, but I swear I figured he was hurtin' Clyde and set to get us crashed in that car."

"Sit back," Clyde said. "Stop breathin' on my neck. I can hear you from where I'm sittin'."

The car cruised slowly along Eagle Ford, passing the small Hamilton house. Clyde parked on the opposite side of the road. Leaving the engine running, he tucked the .45 into his belt, buttoned his coat. "I'm goin' over there," he said, opening the door.

"You want me to go with you?" W.D. asked.

"No, I don't want you goin' with me. Stay put and shut up. If somethin' starts happenin' you get alert." Bonnie slid over to sit behind the steering wheel as Clyde walked across the road.

Up on the porch, he stood at the front door for a couple minutes, several minutes, talking through the screen. Bonnie asked W.D., "You see who that is he's talkin' to?"

"It ain't Lilly," he said. "Could be her sis."

Clyde then turned, stepped off the porch, and quickly crossed the road. "Lilly's not here," he said, getting into the car. "Ray's other sis says laws've been around for Ray's pals. She's scared 'cause of those kids in there. Says laws made her swear not to say they might be headin' back, but she's got a red light in the window. If it's burnin' after dark it ain't safe, and for us to keep on goin'."

"What about the radio?" Bonnie asked.

Clyde shook his head. "She ain't sure he's got it. Lilly's goin' back tonight. We'll drive around till the sun's down."

"Let's stop at my momma's," Bonnie said. "Get Billie Jean and cross the river—get us some sandwiches at the market."

Emma looked thinner, almost sickly, her face creased with concern. She said, "No, I'm just sick all over. I thank God your sister's here." When Clyde asked about the laws' visiting Hamilton's house, Emma said, "They've been back and forth and in and out of here and I'm surprised they aren't sneakin' around right now. For God's sake, y'all better stay outta these parts for now. Where's that boy? Is he tailin' after you?"

"W.D's out in the car," Bonnie said. "We're takin' him a ways."

Driving across the bridge, Billie Jean said, "The cops're comin' back, gettin' up a posse. I think they've got Floyd to find out where the rest of Ray's pals are. Looks like they've cleared out now that they've got Ray in jail, but you can't trust 'em to not be comin' back."

W.D. was elected to do the shopping with Billie Jean. Egg salad sandwiches and soda pops, plus a handful of candy bars. Neither Clyde nor Bonnie left the car until they parked at the tree-thick turnoff to eat sandwiches, and then Bonnie and Billie Jean got out as the sun was setting, but stayed close to the car.

W.D. asked Clyde, "We have to go back to Lilly's?"

Clyde looked at W.D. through the rearview mirror. "If he got the radio he'll be usin' the blades. If he didn't get it, he won't be helpin' us. We're damn near broke and I can't be usin' you."

"Yes, you can, Bud. You'll be seein' what I can do."

"I've seen what you do," Clyde said.

With a mouthful of egg salad sandwich, W.D. said, "You can trust me, Bud. I swear it to you." He looked out the window. "Sun's down now. We gonna go see if the light's burnin'?"

"When it's dark," Clyde said.

Billie Jean got into the car, sitting on the backseat with W.D. Bonnie leaned close to Clyde and said, "Gimme a kiss, daddy." Then she said, "You taste like chocolate. You eat a sandwich?"

"I didn't want one," he said. "The kid's eaten mine same as the one Billie Jean got him. Seems to just swallow 'em without much chewin.'"

After dropping Billie Jean off, Clyde told Bonnie, "Someone's gotta go to Hillsboro. Seems like Ray's got this chance of gettin' out before they fry his ass."

"You think that's what's gonna happen to him?" she asked.

"I know that's what'll happen. Take 'em a while but he hasn't a Chinaman's chance, 'less he gets his ass out of there. Anyone gettin' in there to get him out's gonna be in a war nobody's gonna win."

Bonnie took Clyde's hand. "I love you," she said. "I never want to lose you."

"I love you, too," he said.

Again approaching the house, Clyde slowed for moment. W.D. said, "The red light's burnin', Bud."

"We'll just keep checkin'," Clyde said.

After a visit to the Barrow's Star Service gas station, Clyde followed the back route, off Eagle Ford. He circled once, then twice, looking for anything that didn't belong on the road.

"Ain't no good to see what we need headin' this way," he said, turning off the headlights. "We'll take another drive, cruise past the house."

"No red light!" W.D. said.

Clyde slowed to a stop opposite the house. "There's a couple people movin' in there," Bonnie said. "Those blinds are shut but there's movin' around."

"Could be Lilly and her sis," W.D. said. "I can't see who it is."

"Could be the fuckin' laws," Clyde said, reaching for the cut-stock shotgun with the leather shoulder strap. He opened the car door silently, put his arm through the sling, then into the sleeve of his raincoat. "You get over here and take the wheel," he said to Bonnie. "Get the hell out if you see you gotta take off."

W.D. started to speak but Clyde waved him quiet. He walked across the road, his right arm pressing the hidden shotgun at his side. He hadn't reached the porch when Maggie screamed, "Don't shoot! Think of my babies!"

Clyde had no idea who was in the front room. He threw open his raincoat and swung the shotgun into action. He fired high, and the blast blew out the window. Laws were scrambling on the floor, avoiding a second shot which was delayed as Clyde worked to pry the empty shell jammed in the gun's breech. He could hear someone hurrying from the rear of the house, alongside the building towards the porch. "Get back!" Clyde yelled as the man came around the side of the house, a pistol in his hand that dropped into aim as the spent shell cleared from Clyde's shotgun and the second shell fired.

The man was knocked back several feet as if lifted from the ground. A second man escaped Clyde's third shot by dropping to the ground, as bullets fired from the house zipped past Clyde, cornering him in a cross-fire with W.D.'s shots ringing from the car.

"You're gonna hit Clyde!" Bonnie cried, grabbing at W.D.'s arm. She threw the car into gear and sped away from the gunfire, seeing Clyde running towards the road. For moments he was out of sight as he ran between houses, then appeared again, running and waving at the car.

Bonnie slammed on the brakes as Clyde ran into the road, threw open the driver's door and climbed in behind the wheel. He killed the car lights and sped west over Eagle Ford into the night.

Twenty-Two

"Shit, Bud," Buck said, grabbing Clyde by the shoulders. "Seems like a damn hundred years! I can't say I don't know why you haven't come visitin'!"

"Me'n' them convict hotels," Clyde said, "don't go seein' eye to eye."

"They done signed my butt outta there, so I'm one free man, brother. Got me a genuine Texas pardon, and bought a Marmon automobile, so I'm ready to roll. But what's with you, Bud? Blanche told me what's been happenin' with your havin' a helluva tough time."

"Brother, I'm not havin' a tough time," Clyde said, and glanced at W.D. "We've had times goin' on, ain't that right, boy?"

"That's right," said W.D. "Ain't been so tough. I got me these new pants, and Sis bought me this tie, says it's high class so I can act like a gentleman."

"You need more'n pants and a new tie," Buck said. "Gotta get yourself a woman! Get yourself hitched— "

"—he don't need a woman right now," Clyde said, "'specially one's gonna stick a bridle on his head. Sure don't mean to be sayin' that's you, brother, just this boy's got no time for chasin' cunt since we're headin' up to Missouri. Gonna stop in Joplin and see what's goin' on."

"You mean—" Buck said, holding up one hand like a gun. "That kinda what's goin' on?"

"Hell, that's how we're livin'," W.D. put in proudly. "Livin' by the gun like it says in the newspapers."

Clyde smiled. "Boy here gets to exaggeratin'. Been tight in spots

202

but a helluva lot of movin'. I got laws lookin' in holes for me in half these United States. But listen, brother, you'n' Blanche don't seem to be goin' nowhere in that Marmon, so I'm sayin' why don't you gas it up and follow me'n' Bonnie—all of us'll get a place in Missouri and take it easy. Gotta relax for a spell. Bonnie and Blanche'll be havin' a good time shoppin', gabbin'. Gonna get us a regular apartment, you see. Whaddya think, brother? Y'all want to come make us a family?"

"Listen, don't sound half bad, Bud, but I sure don't want my ass in any of them tight spots, y'know."

"I don't get in tight spots I don't see myself gettin' out of—" Clyde snapped his fingers, "—that fast. No one's gonna get me in a tight spot I'm able to see comin' from a mile off."

"I hear you," Buck said. "You always had lady luck sittin' on your shoulder."

"She ain't sittin' on my shoulder," Clyde said. "She's sittin' in the car alongside me, and bein' my ticket to heaven. We can work good together, brother, and you damn well know it. Haven't we always done that?"

"Sure," Buck said. "We've done that and both windin' up where we didn't figure we'd ever wanna to wind up."

"I'm workin' to do somethin' about all that," Clyde said. "I've got a real education workin' for me that I'm puttin' to use."

In a hushed tone, Buck said, "That's great, Bud, but listen to me, 'cause she don't want me gettin' in a pickle, now's I got a clean slate in Texas. I'm walkin' the fuckin' streets free as a bird. But see, Bud, Blanche and both Marie and Nell're sayin' the same thing, and damn pushin' me to get you to give up this kind of livin'. They're sayin', 'Coax Clyde to get himself clean,' and I'm tellin' 'em, 'I can't do that.' They're sayin', 'Yes you can'—Mom'n' Pop, too, sayin' I gotta show you to turnin' yourself in and makin' a clean slate—"

"—knock it off!" Clyde said. "I follow anyone's thinkin' except my own, it goes in straight to the fuckin' electric chair. Fuckin' laws're yankin' straws to be pullin' that switch and watchin' me fry. That's the only place I'd be headin' hearin' that kind of talkin', whether it's Mom or Pop or you or Jesus Christ doin' the day-dreamin'."

"I know," Buck said. "I know that—"

"—get it through your head," Clyde said. "I stay my way I'm goin' fast and I make a fat score, I'm disappearin' from view—me'n' Bonnie'll be two other folks livin' out their own lives that's nobody's business. If it weren't for Bonnie's mom and family and for my own—and for you, Buck—we'd be in Mexico." He stared at Buck for a moment. "Don't matter what's happened already, you're my brother and we can live like a family, all you gotta do's forget that crap of me turnin' in, or you gettin' on the spot. I'm tellin' you we can do it."

W.D. said, "I can do it with you!"

"That's right," Clyde said. "Boy, you got more beef in your fuckin' blood than fellas twice your size."

"I heard you got the laws lookin' for you," Buck said to W.D., "only they don't know who you are yet."

"I'm not about to send 'em a Christmas card," W.D. said. "Bud'n' me've got too much to do, and there ain't no returnin' address."

"He's right," Clyde said. "No time except right now to get on the move. Get your duds and your pretty wife, and your Marmon and your pardon and we'll all be in Missouri this time tomorrow." He turned to W.D. "Get Bonnie and we'll be movin' on."

"Wait a minute," Buck said. "Hold on and I'll talk to Blanche— fartin' around with that dog in there. She didn't wanna leave it with her stepdad, so I'm haulin' a fuckin' dog. We'll go with you to Missouri, I can tell you that, just to see you settled safe. But I gotta see what she's gonna say...." Clyde nodded. Buck said, "Right now our folks'n' hers are thinkin' I don't know which ducks're sittin' straight, but you know, Bud, you know fuckin' well I know which goddamn ducks're sittin' straight. Am I right?"

That night in a dim roadside diner west of Ponca City, Bonnie, Blanche, and W.D. were enjoying bowls of navy bean soup and cornbread slathered with butter, while outside, Clyde and Buck smoked, strolling near the parked cars while sharing snorts of Oklahoma moon between drags on their cigarettes.

Talking about his troubles in prison, Buck said, "Ma did everythin' a human bein' can do to get my ass outta there. What turned the trick? Blanche stuffin' her dress with laundry to look pregnant, then borrowin' two toddlers from a friend and goin' to the Texas governor beggin' for my release. She told that old woman governor I was the only one who could work a job and keep her and the family from starvin'."

Clyde shook his head when Buck handed him the bottle. "No, brother, I've had enough. That shit you thin paint with...."

Buck laughed. "Y'know what? I get out the joint and was paintin' houses and they send me packin' after two stinkin' hours. You know why?"

Nodding, Clyde said, "Sure, I know why."

Tossing the bottle into some bushes, Buck said, "Couldn't get work haulin' garbage. Son of a bitch laughs and says, 'Send your old lady to the sewin' factory!' You know what he meant?" Clyde nodded. "Whorehouse! Callin' my wife a whore! I coulda shot the fucker. I said, 'And you go fuck yourself, mister 'fore I send you to the fuckin' hospital!'" Buck popped a match with his thumbnail, lit another cigarette, and stared at the diner window where Blanche and the other two were on their feet to leave. "I get sick at times," Buck said. "Can't eat, and that fuckin' grub in the Walls killed my gut. I'm eatin' goddamn porridge like a fuckin' old man."

"Could be worse," Clyde said.

Buck said, "That old lady governor ain't half bad, Bud. She can't've known Blanche was pregnant 'cause I'd been locked away too long to have been able to pop her up. Fact is, unless we're all spongin' off the folks who's got little enough as it is, we fuckin' very well might be starvin'." He laughed a little. "Don't know how those tykes are doin' who acted they was our kids, probably too dumb to know the truth that they wasn't." Taking a deep drag on the cigarette, he said, "Shouldn't've brought that dog—hell, shouldn't have bought the goddamn Marmon."

Clyde said, "You two get in your fancy car, brother, and follow us. You'll have your wife in a genuine mink coat come fall."

Bonnie and Blanche rented an apartment in Joplin, but changed their minds when they saw the stone house—a two-bedroom, living room, kitchen, and bath above two garages separated by a stairway that led up to the second floor apartment. The front door was situated between the two hinged garage doors, with a doorway inside the garage leading up the stairs.

The rental arrangements were made by Blanche and Buck and the family moved in under different names—including W.D., who later said, "They were callin' me Walter, sayin' I was the kid brother. All the way there and gettin' the place, you couldn't say ol' Buck was runnin' for it like a darkie chasin' a chicken, 'cause Blanche wasn't too happy teamin' up with Bud and Sis. But far as I could see, in a few days passin' she wasn't fussin' as much as runnin' to tidyin' after Buck or herself. Or her and Sis goin' shoppin' at Kress, buyin' sheets'n' blankets and dishes and stuff, Sis buyin' a kind of Chinese bathrobe, a bunch of towels and a new dress, a hat, and even a couple glass vases she stuck flowers in. There was a bunch of flowers growin' out back where a separate garage was, and Buck'd made a deal on it to keep his Marmon in. The two cars we had in the garages downstairs were the ones we'd swiped before gettin' into Joplin.

"They'd make lists of what we'd be eatin' since Blanche or Bonnie'd be tellin' the market and havin' stuff delivered. The fella bringin' it would be knockin' at the downstairs door, so Sis or Blanche'd go down to have the stuff brought inside the door, no further 'cause nobody came up into where we all were. Enough it was that Snowball dog of Blanche's barkin' its head off. Got Clyde pissed every time it started a rumpus. I'd go down and haul the grocery boxes up the stairs while they'd be payin' the fella. If Sis went down wearin' that Chinese robe, I'd see that grocery guy's eyes all buggin' out.

"Blanche'd had some idea of keepin' Buck in Oklahoma with her relatives, but Buck said he couldn't find work—couldn't even get a job for a salary that amounted to spare change. She told Bonnie her and Buck'd fought about it and he wasn't gonna stay in Oklahoma. He said he'd never get a pocketful of money living as Blanche suggested, always someone handin' it to him like he was crippled, and what they figured he was worth. It was never enough. He'd said, 'You can't get a man to live like that!' He told her, 'You'll never get Clyde livin' that way, gettin' his hands dirty to make some fat sucker a wad to choke a horse. Bullshit,' he'd tell her. He was gonna take all they got and let the goddamn devil take the rest!'"

W.D. says, "Nights Buck'd be drinkin' whiskey or beer with Bud and Sis, cleanin' guns or playin' poker half the night until they crapped out. Sis'd go to sleep in the bed sighin' how happy she was to be on a regular mattress with clean sheets and pillows and a comforter. I'd lay on top of the comforter on Clyde's side of the bed, 'cause he didn't sleep sometimes, but when he did he'd kick me off the bed. In the tourist cabins we'd stayed in, I usually was sleepin' in the bed with them 'cause there wasn't any place to sleep on the floor."

Bonnie and Clyde had the bedroom that overlooked the rear of the property. W.D. said, "We'd been in Joplin more'n a week, livin' like it was a real place to be, me sharin' Bud and Sis's bedroom, though I was sleepin' on a couple of cushions off a couch. I couldn't get comfortable, my shoulders got in the way no matter how I turned, and my head wouldn't lay down.

"One night I looked up and Sis was starin' down at me from bed, and she says, 'What in hell's the matter with you?' Well, I told her what was wrong, and she said, 'Get on the bed, but don't crowd it up or else he'll be kickin' you back on the floor.' I got on the bed and it was heaven comparin' to the floor. I mean it was a good floor, good, clean, and everythin' about the place was clean and didn't need bein' fixed, nothin' busted like the places we'd been in. Sis did put her arm around me like she'd be holdin' the dog and I said, 'Sis, I sure like bein' with you and Bud,' and she said, 'Shut your trap or he'll be kickin' you outta here.'

"All that time in Joplin was like livin' in a regular person's home, and Sis or Blanche fixin' grub, or doin' it together but always like there was somethin' wrong between them. Sis hardly said much to her or Buck, maybe about the dog shittin' or pissin' somewhere and Sis steppin' in it in a new pair of slippers. I slept on Sis's side of the bed, or on the floor tryin' to get my head layin' even with the rest of me. Bud'd be up early, jigglin' the window shade and checkin' what's outside, even though there weren't much outside except the other house and that other garage where Buck had his car. But he'd stand there a long time, lookin' and makin' me wonder what he was seein' 'cause there wasn't nothin' to see like laws or a posse showin' up. I asked him but he said, 'What the fuck, boy, you think they're comin' wavin' a flag? What the hell, they'll be wavin' a rope for your goddamn neck.'

"I didn't ask him anymore what he was seein', 'cause he'd be up so early the sun wasn't comin' over. He once looked at me and said he couldn't sleep half the night 'cause that fuckin' dog was whimperin' and he said I should give it somethin' to whimper about, like a couple spoons of arsenic.

"He'd go out, shut the door, and then I was enjoyin' sleepin' up on the bed, but if I moved around too much, Sis'd shove me or push me off of the bed.

"She'd stay sleepin' long as she wanted, but Blanche was usually up early and skulkin' in the kitchen like fixin' somethin' for Buck 'cause of his stomach. That was goin' on for a couple days, then she was fryin' bacon the market fella'd brung us, along with the box of other grub and chocolate cookies and soda pop. Blanche'd be fryin' bacon I could smell, and smellin' it I had trouble stayin' asleep.

"Sis could stay sleepin' half the day and then she'd sit in the bathtub so long if you had to piss you'd go down in the garage or straight out around back to pee on the rock wall 'cause there wasn't another place to piss on. Both Clyde or Blanche could go in the bathroom while Sis was in the tub, but neither Buck nor me could go in. Clyde never told her to get out of the tub, and nobody else would, but Blanche'd bitch to Buck, though most of the time he'd tell her to keep her trap shut so Bud wouldn't get mad. When Bud got mad he'd just look at you like you were a rock we'd go down and piss on. Bonnie, sleepin' so late and stayin' in the tub till hot water turned cold.... Sometimes she'd run it hot all over, and that'd get Blanche like to pullin' her own hair out. They got along okay the first week we were there and they had a good time shoppin' at Kress or the other five-and-dime nearby, buyin' all kinds of stuff, or walkin' that dog around.

"If they weren't playin' cards half the night, they'd be listenin' to Bud playin' his guitar—damn good, and Sis would just be smilin' and lookin' pretty or else she'd be readin' one of her poems she'd be writin' when she was sittin' in bed. She did that a lot and I couldn't blame her after all the time she'd spent hunkered down on a car seat or on a blanket in a pile of leaves, then sneezin' and near chokin' on the dirt. She never complained, and told me never to complain 'cause it was weakness—then she'd say, 'You see how Blanche is, don't you? Complainin' from mornin' and damn near all night? So don't complain and be a person like that, 'cause that's a sign of bein' scared, and bein' scared's bein' weak and havin' nothin' worth holdin' still for.'

"I said, 'Well, her and Buck're married and isn't that what she's holdin' to?' Sis looked at me, her eyes kind of gettin' half shut, and she said, 'If you wanna think that, you go on and think that, but keep your mouth shut, or I'll have to smack you.'

"Sis kept playin' with picture puzzles, puttin' together all those little pieces. I remember a big old country road picture of a horse drawin' a wagon in the woods. A lady with the reins and wearin' a bonnet like a pilgrim, and it made me feel real sad. Sis said she'd met a little old lady at the market who was livin' nearby and looked like the lady in the puzzle. She said the lady invited her to have macaroon cookies. So Sis said, "If you behave yourself, maybe we'll go have macaroon cookies with that old lady.'

"We never did, though. Just didn't think about it those couple weeks. Sis could cook up rice and red beans like she did, and chili, and then we'd maybe read her magazines and she'd talk about thinkin', about the power of the mind, how you think hard and hold pictures in your mind and then answers come to you. She said, 'It's like hypnotizin' yourself,' then she rolled over and dozed off. A few times I went around the other side of the bed so's I could look at her face while she was asleep.

"Three different times Bud said to me, 'You stick here with Bonnie and keep that shotgun with you. You understand? We're goin' for some financin'. You stay here and keep a watch.'

"Buck'd get different when he'd go off with Bud, even looked different like how you are when you get excited. He'd hold that other shotgun like it just grew out of his arm, like sometimes how Clyde'd hold the steering wheel.

"One time Clyde came back with a bunch of little diamonds like out of rings and stuff, 'course there were no rings or pins, just these diamonds. We all sat lookin' at 'em, with the big magnifyin' glass Bud had in the canvas bag with the tools and flashlights and spyglasses. He wrapped those diamonds up and stuck 'em away somewhere in Sis's stuff, but then later that night he was hidin' 'em around the apartment. He kept a couple out and one afternoon when Buck was sick again, and after Bud'd sat up half the night puttin' together one of Sis's big picture puzzles which she'd got bored with—showed a big ship with giant sails in the middle of the ocean, all the water blowin' around—he had the two diamonds out that he'd hidden, and then wrapped these careful in his pocket, and said, 'You come on, we're gonna take a ride.' I'd hardly ever asked where we were gonna go 'cause he'd never answer me.

"We took the big Ford out of the garage and drove off. He wasn't sayin' where I was supposed to drive but after a few minutes he started gettin' like ants in his pants. I'd seen him that way only a couple times. 'Turn around and we're goin' back,' he said. I said, 'We forget somethin'?' All he said was, 'Turn around.' So I turned around and headed back and he was really lookin' everywhere, one way and then the other. Didn't say nothin'.

"When we got on our street he said, 'Get out and open the garage doors,' and I got out and then he drove the car in. I was just startin' to close the doors when there's two cars stoppin' on the street, and without warnin' one of them pulls fast as hell into our driveway, blockin' me gettin' the garage door shut. Clyde hollers, 'Laws!' and he's outta the car with the sawed-off.

"Son of a bitch laws is aimin' a gun right at me and yellin' at us, then takes a shot that goes through the garage door window, whizzin' past my ear, bustin' wood and glass. I got around the edge of the garage door but the cop's shootin' until Clyde lets loose the sawed-off, gets him in the shoulder and neck and he goes pitchin' down in the driveway, his legs still kickin'.

"Right then I'm feelin' wet and soakin' out of my stomach, and I yell, 'Bud! I'm fuckin' hit!' The second car's into the driveway like to run through the wall and another cop's already shootin' into the garage. Bud blasts again and's got him in the left side and the face, and one arm's about blown off at the elbow. 'My stomach's hit, Bud! That's where I'm hit—' He hollers to get upstairs, get everyone down into the car. 'Go on!' he yells, 'cause there's a couple other laws firin' from behind the second car.

"I went through the other inside door to the stairs but I couldn't make it. Even hollerin' for 'em to get down in the car made me feel like I was fallin' in half, bleedin' all down myself.

"Buck's comin' down the stairs with the other shotgun. He looks at me. 'You hit? Where you hit?' I said I didn't know. 'My stomach— my side—' He says, 'Bud hit?' I said no, he's pickin' them off. Buck says, 'Get Bonnie and Blanche down here,' then he lunges against the garage door and takes two shots at the laws. One law's runnin' to the far end of the building but Bud fires again, and Buck says he sees a bunch of dust and smoke flyin' off the rock wall at the end of the buildin'—the law's down, got a gun in hand and he's reloadin'.

"Bud says there's one other guy who's gone around the other side of the building. 'No way to get in the back,' Buck says. Clyde says, 'Where's Dub? He gone upstairs?'

"Buck says, 'He's shot'n' sittin' on the stairs.' Clyde says, 'Get the girls down here and get 'em in the car. We're gonna run.' Buck said, 'I hear one of 'em—she's on the stairs.'"

W.D. says, "I got up a few more of the stairs and Sis is comin' down. She says, 'Where you hit?' I said it felt like my stomach. Sis pulled my shirt out and said, 'You're hit in the side. Grab hold of me.' I did and three of us went downstairs. 'I can't stop bleedin',' I said. 'I don't want to fuckin' die bleedin' to death.' Sis said, 'Don't worry, we'll take care of it.'

"Blanche had been grabbin' what she could and looked scared and frantic, sayin', 'Come on, let's go, they're here!' That dog's run-nin' in front of her and almost trips us while Sis is helpin' me to the car.

"Clyde tells Sis, 'Get in the car!' and tells Blanche to help him get the law's car out of the way so we can get past it. Blanche sees the dead cop and his blood and hunks of him on the driveway and she almost faints. Clyde's hollerin' at her and strugglin' inside the law's car to free the emergency brake that's jammed. He's kickin' at it, then jumps out. Him and Blanche are pushin' at it but it won't budge. 'Where's Snowball?' she's cryin' and Bud says it ran past and down the street. Blanche is walkin' casually like in a trance, callin' for the dog.

"There wasn't more shootin' but Bud said the guy around back had for sure called for backup. Buck was draggin' the guy out of the way so he wouldn't be run over and Clyde hollered, 'Let's go!' Buck ran to the car, got in, and Clyde drove forward, rammin' against the front of the law's car. He gassed it and pushed their car out of the driveway, down into the street where it rolled backwards and crashed against a tree. Clyde sped ahead, gettin' us the hell away from that apartment buildin'.

"Halfway down the block, we spotted Blanche. Clyde hit the brakes and Buck jumped out, got her around the waist and brought her inside the car. Then we sped off fast, Blanche sayin' she couldn't find the dog. Sis whispered, 'Good,' then said to Bud, 'You're bleedin' down the front of your shirt, daddy. You've been hit and you didn't say it. How bad is it?' Clyde said, 'Stings. One of those last shots. I felt it hit me. It's a ricochet. Makes me feel like I'm blackin' out.' 'We need to stop,' Sis said, sort of frantic. 'Buck can drive.' But Clyde said, 'Not till we're over the goddamn Oklahoma border and then some, then check all this soon as we get the hell out of Missouri.'"

Twenty-Three

"The motor's overheatin'," Bonnie said. "I smell it steamin'. It's gonna be blowin' out the water."

"We ain't steamin' yet," Clyde said. "I'm headin' off anyway."

"We out of Missouri?" Buck asked from the backseat.

"Plain out of it," Clyde said, slowing down. He gradually pulled off the highway, onto a dirt road, and drove until he couldn't see the traffic on it.

"We're in the damned woods again," Blanche said. "We'll be eaten alive by bugs." Buck told her to shut up.

W.D. said, "I don't know if I'm livin' long enough for the bugs."

"Boy," Clyde said, grimacing in pain, "I'll get you in a minute. Right now I wanna get this slug out of me." He unbuttoned his shirt and Bonnie stared at the wound. "I can feel it right there," Clyde said. "Can you get it with your fingers? Just pull the son of a bitch out."

She dug with her fingernails at the edge of the wound to feel the metal. "I can't get it like this," she said. "Seems like it's pointin' up." She asked Blanche, "You got your nail file?"

"I don't have my purse," Blanche said. "It's all gone, honey. Nail file, purse, everything we owned—everything we bought."

"I got this little weenie blade," Buck said. "It's a souvenir." He handed the small penknife to Bonnie. "Got it the first year we got married."

"That was in my purse, too," Blanche said, and to Buck, "Our wedding certificate, along with your pardon paper."

"And you haven't got any of that?" Bonnie asked.

"I didn't see them carryin' anythin' when y'all were in the car,"

Clyde said. "Everything we had's back there in that place."

"Was—" Blanche said. "Was back there in the apartment. I'm sure by now the law's throwin' a party."

"More like they're throwin' a wake," Clyde said.

Bonnie, digging at the butt of the slug in Clyde's chest, said, "Damn funny goin' in like this and stoppin' when it hits a bone. Could've killed you, daddy."

"It's not that deep," he said. "Had to be a ricochet."

"Sure hard to get at," Bonnie said. "I don't want to push it any further."

Then she said, "Oops! Here it is! Look! Popped out like a bottle cap. You're bleedin' again."

"I'll keep the shirt wadded against it," he said. "We'll get some supplies down the way—soon as it's dark."

As Bonnie handed the tiny, bloody penknife back to Buck, she said, "What about your camera, Blanche? All our pictures we took?"

"I didn't get any of that," Blanche said. "I thought maybe you did."

"Holy shit!" Buck said. "You mean they got our fuckin' pictures?"

"All the pictures we took?" W.D. asked. "With our guns and all that?"

"You got it, boy," Clyde said. "Ain't our guns anymore. Now you gotta get your face operated on like Johnny Dillinger's."

Disgrunted, wincing in pain, W.D. said, "Well, Jesus Christ! The laws got pictures of us—they'll find out who we are?"

"They already know who we are," Bonnie said. "Couldn't make 'em happier. You'll be seein' us all tomorrow mornin' on the front pages."

"Maybe the midnight edition," Clyde said.

"Now they don't have to figure nothin' out," Blanche said. "They just gotta come find us, and then shoot us."

"Don't say that!" W.D. said. "I'm already shot. So's Bud. He's shot, too."

"Nobody's shootin' us," Clyde said, opening his car door. "Boy, get your shirt off and get outta the car. We gotta get a twig or a green branch about a foot long."

"I'll get it," Bonnie said, opening the car door. She got out as

Clyde climbed from the driver's side, telling W.D. to sit on the running board. Bonnie grabbed up a short branch and handed it to Clyde, who said, "Tear me off a piece of that slip you're wearin'."

"I don't want to tear it," she said. "I'll take it off." She went behind the car, removed her dress, and then the slip.

W.D. asked Clyde, "What're you gonna do with a stick and her slip?"

"I'm gonna see if you got a bullet in your hide like I had, or a hunk of lead that's busted off from the rest."

Bonnie handed her slip to Clyde. He carefully wrapped a part of it around the stick, then in a quick move, almost a sleight of hand, he pushed the stick into the bullet hole in W.D.'s side. "Oh, shit!" W.D. yelled. "That's killin' me!"

"It's not killin' you," Clyde said.

"What're you doin'!" W.D. cried.

"See here," Clyde said. "I've done pushed this branch straight through the hole in you, and it's now come out the back side. You see it? Turn your damn head and look at it. Ain't even bleedin' like it was." W.D. yelled again as Clyde pulled the stick out of the hole. "You got no lead in you, boy, and it's just about stopped bleedin'. We'll get medicine soon down the road."

"I gotta drink some water," W.D. said.

"We don't have any water," Bonnie said.

Blanche said, "We got nothin' but trouble."

Ignoring her, Clyde said, "We just sit a spell here and then we'll be on the road. I don't wanna be on that highway in daylight with a bunch of us piled in here."

"This hole's painin' me bad," W.D. said.

"Just keep that shirt bunched on it until we get to a grocery store or somethin' on the roadside soon as it's dark. Gotta get us another car."

"Sun's goin' down," Bonnie said, then to Clyde, "How're you feelin', daddy? Is it hurtin' like the devil?"

"Kinda sick," he said. "I should've pulled it out the minute it hit, but there wasn't time."

"We're all sick," Buck said. "Tomorrow's newspaper's gonna make us a lot sicker. Probably gonna print my fuckin' pardon."

"And our marriage certificate," Blanche said.

"You, kid," Buck said to W.D., "they'll get together and vote you the youngest walkin' dead man."

"Y'all relax," Clyde said. He started the car, drove ahead a half mile, then came to a stop. "You drive for a spell," he told Bonnie. "I gotta stop this bleedin' down the front of me."

Buck said, "Where're we headin', Bud? Where you thinkin' we'll pick up another car?"

"Straight south," Clyde said. "You got any money, brother?"

"Maybe some. What've you got?"

"Not a lot."

Blanche said, "I had forty-seven dollars in my purse—"

"—that's enough moanin'," Buck said. "We've got nothin' so let's forget it." He shook his head. "What the fuck. We got two shotguns here, and the fuckin' laws've got everythin' else we had. Even my car—a Marmon."

"Includin' my camera," Blanche said sadly. "They'll be sayin' I'm a criminal. And I've lost my dog—I've lost Snowball." She started to cry.

Bonnie was looking at her through the mirror.

Twenty-Four

It was hot and wet and near noon that April day in Louisiana as Bonnie was reading the newspaper from ten days earlier, the front page naming the cops who were killed in Joplin. She said, "They're quotin' that Persell fella about what they're callin' his 'kidnapping.'" She looked over at Clyde as he handled the car over the dirt road, dust blowing in through the open window. "He told them who we are, and they're callin' all of us killers."

Clyde said, "It's like I told Persell, it's kill or get killed. Probably shoulda shot his ass, too. Throw that paper away, honey. You had your chicken sandwich wrapped in that newspaper last night." She folded it up. "You've looked at the same paper since last week," he said. "Doesn't do anyone any good you keep readin' it 'cause we gotta keep movin.'"

"I know," she said. "I just think about how my momma feels."

"She knows the truth," he said. "It was us who was raided. You got that map on the floor?" She bent forward—almost fell against the dash. "You alright?" he asked.

"Dizzy," she said, bringing the map from between her feet. She looked at the map. "We're goin' to Bellevue and then east to Ruston. This bank's damn far from Joplin."

"You thinkin' about Joplin a lot, aren't you?" he said.

She stared ahead at the road. "I had a good time there, daddy. We could've lived in that place for a long time. It was private and quiet. Don't you think it was?"

"What I'm thinkin' is we gotta get rid of this car," he said. "Been too long ridin' it. Wake them up. It's like we're haulin' three stiffs. We

217

got work to do."

Bonnie turned, reached over the seat and pushed Buck's knee. He didn't wake up. She patted Blanche's leg. "Blanche? Open your eyes!" She pushed her again. "Clyde says y'all wake up."

"What?" Blanche cried, eyes frantic. "What's the matter?"

"Nothin's the matter," Clyde told her. "Get those boys woke up."

Blanche pushed at W.D., slumped against the left side of the car. "Wake up!" she shouted. W.D. straightened up, then leaned forward to Clyde. "What're we doin', Bud? We there yet?"

"I'm comin' around back of Ruston," Clyde said. "We gotta dump this car and get another one before goin' to work."

"Okay," W.D. said. "I'm ready. What time is it?"

"It's after noon," Bonnie said. "You got a date?"

"Sit back," Clyde told him. "Stop breathin' on me."

Buck was awake. He said, "Soon as we call this one in, brother, and get outta here, we'll grab us some grub—decent grub, 'cause my stomach's shrinkin'."

"Gotta get rid of this car," Clyde said.

As they drove through the neighborhood, Blanche said, "All these old houses look pretty big. Must be nice havin' all the money and a house to live in."

"Right over there," Clyde said to W.D. "That black Chevy across the street? Go get that one."

Clyde stopped the Ford, and W.D. climbed out. He trotted across the street to the Chevrolet, parked in front of a boardinghouse. After sticking his head in the window, he opened the door and got in, then signaled to Clyde who gave a signal, his finger moving in a circle which meant "See you around the block." Clyde then drove on in the opposite direction. W.D. drove away from the boarding-house, but Bonnie said, "Someone's runnin' after him!"

A young man had charged out of the boardinghouse as W.D. was heading to the corner. Hearing the young man hollering, W.D. gassed the Chevy into a fast turn and sped away. Clyde made a quick turn off the street, just as Bonnie caught sight of a young woman running after the Chevrolet.

Maneuvering swiftly through the neighborhood streets, Clyde spent several minutes in search of W.D. "Where the hell'd he go?" he said angrily. "Should've come around this way, headin' where we are."

Minutes later, Clyde turned east on another road, then south toward the highway into the middle of Ruston. "He's nowhere!" Buck said. "Goddamn kid's taken off. There's some folks parked up ahead. You think they seen that Chevy?"

"I see 'em," Clyde said. Driving slowly, he angled off the road towards the rear of the parked car. He stopped, got out and approached the driver's window. "Say, fella," he said, "you seen a black Chevrolet go?"

The driver stared at Clyde, surprised. "I sure as hell haven't, but that's what I'm lookin' for! That's my car and they just stole it—"

Clyde jerked open the car door, grabbed the shocked young man and pulled him out of the car. "I've got a gun so just do as I tell you." The young woman in the passenger's seat started to scream, but Buck was at her door, pulling it open and grabbing the girl. He said to Clyde, "Let's kill 'em both!"

Clyde pushed the dazed driver onto the backseat of the car as Buck said, "Whatta we do with this dame?"

"Put her in here," Bonnie said, climbing out. "Put her between me 'n' Clyde."

The young woman was ushered onto the front seat, Bonnie following her in and pulling the door shut. Her companion sat stiffly squeezed between Blanche and Buck, who had his gun in hand but was fishing with his other hand past the guns on the floor until he found the pint of rye. All jerked back and forth and against one another as Clyde drove swiftly, wheels jouncing in potholes, narrow back roads, turning sharp and heading in a wide circle of the area, Bonnie's newspaper pages rattling apart in the wind or blowing around the sandwich wrappers and dust. Both captives sat in silent fear as the car zigzagged over back roads, swaying as if to capsize, then racing ahead.

Gradually he slowed down, his anger at the blunders subsiding as Bonnie cheerfully chatted with their latest kidnap victims. His name was Dillard and his "sweetheart," as he called her, was Sophia. "What you've done," Bonnie said, "is give us a mess of trouble, 'cause we're just chasin' around instead of doin' what he came to do."

"Like I said," Buck mumbled, "tie these two up, blow their brains out and stick 'em in the swamp."

"That's not what we came to do," Bonnie said.

"We're not gonna blow any brains out," Clyde said, "or stick 'em in a swamp. We've lost the boy and we're gettin' our asses outta here."

The air was thick, hot, and wet. Sophia asked, "What about us? What're you gonna do with us?" Bonnie shrugged and gave a smile. Sophia asked, "Who are you? What did you come here for?"

Nonchalantly, Bonnie said, "To rob a bank. These gentlemen are bank robbers." Sophia began to wring her hands. She had a home demonstration business, she said, a mother and father to worry about, and lots of people depending upon her.

"We got a lot of people worryin' about us, too," Bonnie said.

Dillard cleared his throat, and said to Bonnie, "I heard you call the driver 'Clyde'...."

"That's right," Bonnie said. "His name's Clyde."

"And your name?" Dillard asked.

"My name's Bonnie," she said. Dillard stared at her. "What do you do?" she asked. "You also got people dependin' on you, too? Worryin' about you?"

"They don't do much worryin'," he said. "I work in a funeral parlor."

Bonnie laughed. "A funeral parlor? What do you do in a funeral parlor?"

"I'm a state-licensed undertaker," he said.

Blanche said, "This isn't funny! It's a bad omen!"

Dillard said to Bonnie, "Your friend could be right."

Bonnie looked around at Dillard and said, "When we're all taken care of and tucked away, will you come and make us look pretty?"

The young man said, "I'll definitely keep that in mind."

Still in Louisiana, Clyde drove off the road and stopped. He told the couple, "I'm gonna stop for gas at the station I see up the road, and I'm gonna put you on the floor and cover you so nobody sees you when we're gettin' gas. If you do any yellin' or shoutin' there'll be some trouble you won't like."

Buck said, "There'll be a bloodbath!"

With a full tank of gas, and Dillard and Sophia crowded onto the backseat with Buck and Blanche, Clyde drove a back road across the Arkansas state line. He stopped just outside the town of Waldo, and said, "You two're gettin' out here. Let 'em out, Buck." He then told Dillard, "Come here," and handed him a five-dollar bill. He said, "Call the sheriff of this here town and get you a ride back."

Bonnie waved goodbye to the couple.

On the hunt for the real Clyde and Bonnie—as though all we shake out are shreds of ghosts—I sought, bargained, and cajoled all I could from any source I'd tracked, no matter how distant, who could offer some kernel of truth, a view, a memory. I made contact with Billie Jean (Parker) and Blanche Barrow. I talked to W.D. Jones, who carried sadness for Sis and Bud, as he called Bonnie and Clyde. Still holding a tarnished reverence for the pair, and who was reluctant to talk until I shared with him my two conversations with Alvin Karpis. Once Public Enemy Number One, the handsome man whose intense eyes could bore into you had earned the nickname "Creepy" Karpis. He was a record-holder, having spent one of the longest terms in Alcatraz. He played a key role in the Karpis-Barker gang, one of the most notorious in American history. He robbed banks the same time as John Dillinger, Pretty Boy Floyd, Baby Face Nelson, and Clyde Barrow, though none of their paths ran necessarily parallel.

My talks with Karpis occurred after he'd left Alcatraz, spent time at McNeil Island before his release, and his exile to Canada. He felt that while in McNeil he'd invested too much time teaching Charles Manson to play guitar—to the point, he said, of "having been conned by Charlie." On my second chat with Karpis, the once-notorious Public Enemy Number One told me about a bank Doc Barker had once "discussed hitting," but the bank had already been hit by Clyde Barrow.

Karpis said, "And with Barrow's history, he could've been sitting on the rock as well, or long-since fried, gassed or hanged, depending on which state caught him, if they'd ever come close to catching him. He was the slickest damn weasel you could've run into—only you didn't run into Barrow since he was nowhere long enough for anyone to lay a hand on him. You'd think nobody in their fucking mind could've spent the amount of time running like that boy did. And fast, like a fox on fire, and a master of hit-and-run no matter how fast you're playing it. He's here, he isn't, then God only knows where the hell he is. He was a fucking rumor. Was he real? Here's a bunch of feds, barnyard lawmen, and cornfields of hicks chasing him, and you can bet some close enough to breathe on his collar, then fast as you're on top of him, he's gone. I say he had all he wanted. He had his guns and he knew how to get more and he had his gal—that little Bonnie gal, no bigger than a tyke (neither was Barrow much bigger than her, but you would've thought he was a giant, dealing out that vanishing act). He'd had a new set of wheels sometimes three times a damned day, and you have to hand it to him—nobody else was like that roadrunner in the cartoons more than Barrow, that coyote chasing up one mountain and down another and shooting from every angle, always thinking he's got his bird, when all he's got is himself being made a fool out of."

W.D. Jones listened to the Karpis rendition of Clyde with reverence, as though we were talking about a saint. Jones said, "I don't like to be interviewed because nobody gets what I say right. They get it backwards; things I didn't say or never woulda said but they've got me sayin' it. Also you might understand the trouble with these limitation laws, though I don't give it much mind 'cause it's too far back—it's old stuff that's got nothin' backin' it up." I said I understood. He said, "Well, you sound like you do, but I don't have much to say that's not been said by someone other than me."

He wanted to know more about Karpis, and I said it was one of the regrets that still stung me because of what I was involved in at the time Karpis wanted to share his life story—said he'd maybe find a writer to do it, as he wasn't sure he had the ability to take it on.

In time, Karpis left the country and was living in Spain where he died from an overdose of sleeping pills and booze that I've suspected was more intentional than mishap.

Jones said, "I got enough fuckin' trouble without knockin' myself off. What's written about me nobody's quotin' what I've said, and they pick up stuff from what others said, and from police stuff, but you understand some of that was necessary bein' in a position to do with myself stayin' alive after all of what happened back then, and half of 'em so far back nobody gives a hoot—especially me."

W.D. kept driving, he said. "I kept drivin' and thinkin' it'd come to me where I was headin'." Once he knew what he was doing, he ditched the Chevrolet and "hobo'd it back" to Dallas, thinking he'd find Clyde and Bonnie right where the laws would've anticipated they'd never be found. "It was like a knack someone's got at cards and tricks like magic where the guy's got an empty hand and next you're seein' he's holdin' up a rabbit.

"I told his folks I'd be gettin' back with them, but his dad and Cumie, even his sis and brother L.C. told me to go the other way. He warned, 'Don't find Clyde!' They were sayin' they knew he'd take me right along and the only place we were really headed was to the electric chair. His sis Nell said, 'That's what's goin' to happen to Clyde and Buck—my two brothers are goin' to be executed soon as they catch them.' His ma said, 'They don't kill the boys the minute they get their hands on them. You gotta follow the American Constitution and be tried by peers, and that's the United States law and the way it's done in Texas, so nobody gets rushed into any electric chair without bein' tried by ordinary citizens in the Texas court of law.'

"Nell said to me, 'You've got a choice, boy, you can keep movin' on or get hanged or fried,' and his dad, ol' Henry, sat lookin' at me and rubbin' his hands and then he said, 'You take your pick, boy, they don't necessarily get you hanged, but they sure got that chair juiced and waitin' for you, 'less'n you high-tail it out of Dallas and out of the state of Texas. You get your name changed to somethin' nobody knows and grab a little wife and go be livin' in Nevada or

Cheyenne where nobody'll know who you are. Otherwise,' he said, then he drew his finger across his neck.

"I said, well, I had obligations to Clyde and Sis who were better'n any sister and brother to me, and I had to see 'em even if it was to be sayin' so long.

"They asked me if Blanche had ever done harm to anyone, and I had to laugh, and said she just loves Buck and has her livin' all wrapped around his; it's the same with Bonnie, who's smarter with her mind than the rest of us, but she's never done harm to someone, never done anythin' like they're sayin' in the newspapers. That's all lies. I said you read all them papers and they're makin' up half of what they're sayin' Bonnie's done 'cause they don't know what to be puttin' in them papers unless they're told by the laws, and there's never been a single instance when Bonnie's shot at anyone or hit 'em in the head, and she's like Clyde's wife, and there's nothin' neither wouldn't do for the other. It's just that Clyde's like that cartoon put in the paper showin' how he's like a gopher and you never know what hole he's goin' in or comin' out of, but whatever it is, it's sure out of reach every time. I tried to tell the folks I had an honest dedication to Clyde, and I knew there were people all over who figured he was doin' what came natural, but Bonnie wasn't like him that way—like I said Sis was smarter, and her writin' and drawin' pictures, but there's nobody smarter than Clyde at gettin' away from the laws, and takin' care of us who're close. Better'n any family I've ever known."

Having successfully escaped Louisiana and Arkansas, and feeling only half-safe in Texas, W.D. did all he could to avoid being spotted. He'd raced off without knowing where he was going, other than he'd lost Clyde and Bonnie, who'd failed to find him in their pursuit. Years later he'd say, "It was then that I started calling upon 'mental' resources, or I'd just get blinded in my thinkin', and lookin' to see if Bud was gonna catch up, but I didn't know where the hell they'd gone. I knew at the same time I couldn't come to any stop without the laws catchin' me and once that would've happened I coulda just jumped in the lake, pulled down the window and called it a night. I knew what I'd tell the laws, though, and I had it figured."

He knew he could probably get away with it. To some degree it was reasonable and might've satisfied the law. His story was that he'd escaped from Clyde Barrow who'd held him a "prisoner" the whole time—threatened he'd track him and kill him or have him killed no matter where he ran off to or who he wound up with. "I was hopin' I could get away with it," he said, "since it wasn't likely they'd get Clyde—he was too fast, too smart for 'em."

Twenty-Five

    I traveled from Louisiana to Memphis, from Frisco to New Orleans, then Texarkana for a visit with an old man who'd once encountered Clyde Barrow and rented a cabin to Bonnie. "I knew it was her," he said, remembering her vividly, and the car she arrived in driven by Clyde. "That car, a couple-year-old Ford, had one nearly flat rear tire. I rapped on the window and he rolled it down. He had a hat on and round dark sunglasses. I said, 'Your back tire's about ready to go flat on you.' He looked around but I said, 'The other side, the back left tire.' He said the car'd been ridin' lopsided, and thanked me. The girl had rented the cabin. She had a funny little red hat on, sat up on top of her head like a candy box. The blouse she had on was shiny like black silk, only the arms were made of lace. Just lace all the way from her shoulders to her wrists, and though I'm not jeweler, the ring she wore had a pretty big stone that looked like it cost a bundle.

    "They were a married couple, she said, Mr. and Mrs. Jack Beatty. I was told they'd be stayin' two nights, maybe three. I gave him the cabin and he drove down to it, parked right in front of it.

    "After dark, the young fellow had the car jacked up and that bum wheel off. I asked if he needed any help and he said no. Then I asked if he was any relation to Clyde Beatty, the circus lion tamer. He laughed a little and looked up at me. He said he wasn't any relation to Clyde Beatty but said he'd seen Clyde Beatty and the lions in a picture show or a newsreel. He stood up, brushin' at his hands, and said he'd pay me some cash to take his wheel to an all-night service station he'd spotted a few blocks south. I said I could do that. I'd drive it down there, get it fixed pronto since I knew the guy workin' nights. Then he said, 'You'll get it right back?' I told him yes. He said soon as I got it fixed he'd appreciate my puttin' it back on his car, and he handed me a few dollars, then went into the cabin.

"When I got to the station, I waited while the boy I knew patched the leakin' tire, and I asked if he knew anythin' about the Barrow gang that'd been in the papers and some wanted posters goin' around here and there. He said he'd read about the bank robberies and stickups, and I said, 'Well, what if he came in here? Stuck you up?' I asked if he worried about gettin' robbed and he said he'd get paid the same if someone pinched the sales money or not, and he'd make not a nickel more or less.

"I wanted to tell him about the fellow at the cabin bein' Clyde Barrow, but I didn't. I had no proof he was a bank robber and wanted for murder, and since they'd be there maybe two days, I thought maybe I'd have a chance to find out by goin' to the sheriff. I drove his tire back, put it on the car and left the jack and tool on the runnin' board of the car. I didn't want to open the car door or get at the trunk. I was right in front of the cabin and they had the blinds shut tight and no lights on.

"It was before dawn the next mornin', I heard the car start up and back on out to the road, then head off goin' north. I hadn't seen who was in the car, and I went to the cabin, thinkin' maybe the girl was there. But nobody was there. Both blankets were missin' off the bed, and they'd taken one of the pillows. The towel and a washcloth was gone and so was the soap. My goin' to the sheriff sayin' Clyde Barrow and the Parker girl were in the cabin, and that Barrow had me haulin' his flat tire down to the service station, then puttin' it back on his car would've had me lookin' like a damn fool goin' in there with such a tale."

Next stop for me was Joplin, then back to Louisiana—a circuit of grabbing for some key from the chaos of three-fourths of a century's American newspaper blunders and flawed information.

No way of knowing where Clyde and Bonnie were, or when or how they'd pop up next, in which state, country or city; only splinters of fact scrambled into newspapers or magazines more fanciful than factual.

They drove night and day, endless roads like capillaries in a vast body blazing in the summer and freezing through winter. Cold rains—invincible mud. Radiators overheating. The stink of cheap gas and burning rubber, and the smell of Bonnie's perfume that was never cheap. She'd buy it over roadside drug counters or cosmetic slots, or in the brief shelter of a downtown store, her manner and dress so far from a clerk's idea of a gunman's moll.

Bonnie Elizabeth Parker had never been a problem for me. I knew almost everything she was and how she got the way she did, and why she made the deliberate choice to spend her life, short as it was, locked emotionally to Clyde, who could walk the walk and talk the talk, and who held faithful to the little gem wedged into his life like a painless sliver. That was Bonnie.

It took a while for me to draw a bead on Clyde, but once I got him in my sights, I believed I could see who he actually was, and what he was like: young and desperate beneath the chill of his manner, and so controlled and methodically determined that he could almost predict every turn of his life, or at least take charge of it. And though physically small, he was feared by larger, less exact men. Clyde took charge of all situations. Organized almost to the point of meticulousness, and far smarter than Pretty Boy Floyd or Baby Face Nelson or so many operating outside the law, Clyde carried a solitary view of his shrinking world. He was devoted to guns, to the oily slickness of metal, the quick snap of the firing pin on a bullet's bottom spoke louder than his words.

He carried a concern about going deaf, and passed this on to Bonnie. During a secret family get-together in Dallas on Dog Town Road, Bonnie told her sister she too was having hearing trouble. "All the noises I hear bump together," she said. "What you're sayin' gets stirred up in all the other noises." She asked Billie Jean to speak louder, "So," she said, "I'll hear your voice above the ruckus." While the group was having their secret picnic, Bonnie asked Clyde to tell Billie Jean about a bank robbery in Minnesota.

Clyde grinned. He said, "Buck busted out a back window and

we climbed in over the broken glass, and hid until sunup." Clyde said he slept in a swanky chair, the shotgun on his lap, while Buck lay snoring on the floor. First thing the next morning when the manager opened the door, Clyde was there to greet him. "I said, 'Good mornin', sir,' and stuck the shotgun against his stomach. I told him to lock the front door up again, and open the back door."

Bonnie said, "I brought the car up the alley behind the bank. Blanche was on the backseat, waitin' for the boys to come out."

"That man gave me no trouble," Clyde said. "He was a pleasant fella and did what I told him. We didn't have no mix-up except for Buck carryin' that bag of silver change that was heavy as a hog." Clyde said he'd snatched over fourteen hundred dollars from the safe and told the manager, 'Now you go on and sit in that comfy chair I was sittin' in waitin' for you, and tell anyone comin' out after they'll be gettin' a load of buckshot.'"

Bonnie's mother gave a nervous look as Clyde went on, saying how Bonnie scooted over so he could climb behind the wheel, Buck hardly getting the car door shut as Clyde sped out of the alley.

"All of you know the crap that goes on in the newspapers," Buck said, "sayin' we shot up the town gettin' out of there, and gals were shootin', but none of that's what happened."

"They just make that up," Bonnie said. "They get everythin' wrong so people get excited and go buyin' papers everywhere they see 'em."

"I knew it," Cumie said. "Then y'all came straight on?"

"Through Iowa, Kansas, and Oklahoma," Bonnie said. Clyde said they had to change cars a couple times, once across the Nebraska border, then again north of the Texas line. Bonnie squeezed his hand. "We had a good time, though, didn't we, honey?"

Her mother said, "Bonnie, come walk with me a little ways. My legs are so stiff I can hardly bend my knees." They strolled a short distance from the rest of the family until Emma stopped walking. Almost whispering, she said, "Honey, you still got a chance of savin' yourself. You give yourself up before it's too—before somethin' awful happens to you."

"You mean like dyin'?" Bonnie said. "Like before I get myself shot?"

"Yes, for the love of God," Emma said.

"Clyde's name's up, Momma. He knows he'll be shot sooner or later 'cause he's never gonna give himself up, and he's never gonna surrender so they can plain execute him in that electric chair. They know it. But I'll be with him till the end, Momma. I love Clyde and when the end's comin', I'll be dyin' right alongside him. I'm in as big a spot as Clyde, and my name's up too. I know it sounds bad to you and the rest of the world, but I'm happy bein' with Clyde no matter what comes." She hugged her mother and said, "Momma, I got some money for you."

Clyde also had money for Cumie. He handed her an envelope of cash while Buck doled out silver dollars to everyone in the family. The group clung together a few more minutes. Buck and Clyde made a plan of meeting across the Oklahoma line the second weekend in June. Late at night. "The bridge we'd spotted," Buck said.

Clyde nodded. "That's it," Clyde said. "I'll give a couple honks on the horn and you answer. I'll flash the headlights, and you flash back three flashes."

As Buck and Blanche drove off in a separate car, Billie Jean told Clyde, "W.D.'s in Dallas and wants to go with you. I think he's crazy, but he's swearin' that's what he wants to do."

"He's not crazy," Clyde said. "What he is he's a pain in the ass."

"Accordin' to him," Billie Jean said, "you're just about the most important and famous fellow in the world. He told me to tell you he'll be waitin' for y'all right now."

The trail from the family get-together to a tourist camp in Vernon, Texas, with W.D. on board, grew vague and clouded as time rolled into June. Bonnie would later tell her sister that Clyde frequently talked about his dead-set plan of "bustin' into Eastham prison." She said, "Nights in the cabin he keeps a weak lightbulb burnin', sometimes shinin' right into his face." To block the light,

Bonnie slept with a blouse, a towel, or another sheet covering her face. If Clyde fell asleep, she'd unscrew the bulb. "When W.D.'s not sleepin' on the floor on that mat we got off a swing," she said, "he'll be sittin' at the window, the shade angled so he can see out, and feelin' he isn't any longer a pain in the ass."

If instead of a cabin, they stayed hidden in the woods, Bonnie would later tell her sister, "The only light's comin' from the moon or stars while we're sleepin' in the car, way deep in those woods. You hear the night critters makin' sounds, lonely sort of sounds like they're lost out there. Sometimes that's the best of times, the moon bein' full and so bright through the trees. All them stars shinin' like a ceilin' of jewels. Those times nobody knows what I'm thinkin' or feelin', and that's the way I like it. Last week I woke up with a deer stickin' his head in the window. My sittin' up and touchin' his nose scared him. He banged his antlers on the top of the car door like he couldn't get himself free, yankin' his head like he was, and pullin' back. Clyde'd jumped up and got the shotgun, thinkin' the laws or someone's on us.

"Sometimes I'm drivin' so Clyde'll shut his eyes, but most of the time he's drivin' and we're travelin' those back roads like a devil shot right outta the heavens."

Billie Jean had said, "Honey, you now seein' yourself as a devil?" Bonnie stared at her sister and didn't say anything.

Saturday night, ten days into June and speeding north on the Texas highway they raced past the town of Wellington, holding the five-window V-8 coupe at an even eighty, Bonnie's head had bowed, her chin at her chest and both hands in her lap, fingers curled inwards. Clyde glanced at her. She'd dropped off talking about her mother and what she'd said during the visit with the folks.

W.D. was asleep on the rear seat, three guns on the floor, and two rifles in the trunk. Clyde's eyes were getting heavy. He thought of pulling over, waking W.D. and letting him get behind the wheel for a while. He'd put Bonnie in the rear so she could sleep better. There was still time before meeting Buck at the Oklahoma border.

He felt a sting in his left eye. Rubbing it, he found something had blown in and struck the far corner of his eye. Again he turned his head and looked over at Bonnie. He'd later say he hadn't seen a detour sign or where the earth had been excavated for a new bridge to reach across the Red River. It was fast, the highway veering to the old bridge, and racing straight ahead, Clyde missed the detour.

Too late he saw what he'd done, but hit the brakes, the car swerving, skidding, then sprung from the road and seemed to hang in the air sideways for a second, then plunged a dozen feet towards the dry riverbed.

W.D. was flung out of the rear seat, seemed to hang wedged against the inside of the roof for a moment, then the crash. Dirt, dust, smoke and gasoline spewed everywhere. The car caught fire. Bonnie cried out, pushed half-forward with her legs somehow stuck beneath the dashboard. Fire was erupting inside the car, and Bonnie screamed, "It's burning me! Get me out! I can't get out!"

Smoke, fire and the biting stink of battery acid filled the interior as Clyde struggled to free Bonnie. A moment later he saw two strangers scrambling down the embankment and running to the car. They began pulling at Bonnie's door that was stuck. Clyde felt for the shotgun, but then reached across Bonnie and unlocked her door. It was damaged—hard to open. Bonnie kept screaming. Clyde thought she would've called the appearance of the two men "a stroke of magical luck."

They yanked and pried at the damaged car door while Clyde struggled out on the driver's side, came around and helped the men working Bonnie free from beneath the burning dashboard. W.D. had squeezed out of the wreck, staggered back half conscious from his collision with the inside of the car's roof. He quickly rescued the guns and ammo from the car, then opened the trunk and gathered what he could carry.

Bonnie was screaming that her leg was "fryin'."

Clyde cried, "Hurry up! Get her out!"

One of the strangers noticed the guns W.D. was gathering from the sprung-open trunk of the car. Clyde kept yelling, "Get her out! Get her out!"

Then they had her. She looked like she'd passed out. All three managed to free her as the smoke and fumes thickened, and as they lifted her to be carried, she started struggling and kicking. "It's alright!" Clyde told her. The skin of her leg was reddened and blackish from the burn and the flesh looked torn. He then looked at the two men. "Where'd you come from?"

"We were on the porch of the house when you went off the road," one man said. "We're right up the slope. We'll fetch a doctor—"

"No doctor!" Clyde said. "We'll take care of her. Let's go—let's get her to your house."

Both men carried Bonnie up the embankment, but kept glancing at the guns W.D. struggled to carry until they reached the small house overlooking the riverbed. A few scant trees surrounded the porch where two women were waiting, one holding a baby that was crying. The older woman stepped off the porch, and seeing Bonnie sagging in their arms, cried, "My God! Bring her inside! This girl injured bad."

Moaning and jerking, Bonnie was placed on a bed in a small middle room where the only light flickered from a kerosene lantern on a table. Clyde looked at the others: the younger woman with the baby, and a third man. "What's your name?" he asked. The man said his name was Alonzo. Clyde reached out a hand, but seeing the guns overloading W.D., the man stiffened and stepped back.

Clyde didn't answer. He turned to the woman at the bed with Bonnie. "Mister," the woman said, "this girl's burned bad, and needs a doctor—"

"—no doctor," Clyde said. "You take care of her, fix her with whatever medicine you got. We'll handle the rest as soon as we get out of here. Just attend to her as best you can."

Alonzo said, "She could lose her leg with that kind of damage."

"You two ladies ease her pain," Clyde said, "and we'll be on our way. All we need's a car. You got a car?"

"Who are you?" the younger man asked. "What are these guns

for?"

Her face straining with pain, and almost incoherently, Bonnie cried out, "You know who we are? This is Clyde Barrow you're talkin' to! That's who he is…."

Clyde grabbed the shotgun from W.D. "Nobody's gonna get hurt in here," he said. "The rest of you stay put in that room and nobody make any funny moves." To Bonnie, he said, "You hold on, sugar, and let these ladies get you cleaned up."

Looking up at Clyde, the woman cried, "This is an awful burn on this girl, she's got a terrible gash and's needin' more than cleanin' up."

"We'll get her fixed okay," Clyde said firmly. He placed his hand on Bonnie's forehead. "Lay here, honey, and I'll figure this out. The damn road—"

"—we missed a detour sign," W.D. said. "We messed up."

"Shut up!" Clyde told him, and turned to the others in the front room. He looked at them, then toward the kitchen. "Where's that other guy who was standin' over there?" The men didn't answer. Clyde said to W.D., "Go find that fella." To the men he said, "No one else goes anywhere." Holding the shotgun, he asked Alonzo, "Where's your car?"

"My car don't run," the man said. "There's the other one around the back."

"That other guy's gone for the car!" Clyde told W.D. "Go stop him! We need that car."

W.D. hurried through the kitchen and out the back door. Clyde went into the front door, gripping the shotgun. Struggling, Bonnie tried to come off the bed, her bloody dress soiled and burned. Blood was leaking down the lower part of her leg. The woman tried to hold her down, but dazed, Bonnie said, "What's happened to me?"

"Lay back down," Clyde told her. "We're gonna get your leg cleaned and fixed and gettin' out of here."

Coming up the porch and through the front door, W.D. said, "No car, Bud. Nobody out there. I didn't hear any car."

"He must've pushed it to the road and jumped it," Clyde said. "Bonnie can't walk and we can't get outta here carryin' her. Gotta figure out where we'll carry her to."

"We'll get a car," W.D. assured. "Maybe he's gone for a doctor."

"Like hell he has," Clyde said. To the older woman he said, "Where's that boy gone? Where's he run off to?"

"I don't know," she said. "A neighbor's. He don't like guns." She looked up at Clyde. "None of us like guns, but I'm tellin' you this girl better get to a hospital. I'm near seein' the bone in her leg."

"Clean it!" Clyde said. "Fix her and we'll wait. Bring what medicine you got in here and bandages or clean cloths."

"I can't fix her!" the woman said. "I'm no doctor."

"You got bandages, don't you?" he said. "You got some clean towels or somethin' for bandages? Now do what I'm tellin' you." He turned to the others. "Y'all stay where you are and keep quiet. We'll leave this lamp here while she's fixin' the girl."

Turning back to the women, he said, "Get all that battery acid off her skin and get me some string and a big needle like you use on a turkey. She'll be okay. I guarantee you." He stepped to the bed and asked Bonnie, "How is it, sugar? I'm sick as hell over what's happened to you and us gettin' trapped out here. Just rest now, let these ladies get you cleaned and we'll get help when we get outta here."

"I just hope I got a leg left," Bonnie said. She moaned painfully. "I feel like I busted ribs, daddy. I'm not dyin' yet, am I?"

"You aren't gonna die no how," Clyde said, then asked the woman, "What's your name, ma'am?"

"We're the Pritchards," she said. "Myself and my husband, and our son-in-law—"

"—who's run off?" Clyde said. "Where's he gone to?"

"Mister," the woman said, "I don't know, but yes, this girl could lose her leg if she isn't attended to. I can't fix her like you're sayin'. We can wash her with towels and water and I've got ointment and baking soda—"

Bonnie cried out. Clyde told the woman, "Bring all what you've got, you and this lady helpin'. Get me that needle and cord and the rest in a sack. You got a sack?" She nodded. "Well, get it, then! Don't just sit here belly-achin'." He touched Bonnie's cheek. "You got dirt all over you, honey. You hold still till these ladies get you cleaned off. I'll fix where you're hurtin' soon as we get out of here. That damn road coulda killed every one of us. We're lucky as hell your two fellas climbed down to help us."

The women bathed Bonnie's leg, her face and her arms, and kept cool-soaked cloths on the burned skin. Her upper leg was swelling and blistered to her knee.

When the women had done all they could for Bonnie, Clyde ushered them into the front room where W.D. was standing guard, watching the man and the baby. Clyde returned to the bed, sat on the edge for a moment and took Bonnie's hand. "It's goin' to be alright, angel. I'm goin' to see you're taken care of proper soon as we're outta here. Shut your eyes now and rest."

"It hurts too much to rest," she said. "I never felt any pain like this...."

"It kills me to see you hurt," Clyde said. "Just kills me in my guts."

He stayed on the bed with her, stroking Bonnie's head. She kept wrinkling her face in pain and cried out when Clyde moved from the bed. He went to W.D. in the front room and said, "You've gotta go for a car, and nobody's goin' to be hurt. You go down to that road and flag us a car. Bring it back here."

"What about the people in the car?" W.D. asked.

"You got your fuckin' gun, so get 'em here with the car. We'll leave them with these folks." W.D. started out the door but Clyde suddenly grabbed him, yanking him back inside. "Listen—" he said. "That's a car we're hearin' right now."

"Maybe that guy's come back," W.D. said.

They both listened to the sound of the approaching car. Moving against the wall, Clyde glanced out the corner of a window. "Headlights are turned off," he said. "They're goin' around the house to the back door. Let's get out of this room," They heard the car stop beyond the kitchen door. No more sounds.

W.D. whispered, "They're gettin' outta the car."

"Fuckin' laws," Clyde said, then whispered to the others, "You folks, sit quiet, say a lady's been hurt in the car, and don't say nothin' else 'cause we're right outside around front and drawin' a bead on anyone talkin'. I wanna get out of here with nobody else gettin' hurt."

Clyde handed W.D. the shotgun, withdrew the pistol from his belt and pulled W.D. through the front door. Outside, they backed against the side wall as two men stood for moments in the kitchen, then entered the front room. For a moment they stood staring at the others in the room. "Hello," one man said. "I know you folks, you know me. Where's the folks who were down in that wreck?"

Alonzo pointed to the middle room, saying, "I know you, Sheriff Corry. The girl that was in the accident's restin' in the room there."

Mrs. Pritchard said, "She's on the bed, Sheriff, and she's hurt bad."

Looking strangely at the people for a moment, the sheriff and the second man went into the middle room.

From outside, Clyde watched through the window as the sheriff asked Bonnie, "How bad you hurt, young lady?"

Moaning, Bonnie said, "My leg's hurt…"

The sheriff lifted the bloody sheet and felt Bonnie's pulse. He asked, "Where did your friends go, young lady?" She moaned. The sheriff said, "You had two fellas with you?" She didn't answer. He looked at the second man, then said, "She's not conscious."

"Jesus," the second man said, "she's got some damage. She better get to the hospital." He looked back into the front room. "Where's the other two fellas who were with this girl? She's in too much pain—passin' out."

The second man lifted the kerosene lamp from the table and both returned to the front room. He asked the Pritchards, "Where's the two fellas?" The baby started crying again. No one said anything.

Pritchard looked toward the front door. "They've gone outside."

The man holding the lantern raised the light as the sheriff opened the front door and stepped outside, followed by the second man. They looked to the far side of the house but then froze as Clyde said, "Hands up, boys," and pressed the pistol against the back of the man's neck. "Don't move," he said. "You're both covered."

"We're not movin'," the sheriff said. "Nobody's movin'. Take it easy—"

"—shut up!" Clyde said, and told W.D., "Frisk these boys—this sheriff's got a gun in his holster." He carefully took the lamp out of the man's hand and set it on the porch.

W.D. lifted the sheriff's gun and got a revolver from the second man, saying, "This one's got a marshal's badge, Bud."

"Who're you?" Clyde asked the man,

"My name's Hardy. I'm the marshal."

Clyde said, "Boy, get their handcuffs. Now, fellas, bring your hands down slow and this boy'll cuff—one to one. Make any fuckin' move besides what you're told, you'll be meat for the crows." Clyde stuck the sheriff's pistol into his belt, and told W.D., "Go get Sis off that bed and get that old fella to help you bring her out the kitchen to these boys' car in back."

W.D. nodded, cradling the shotgun, and went back into the house, carrying the kerosene lamp.

Clyde could hear W.D. telling the man to get up and help him bring the girl out back. "Now," Clyde said to the marshal and sheriff, "you boys just keep lookin' straight ahead and lead the way to your car." He pushed the muzzle of the pistol between the marshal's shoulder blades, and said, "I've just pulled the hammer back on my revolver, and damnit to hell, this one's a hair trigger you gotta not breathe on, so you fellas walk easy and live a little longer."

"What've you got in mind?" Corry said. "What're you gonna do with us?"

"I'm gonna put you in your car, both of you in the backseat since you're now Siamese twins with your cuffs, and we're all goin' for a ride."

Bonnie was at the back door, held up by W.D. and Alonzo, who was also holding the sack. Bonnie looked hazy, suffering, her face pale and pained. "Get her in the front," Clyde told W.D., "and these boys in the back. You help Sis but keep a bead on these two. Give me my shotgun."

Bonnie moved painfully into the car, helped by W.D. and Alonzo, each step on her injured leg causing her to whimper in pain. She collapsed onto the car seat, and W.D. placed her in the middle. Her head was drooping forward. W.D. said, "Keys are right in here."

Alonzo said to Clyde, "You aren't takin' me with you?"

Clyde said, "You wanna go for a ride?" The man shook his head. "Go on back in your house," Clyde told him. "Thank your wife and the other lady for helpin' like they did."

Alonzo hurried into the house and shut the back door. W.D. was holding Bonnie up while Clyde got into the car. He quickly started the engine, and as he backed up away from the house, Bonnie slipped against Clyde. "She's shivering," W.D. said.

"There's a blanket in the trunk," the sheriff said.

Clyde looked around at the sheriff, nodded, then told W.D., "Go get the blanket the sheriff's talkin' about."

"What about what we got in the wreck?" W.D. asked. "You think it's all burned to shit?"

Clyde put his arm around Bonnie, her head cradled at his shoulder. "I don't think she's wantin' to smell any smoke, boy."

W.D. took the keys and went around to the trunk. The sheriff said, "That girl's in a bad way. What're you gonna do? She needs help—she could die."

"I'm fixin' it soon as we get where we're headed," Clyde said. "I won't let her die." The trunk lid closed and W.D. got into the car with the blanket. "Get it around her good so she's warm. Give me this side of it, and we'll get her covered up. You hold her so she don't fall over. Any trouble either of these boys give us, you finish them both off."

W.D. smiled, turning on the seat to stare at the two lawmen.

Twenty-Six

Clyde's eyes darted to the rearview mirror as the two lawmen shifted nervously. "Just take it easy back there," he said. "Enjoy the ride."

"Where are we goin'?" the sheriff asked.

"Got a meetin' in a spell," Clyde said. "A fella who hates talkative laws."

"We gonna shoot 'em?" W.D. asked. Clyde glanced again at the lawmen, their eyes glued to the mirror. "I don't mind none," W.D. said. "Shoot their balls off first."

"Shut up," Clyde told him as Bonnie stirred, moaning. She pressed her face against Clyde's shoulder, muttering that her body was burning. "Daddy," she said, "I'm burnin' on every part of my body." Her eyes opened wide as a car approached from the opposite direction, the headlights cutting across Clyde's windshield. He veered deliberately to the left, edging into the oncoming lane. He heard one of the laws gasp.

"Where do you suppose that bastard ran off to?" W.D. asked.

"You can ask these boys," Clyde said casually. "They're the ones he shot his mouth off to. If I ever see him, I'll kill him."

"You'll never see that son of a bitch," W.D. said, tensing as the oncoming car swerved right to avoid a collision. It always worked, forcing their attention to the right side of the road instead of getting a glimpse of a face behind an approaching windshield.

Bonnie used to laugh about it. Now, eyes squeezing shut again, she kept moaning that the pain was turning her inside out. "If we weren't havin' to run our asses off," Clyde said, "we wouldn't be in this fix and she wouldn't be hurtin' so bad." Again he glanced into the mirror. "You boys're gettin' a nice ride, aren't you? Sure wouldn't want to see no discomfort comin' your way."

The marshal nodded vaguely. He cleared his throat, and said, "These handcuffs are shuttin' off my blood."

"Probably won't matter none," Clyde said, "least where you're goin'."

W.D. chuckled. "He won't need nothin' but some feather wings like you shake off a chicken."

"Stop alarmin' these boys," Clyde said, slowing to the far right side of the road. A quarter mile further and he turned off the highway onto the dirt apron of an all-night gas station. "You boys don't hold to keepin' much in a fuel tank, do you?" he said.

The sheriff said, "We weren't plannin' on a trip tonight."

"This whole time," Clyde said, "shows a body how you never know what's comin' your way...." To W.D., he said, "Go get us some gas, then take the handcuffs off these fellas." W.D. got out, and as the tank was getting filled, Clyde said to Hardy, "Soon as he gets the gas and unlocks you, you're gonna get up front and you'n' the boy move this girl in the back so she can get her leg off the floor." To Corry he said, "You're gonna move over or get her feet up on you."

W.D. and Hardy lifted Bonnie from the front seat. "Real easy with her, boys," Clyde said. They placed her onto the rear seat lengthwise, her feet on the sheriff's legs, and covered her carefully with the blanket.

The marshal sat uncomfortably alongside Clyde, and said, "What're you fixin' on doin' with us? Why are you kidnappin' us?"

Clyde turned his head and looked at him. "Would've had to shoot you if I'd left you back with those folks. You're doin' alright so far, aren't you? Long as you sit quiet without pullin' any shit."

"I'm not pullin' any shit," Hardy said. "I don't want to get shot—"

"—that makes two of us," Clyde said. "But any shootin' to be done, it's better I'm doin' it than you. You see how it is."

Hardy said, "I know who you are," and said nothing further.

W.D. got back into the car, stinking of gasoline, and Clyde said,

"Open your window and get blown off so the smell of you don't make her any sicker. She's the one we're worryin' about first."

"She needs to get to a hospital," the sheriff said.

"Then we're all takin' a trip to your stinkin' jail," Clyde said. "You probably got a wife, and would you dump her somewhere and run off into the night—go hidin' somewhere? You know damn well you wouldn't. So just shut up and maybe you'll get out of this stayin' alive."

Close to three in the morning, Clyde stopped the car before an old road leading across the Oklahoma state line. He followed the road to a narrow bridge on wooden piers and honked the horn. Moments later, another horn honked the signal, and the lights flashed. "That's him," Clyde said, returning the flash.

He ordered the two lawmen out of the car as a second car came forward, the headlights off, slowly crossing the bridge. "What're you goin' to do?" Hardy asked. "Who's this comin' at us?" Clyde told W.D. to handcuff the two laws, and then raised the shotgun. The sheriff's face flashed a look of fear.

Buck brought the roadster to a stop, climbed out, and seeing the lawmen, said, "We gonna shoot 'em?"

"I don't think so," Clyde said. "Get Blanche in this sheriff's car 'cause Bonnie's hurt. We'll take care of the fellas. They aren't half bad, but let's walk 'em a ways under the bridge." He told W.D., "Go find something to bind these laws."

Buck said, "There's cuttin' pliers under the seat."

Motioning with the shotgun, Clyde moved the handcuffed sheriff and marshal off the road, and down to the bottom of the bridge, at the edge of a narrow river. He then pointed the men toward some trees. "That's far enough," he said. The men stopped walking. Both looked sick as Clyde stared at them. He said, "What're you gonna do if I let you go?"

After a tense moment, the marshal said, "Find our way out of here."

"You'd run your ass to the nearest phone!" Buck said. "We oughta shoot 'em. It won't make much difference—they're gonna be in our hair. Should've shot 'em and let the coyotes fuckin' pick 'em clean."

Hardy said, "You don't have to shoot us. You got the drop on us—"

"—that's for damn tootin' sure!" Buck said, hands antsy with the shotgun. He looked around quickly as W.D. trudged down the slope, half-tripping on a long length of barbed wire.

"We can wire these fellas to the tree," W.D. said.

Buck pressed the barrel of the shotgun up beneath Corry's neck as W.D. and Clyde strung the wire around the men to the trunk of the tree. "You're two lucky laws," Buck said. "I'm personally itchin' to shoot you full of fuckin' holes."

Clyde grunted, "Leave 'em be." He came face to face with the men, and said, "Ain't any graces we're showin'," he said. "You can thank that achin' girl I'm walkin' away instead of doin' what this boy's all itchin' to do." Neither of the lawmen spoke. Clyde's face came within inches of the sheriff's. "If she wasn't hurt and bleedin' and sick," Clyde said, "I'd probably as soon let him put you in the mud, but like this boy's said, you haven't got any drop on us, and I've never put a body on the spot who hasn't." He stepped back, nodded to Buck and W.D., and said, "Leave 'em. Let's go."

Bonnie was still curled on the backseat of the sheriff's car, moaning with each breath. Blanche had climbed into the car and was holding Bonnie's head on her lap, stroking her hair. She said, "She's all congested, Clyde. What's gonna be done about her leg? That's somethin' frightful."

He said, "She's burned bad, and I'd as soon cut off my own leg and give it to her if I could, but I can't, Blanche, and you know it. We'll get her fixed soon as we get far away from here."

Blanche said, "I know it, but we don't want her gettin' pneumonia. Where'd you take those laws?"

"They're wired to a tree," he said. "Let 'em start hollerin' in the mornin'." He told Buck, "Let's get our ass outta here before a posse gets on out lookin' to hang us."

Twenty-Seven

Not long after Clyde followed Buck's Ford convertible away from Erick and the laws wired to a tree, he found another car and ditched the lawmen's vehicle off a Texas highway.

It was Sunday. The two cars had driven back roads deep into the Texas panhandle. They stopped at roadside diners and highway markets, sending in W.D. to stock up on supplies. To Clyde, the important thing was relieving Bonnie's pain. She was in a bad way, crying, "Shoot me!" and "Cut my leg off!" and, "Oh, daddy, put me out of my misery!"

There were few options to ease her suffering without seeing a doctor. Kidnapping one crossed Clyde's mind more than once, but when he voiced the plan, Bonnie shrieked, "No! We can't do that!" Taking her to a hospital was out of the question, though Clyde knew it could come to that very soon.

Late that night, both cars pulled off the highway onto a side road that led them a mile into the woods. Clyde held the bottle of whiskey to Bonnie's lips and coaxed her to swallow as much as she could. W.D. stood guard while Clyde cleaned Bonnie's injury with hydrogen peroxide and alcohol. Then, soaking the string in alcohol and heating the turkey needle with matches, he attempted to stitch a deeper part of Bonnie's wound while she squeezed Buck's and Blanche's hands in each of her own. They kept her covered, warm, and supplied with whiskey the rest of the night. By morning she appeared to be sleeping quietly.

Two days later, the cars crossed into Kansas. On Wednesday, four days since the wreck, Clyde got rid of the car he'd picked up in Texas, and stole a Ford V-8 sedan in the town of Hutchinson, then drove straight through to Arkansas.

Blanche said, "Bonnie isn't sleepin'. She only looks like she's sleepin', but she's got her eyes closed and she's sufferin' and droppin' in and out of bein' awake. She won't eat and if we don't take care of her soon, she's gonna up and die on us."

"She ain't gonna die!" Clyde said. "Don't worry. We're gonna take care of her." He looked around, saying, "You're doin' a good job, Blanche, and she's gonna be okay. We're gonna be okay—"

Blanche was shaking her head. "Unless we do somethin' pretty damn soon, it's the shock gonna kill her. She keeps passin' out."

"We're gonna get us somewhere to get settled," he said. "We'll get her taken care of soon as we get settled. You're a blessin', honey, and we couldn't do this without you."

Bonnie let out a shriek as the morning sun struck the windshield. Soon as they hit Van Buren, crossing the bridge over the Arkansas River, Clyde pulled to the side of the road. Buck eased to a stop behind him, as Clyde climbed out and walked back to the car window where Buck asked, "What's wrong, brother?"

"Bonnie's not good," Clyde said. "She's not eatin'. Just wants those popsicle ice sticks. This is damned Thursday already, and we gotta get a cabin fast—lay low so she can get on her feet."

Buck nodded, saying, "I seen that sign the other side of the bridge—cabins with indoor plumbing and hot plates—"

"—mattresses on the beds," W.D. said.

"And closed garages," Clyde said. "We'll get us one. I'm sayin' we're a family that's campin', and a stove blew up and hurt her leg. No one gets confused." He climbed back into the car, then pulled ahead as Buck followed.

Not far from the county line was the Twin Cities Tourist Camp. Clyde told the manager, "We got others in our party and we're needin' two cabins—side by side. My wife's had an accident with a damn camp stove that blew up. Burned her leg bad and she's in need of attention. I'd be thankful for your steerin' me to some help."

The manager introduced himself as Sid, and came out to the car with Clyde to look at Bonnie's leg. "My, my!" he said. "That's bad. I know Doc Walter Eberle, and I'll ask him to come see her, but maybe the hospital—"

"She won't go to any hospital," Clyde said. "She's got religious qualms."

"Then she ought to have a nurse," Sid said. "You don't want her gettin' infected, and let's hope she hasn't got any yet." He told Clyde he and his wife, Ida, had a daughter who'd worked in a hospital attending burn patients. "She'll be more than happy to change that dressin' on her and see what can be done."

Clyde sighed. "That would be a blessin', sir. I'd be indebted to you."

While waiting for Sid's daughter, Bonnie whispered to Clyde, "Maybe I'm dyin', honey. My whole body's burnin', even in my arms and my ribs. I don't even feel like I've got a leg on my body. I'm scared, daddy."

Outside the cabin, Clyde said to Buck, "This fella's daughter comin' to take care of her could be liable to get wise to us, so you and Dub better lay low. Bonnie's gettin' outta her mind and could be talkin' about stuff."

Blanche said, "I can't tend her no more. I don't know how. You say this girl's worked with burns, so let her do it."

For three days while W.D. and Buck kept the cars closed in the garages, Clyde stayed close to Bonnie. Sid's daughter, Hazel, changed the bandage, treated the burn with medication, and said the "emergency stitches" were "pretty well done." Clyde said some hunter "that'd had medical trainin' did it."

Bonnie never left the cabin. Hazel brought her lemonade and ice cream to cope not only with the heat of the burn and fever, but of the cabin itself, holding at one hundred degrees from morning on.

Though low on money, Buck and Clyde drifted into town to buy a fan to keep the room cooler, also checking the town bank. But Clyde said, "Can't do nothin' here. Too close. We'll get over to the next county to be makin' any withdrawals."

Edgy and concerned, Buck told Clyde, "That Hazel's gonna get smart, brother. She's no cluck and she's gonna know who we are if we hang around much longer."

"She's not gonna know," Clyde said. "She's too busy bein' Florence Nightingale, and not around us that much anyway. I don't like sittin' anymore than you do, but that's what we gotta do."

"Each mornin' while Bonnie was laid up," W.D. would later say, "Clyde and Buck drove into the town for supplies, Clyde worryin' about the cabins and scared to be movin' Bonnie in her condition. He got the idea that Pretty Boy Floyd could get us all a hideout and fix it so we'd all be taken care of. Clyde wanted to see Floyd and make contact, anythin' to find a place for Bonnie bein' on the mend.

"Then we found out Floyd wasn't in the area, and on top of that, the worst part, Floyd wasn't goin' to give Clyde any help. The rotten guy was tellin' all the people he knew not to help Clyde, and I thought it was pretty bad of Floyd to say that Clyde was a punk goin' around shootin' everyone. I got to thinkin' that the way the newspapers were talking about Clyde, it was takin' a little shine off Floyd, least that's how I saw it, so we weren't gettin' any help and damn fast feelin' like a bunch of sittin' ducks."

Two days later, Bonnie's condition grew worse. Clyde told Buck and Blanche that "Florence Nightingale's sayin' she's done all she can, and now seems drawin' up into herself, like suspicious of us holin' up. Somethin' has to be done to take care of Bonnie until she's better. Cryin' half the time to see her mother. Wants to be with her mother—have her takin' care of her. We can't do that, but I've gotta go home and see what can be done."

Buck said, "The law's gonna be all over her mom's house as well as our folks'. They're stickin' like bees to a honeycomb. They're perched on the damn roof waitin' for you or me."

"Laws don't worry me," Clyde said. "Not half as much as Bonnie bein' hurt. I'm goin' back down and see what I can fix."

That afternoon, Clyde took off for West Dallas, alone in the Ford with the shotgun at his left side, a .38 on the passenger seat, and a .45 automatic in a paper sack on the floorboard. All he could think about was Bonnie. Every pain she felt ricocheted inside him. He said he loved her more than anything, maybe even more than his own life. Nothing was going to be right until Bonnie was okay, up on her feet, no pain grabbing her body and mind. Clyde kept his foot pressed on the gas, closing the gap between Arkansas and Texas.

He saw one law car. It came approaching in the opposite lane, hitting a good pace. His left hand inched for the shotgun, but the cop didn't even notice Clyde's car. The sun was down and he felt better. Nobody was going to stop him.

By eight o'clock he was cutting over the dirt roads heading to Dallas. Ditching the car where no one would spot it, he stuck the .45 into his belt and snuck into West Dallas to meet with his folks.

Cumie, surprised to see him, said, "The laws have been here today, lookin' for you." She said she'd go back to Arkansas with him. "My two boys bein' trapped in Arkansas, and poor little Bonnie hurt and sufferin', needin' her own mother or myself."

Clyde said, "No, I can't have you or Bonnie's mom gettin' arrested or bein' in a line of fire. For the love of God, you know that's bound to happen." She stared at him, tears gathering. "I got an idea Billie Jean'll come with me."

He arrived at Bonnie's a little later, and told Emma the same thing he'd told Cumie. Too dangerous for a mother. It was Billie Jean he wanted to talk to—Billie Jean he'd come for. It was impossible for their mothers to join them, and he couldn't trust anyone else. "Billie Jean's at a movie," Emma told him. "She'll be back around eleven o'clock. You stay until she gets back, Clyde. You stay here 'cause it won't be safe for you on the road." She then began to cry and left the room.

Laying on the couch he'd slept on when Bonnie was at home, Clyde felt his muscles falling loose from his bones. He could smell Bonnie's perfume on the couch. He could smell her body when he closed his eyes. He dozed in a gray haze, then jerked up, grabbing the .45 when the front door opened.

"Billie Jean!" he said. He told her what was happening, how Bonnie'd gotten hurt and was now crying for her mother.

"I knew she'd been hurt and nobody told me," Billie Jean said. "I have to go—I gotta be with her. I've been scared for her, Clyde. I've been so scared for all of you."

"Get what you need," Clyde told her, getting up from the couch. "I'll be back for you in a few minutes, 'cause I gotta get the car."

"Be careful," she said. "Laws are up and down Eagle Ford all the time now. They go up and down, damn near smellin' the dirt like dogs."

Twenty-Eight

Recalling that last day at the Twin Cities cabin, W.D. said, "It was a long time before I stopped shakin' over how dumb and fucked up Buck'n' I'd been, runnin' on our own without Clyde. Robbin' and gettin' nothin'. Shootin' a goddamn sheriff and other laws, then losin' the car we lifted and walkin' all the way back in the hills, leavin' the cars we had at the roadsides so as not to get tracked, but dammit, we got tracked all the same. They didn't catch up with us. Though Clyde blew his top, and I'd never seen him mad as he was; he had poor Billie Jean shrinkin' and scared. It was such a mix-up. Buck shootin' that old sheriff guy way over the hill and bustin' us gettin' outta there, gettin' back with twenty stinkin' bucks.

"Bonnie just kept sayin' she knew it'd happen—we shouldn't've gone like that, thinkin' we could do somethin' we couldn't do. Buck was arguin' back that it wasn't his fault, though he didn't blame me for it. Clyde knew Buck'd fucked up and instead of helpin' Bonnie and him what we'd done was get all of us on the run with laws now diggin' around every bush on our trail. 'We gotta get the fuck out of here,' Clyde told us.

"Buck and Clyde went outside the cabin, and Clyde told me to go check the car and make sure it's runnin' good, check the tires, the water and oil. He said then fetch Billie Jean's belongin's and all of Bonnie's stuff, and pack it in the trunk. Him and Buck were gonna load guns and ammo on the second time.

"I asked, 'Second time for what, Bud?' He said we can't get six of us in the coupe so we were goin' in shifts, and 'Right now!' he said. He was gonna run Billie Jean to the train and get her headed back to

250

Dallas, then run Sis and Blanche to a hidin' place 'way the fuck outta here,' he said, then comin' back for me and Buck.

"The car was parked right at the side door, and I said okay, and started checkin' the car. Must've been only a few feet from the cabin door and I could hear Blanche's voice comin' through it, sayin' to Bonnie, 'Don't you ever think of gettin' out of this?' and Bonnie sayin', 'What the hell're you talkin' about? Gettin' outta what?'

"Blanche said, 'Breakin' free's what I'm talkin' about, livin' free and stoppin' this runnin' that's got no end to it—goin' back and forth without any sense—you gotta know that?'

"Bonnie started coughin', maybe tryin' to move around, coughin' weak but she said, 'I know what I know, Blanche, and you know Clyde can't go free any more than Buck can who's now bein' seen for puttin' some sheriff on the spot this afternoon, whoever they're talkin' about, but it's too late for that 'breakin' free,' 'cause we're all wanted now, and you know that.'

"I could hear Blanche gettin' up on her high horse, and she's sayin' she hadn't killed anybody!

"Bonnie said, 'Buck's wanted along with Clyde and you gotta resign yourself to it, honey, long as we're livin' there's no way out to runnin' around bein' free. Buck got his chance of bein' free and see where's it got him.'

"I was checkin' the plugs, close to the door and hearin' plain'n' clear. Blanche sayin' there was a way out by goin' to Mexico. Bonnie stayed quiet for a moment, then says, 'So why don't you go to Mexico?'

"Kind of a little hysterical as she's talkin', Blanche says, 'Buck'd like to go but he doesn't wanna leave his family. You gotta know Clyde's worse than Buck at bein' sorry to leave the family, though even in prison the family comes to see you. Even if they got you on death row the family's gonna come see you.'

"Bonnie coughed again, spittin' something up, and I hoped to hell it wasn't blood. She said, 'Why don't you shut up a spell? You talk too much, Blanche, and sound dumb most of the time. You want to talk about Clyde, you go talk to him. You talk to me like that

I oughta hit you in the teeth!'

"Blanche says, 'I'm tough, too, Bonnie girl, and don't think I'm not.' Then Bonnie's soundin' mad and I know it ain't no good for her. She said to Blanche, 'You're not as tough as I am, Blanche girl. Ever hear me talkin' like you're talkin'? Dreamin' up ways of gettin' out of here and leavin' others behind? Death row? You're livin' on it right now! I ought to bust your nose so you see you aren't as cute or pretty as you think you are. I'm pretty and everybody knows it, and I'm tough like they're reportin' me in the newspapers, sayin' I'm a gunmoll and a gangster—'

"'—and you are a gangster,' Blanche is sayin'. 'You're a gangster the same as Clyde!'

"Bonnie says, 'And what the hell are you, bitch? What the hell's Buck—just a big dumb clud with his kid brother shootin' the way out for him. You sound like a rat, Blanche, that's what you sound like. A rat!' She's coughin' again—not good. It's gettin' me mad. Where the hell's Billie Jean?

"Blanche is sayin', 'If you weren't so hurt I'd hit you for sayin' that!' That gets Sis mad now, and her voice gets hoarse as she's sayin', 'You pull somethin' on me and Clyde's takin' care of you if you did. Anybody puts a hand on me they're fuckin' dead!'

"Blanche was comin' to the door, sayin', 'I'm gettin' outta here!'

"'Good! Give a holler,'" Sis says. 'Run and you'll see there won't be no end to your runnin'!'

"The cabin door opens and out Blanche comes all bustlin', all chuggin' and sweatin'. I got my head in the engine, and she says, 'How long you been out here?'

"'Just a minute or so,' I tell her. She says Bonnie's arguin' with her, and I ask, 'Where's Billie Jean?'

"'She's out back by the cabins, cryin' and horsin' with someone's dog. You better go fetch her.'

"When I went around back of the cabins I see Billie Jean sittin' on an old wood chair. Just sittin' there. I said, 'Billie Jean, did you get your stuff ready to go?' She said her stuff was sittin' in a couple bags at the foot of Bonnie's bed. I told her I'd go get her stuff and get ready.

"We went around to the cabin and Billie Jean went into Buck's cabin where Blanche'd gone. I gave a knock and went into Clyde's cabin to get Billie Jean's stuff. Bonnie was layin' there with the back of her hands on her forehead. I said, 'Sis, are you alright?'

"'I'm okay,' she said. 'Where's Bud?'

"'Him and Buck're in the cabin cookin' up some kind of plans. I'm gonna put Billie Jean's stuff in the car and load a bunch of this other stuff out of here.' She nodded. She asked me to step close to her. I did, and she took hold of my hand and said, 'You must've had a rotten day.'

"'I guess I did,' I said. 'Bud's got a right to be mad, you know. Weren't no good reason for what went on. Buck's older so I figured he knows, but Sis, he don't know too good at all.'

"She was looking at me sad-like, and she said, 'Do you think I'm a pretty woman?'

"I brought her hand up to my face and kissed the back of her knuckles. 'You're as pretty as a princess I saw in a book once. Sis, you're as pretty as one of those movie stars in the magazines you're lookin' at. I honor you, Sis, and I kiss your hand like I just done.'

"I got Billie Jean's stuff in the car and some bags Sis had, then Clyde came out and got me and says, 'Blanche's comin' so we'll put Sis in the car next to me. The other two'll sit together.' I asked where he's takin' them but he said, 'Same place I'm takin' you and Buck soon as I get back.'

"I said goodbye to Billie Jean, hugged her, and she got in the car on Blanche's lap. I nodded to Sis, and Clyde drove off, not speedin'—just a casual drivin' off.

"Buck said to me, 'Well, boy, we sure fucked the day, didn't we?' I felt like sayin', 'You were runnin' it today, stupid.' But I didn't say nothin'.

"I got my pockets full of ammo, had the .38 in my belt and waitin'. Buck was nippin' at another bottle, gettin' fuckin' drunk, and every minute I'm thinkin' how those deputies and laws chasin' us could track us over the hill and here we're sittin'—like those tin ducks Clyde told me about.

"It wasn't a real long time but sure as hell seemed like it, and maybe it was a long time. I just couldn't tell nothin'. Bud must've been crankin' that coupe's limit to the top, just goin' mad as a racin' car. Me'n' Buck just stayed outta sight like it was any other night, me with the .38 and him with the shotgun.

"Clyde wanted to take Billie Jean to the train, but then drove way in the woods, droppin' Blanche, Billie Jean and Sis in a hidin' place. 'C'mon!' Clyde was yellin' at us. We took off. I felt sick in my gut. I was more pooped than I ever was anywhere. I figured if we got stuck and shootin' started, I was just gonna lay down and die."

Twenty-Nine

It was late night when Clyde drove past the Twin Cities cabin, catching a glimpse of W.D. at the window. He turned the car around, killed his lights and stopped at the side of the cabin, the engine running. Quickly, W.D. came out of the cabin with a canvas suitcase. He climbed into the car, saying, "Buck's gettin' his stuff." Moments later, Buck appeared, his arms loaded with belongings he'd bundled into the cabin blanket. He pulled the car door shut and Clyde drove ahead to the highway, then made a sharp turn and disappeared into the night.

"We gotta have another car," Clyde said. "Can't fit us in this fuckin' car. We'll get one tomorrow, soon as Billie Jean's on the train." To W.D., he said, "We get in the woods you get Bonnie on the car seat, and see she's restin' okay."

W.D. said, "She likes sleepin' in the car. She told me she don't like bugs and snakes."

"She's not worryin' about bugs and snakes," Clyde said.

Buck said, "Blanche frets about bugs, but she's sure not nuts about snakes." He shook his head, and said, "What a mess this day's been, Bud. I'm glad it's night and I'm glad we're outta that cabin—no more shootin' tonight. Whatta fuckin' mess. Fucked up good."

"Brother," Clyde said, "you're cryin' over spilled milk."

W.D. laughed. Clyde glanced at him.

"Just sleep," Buck said. "That's all I want to do tonight."

"Welcome to bugs and snakes," W.D. said.

"Fuck the bugs and snakes," Buck said, and W.D. laughed again.

Clyde said, "Boy, you sittin' on a bag of bugs that're ticklin' your butt?"

"Naw," he answered, "I'm just sayin' goodbye to today. That's all I'm doin'."

Leery of drifting too far on the main roads, cautious about markets and roadside diners, Clyde stayed nervously alert the following morning as he and W.D. drove Billie Jean as far as Sherman, Texas, to catch a Dallas-bound train. He told her to see the folks and talk about another meeting in "maybe a couple weeks from now." Then he stopped at a drugstore and sent W.D. in for peroxide, gauze and bandages, and rubbing alcohol.

Closer to the woods, he stopped at a gas station, also serving as a small market. "We're gettin' gas," he told W.D., handing him some money, "and go on in the store for a couple bags of eats, some cookies and bottles of soda pop. And get some smokes and matches."

Later, without success at stealing a bigger car, they carefully made their way back into the woods where they would not be seen. Bonnie was still on the blanket, cushioned by leaves beneath her that W.D. had piled earlier that morning after helping her from the car.

Clyde switched the license plate on the car, then joined Bonnie eating cookies and drinking soda pop.

Buck was sitting on the ground, his hands to the sides of his head as Blanche sat alongside him, saying, "I swear it's every one of us caught in a damn hole, and we're like ducks to be picked off by any hick with a gun."

"No, we're not," Clyde said. "We're okay here. There's nobody around for miles."

"Ain't that a damn fact!" she said.

Clyde smiled. "You're eatin', you're sleepin' on a cushion. You gotta go to the toilet, you go in the bushes. We got toilet paper and soda pop—"

"—and we still got a bottle of rye," Buck said.

Clyde said, "So no point in gettin' huffy and bothered, Blanche."

Bonnie said to her, "You're sure as hell better off than I am," and groaned a little as she turned to her side. "Clyde's doin' all he can to take care of us—"

"—I didn't ask Clyde to take care of us!" she said. "I'm supposed to have a husband to take care of me and look where I am—sleepin' in the goddamn woods and crappin' behind a bush!"

"Be quiet!" Buck said. "Quit shootin' off your mouth. It's hard on every one of us. You married me and we're in a jam and there's nothin' my brother or anyone else can do about it. We gotta lay low."

"Well, get more food for us!" Blanche said. "I gotta eat somethin' besides goddamn beans and dried-up jerky and cookies. I'm gettin' sick!"

"Blanche," Clyde said. "We're not gonna be livin' here till doomsday—"

"Who says!" she cut in.

"I say it," he continued. "Doomsday ain't around any corner 'cause we've got plans for more than this. We'll get other cabins— one for each of us like we had, and we're gonna lay low till Bonnie's movin' around better'n she is. We aren't down to eatin' grass and crickets, 'cause we got money, but what we ain't got's the guns and ammo to get us more."

"I'll tell you," Blanche said, "get some shotgun and shoot these damn birds 'cause they're drivin' me crazy."

"Maybe you are crazy," W.D. said.

"Kiss my ass!" Blanche spit out.

W.D. said, "I don't mean you are crazy, Blanche. I don't mind bein' here, bein' in the nature we've got that's dead as hell except for the birds. But like Bud's sayin' when we got in here, you see a bunch of birds bustin' out of the bushes, then you've got a whole bunch of watchdogs. Makes me comfortable with them sittin' overhead."

"And shittin' right on top of you!"

"Why don't you all shut up about shittin' and birds runnin'," Bonnie said.

"We're just waitin' like we're in a train station. Isn't that right, daddy? We're like Billie Jean sittin' in the dinin' car of that train."

Clyde nodded. "That's right, honey. We aren't in any pickle here, so no one's got reason to be complainin'. Anyway, we got work to do and we gotta get movin'. So, Blanche, you're gonna feel just right, you'n' Buck in a cozy nice cabin."

"Suits me," Buck said. "We know what we're after. We're huntin' the prey—a bank job, smooth as butter, no fuckin' in and out of it, and one not big enough to be armed to the teeth. Hell, we got gasoline stations and markets instead of sittin' here eatin' beans and chasin' flies."

W.D. gulped at the neck of a soda pop bottle, looking at Clyde as he tipped the soda and drained it. Wiping his mouth, he said. "What if your dad's fillin' station gets held up? Whaddya think about that, Bud?"

"I don't think about it," Clyde said.

Buck said, "Anybody dumb enough to rob Star Service's gonna get himself filled with lead. Ain't that right, brother?"

Clyde smiled. W.D. said, "I got the feelin' that's what they're thinkin' about me. Gonna fill me with lead. Some mountain boy comin' down after my ass for robbin' his folks' gas station."

"Nobody's got a gun in your ass," Clyde said.

"No, sir," W.D. said, shaking his head. "Nobody's got a gun in my ass except the laws, and you think we got a chance of livin' where they aren't breakin' our necks? I can't help thinkin' about that. Can you help thinkin' about it?"

"I don't think about it," Clyde said.

Annoyed, Bonnie said, "Nobody's thinkin' about it. They got our death warrants signed, and that's it."

"Nobody's signed my death warrant," Blanche said. "I didn't shoot anybody."

"They got mine signed," Buck said, "and they got yours, boy— tied up with a pink bow like a Valentine's box of sweeties. Soon as they find out who the hell you are, then you might as well go swipe yourself a headstone."

"I don't like any of this talk," Clyde said. "Gets bad without all this moanin', and the truth's that it doesn't make a shit of difference. W.D.'s got no choice anymore 'cause they'll get his name on the hot seat. That's what you got to be lookin' forward to—all of us, whether you like it or not, or gettin' buried out here in the weeds with a bunch of critters pickin' at our bones—"

"—stop talkin' all this kind of talk!" Bonnie cried. "I'm blowin' all up over my body—swellin' and I'm walkin' like a crippled person. I can't even feel my leg's a part of the rest of me, and these flies are really awful—" She started coughing and Clyde stared at her, worried.

Buck said, "I'm still thinkin', brother, we ought to find Pretty Boy and him gettin' us a place to hole up so Bonnie's fixed right. Some place we can all take it easy and won't be gettin' our heads beat on."

"Some joke!" W.D. said. "Mister Floyd won't do nothin' for Clyde Barrow 'cause he's jealous as a green-eyed jackass—and people go askin' what's Pretty Boy jealous about? The answer's 'cause they're scared of Clyde Barrow. All those big hotshots and they're all scared of Clyde Barrow!"

Thirty

Blanche was throwing up. "Can't help it!" she cried. "I'm sick of this jerkin' and bouncin' around. Can't we get on another road? I'm goin' on my knees and sayin' a prayer to Jesus'n' his virgin mother that soon as I'm outta here I'm gonna keep prayin' to stay alive!"

Bonnie groaned. "Maybe you wouldn't be prayin' and pokin' so much, Blanche, if you kept your mouth shut."

"How 'bout you all shuttin' up?" Clyde said. "Road's bad enough without all the bullshittin'. Soon as we're outta here we'll stop and see how to keep y'all from pissin' an' moanin.'"

"I ain't said a fuckin' word," Buck said.

Clyde glanced at him through the mirror. "You just did, brother. Let's keep it down till we get the fuck outta here."

They slept in the woods again. Clyde had a plan. He wanted to raid the First Battalion Armory on the Phillips University campus. He'd told Buck and W.D., "We hit it late night, get all we can carry outta there. You stay in the car, boy—never know if those fuckin' patrols are snoopin' around. Then we get outta Oklahoma."

"North into Kansas," Buck said. "A couple banks."

Clyde nodded.

Two nights later, Clyde and Buck carefully removed a pane of glass from the rear entrance to the armory on the Phillips campus in Enid. Inside the armory, both began assembling an impressive pile of thirty-five Colt .45 automatic pistols, eighty magazines, a hefty supply of ammunition and several Browning automatic rifles. Clyde brought several weapons and pairs of army field glasses to the car waiting at the rear entrance. W.D. quickly climbed out from behind the steering wheel and helped load the weapons and ammunition into the trunk of the car. The automatic rifles were stacked on the floor of the backseat. Clyde said nothing as he sorted the cache, his eyes dancing with excitement.

Deserting the armory, broken glass inside the door, Clyde and Buck got into the car and drove slowly for the exit from the university grounds, cautious of alerting anyone. Clyde said to everyone in the car, "Nobody do any bitchin' or pukin' 'til we're fuckin' clear of Treasure Island."

W.D. chuckled, "I've never seen such a haul."

Buck said, "It's a beauty. They gonna miss those BARs."

On the highway in minutes, Clyde then bypassed the main road to Kansas, and hit the graveled back roads again, heading north. Driving at a reasonable speed, he said, "We'll be out of Oklahoma in minutes. You okay, Blanche?"

"I'm okay," she said.

He said, "We're outta Oklahoma and less than an hour we'll reach the outskirts of Wichita and get a couple cabins."

For days the group traveled through Kansas and Nebraska, robbing gas stations. More robberies in South Dakota, then into Iowa and south to Missouri, Clyde staying close to state boundaries. Clyde drove into a service station a few miles south of Platte City, and stopped past the pumps. As the attendant approached the car, Clyde opened his door and got out. He was looking across the highway at the Red Crown Tavern and Café. "I'd like to see a couple cabins over there," Clyde said. "My wife's not feelin' too hot, and my mother-in-law's with us."

The attendant told Clyde the cabins were part of the Red Crown Tavern. "They got a restaurant and ballroom," he said. Clyde thanked him and got back into the car. He told Blanche to go get adjoining cabins for them, with the garage in the middle.

While Blanche secured the cabins, Clyde pulled across the road and waited. She came out and nodded, showing she had it taken care of, and waved the keys. The manager was watching through the office window.

Clyde lifted Bonnie from the front seat. "I'm a fuckin' cripple," she said.

Clyde shook his head. "I don't mind carryin' you, honey. You're gonna be okay, 'cause you're gonna heal up like you were."

The car was hidden in the garage separating the two cabins. The door to Clyde and Bonnie's room was the only door from the garage. "Several times the garage door was opened and closed," said Neal Houser, the Red Crown manager. "A lot of foot traffic from one cabin to the other, though they looked like a bunch of college kids gonna be having a wild time. The one girl I never saw—she remained in the cabin with the shorter fellow and the kid, the young one." After unloading some of the weapons and ammo, with the garage door shut, both Clyde and Buck checked the cabin windows to make sure no one outside could see in.

Early the next morning, Blanche and W.D. paid for the breakfasts, which Buck and Blanche shared with W.D. before he carried two more breakfasts back to the cabin housing Bonnie and Clyde. W.D. returned to the restaurant to buy newspapers.

Clyde gave Blanche some money to drive into Platte City for some supplies at the drugstore. W.D. later said, "Clyde was eatin' his breakfast, Bonnie was eatin' hers, in bed readin' the newspaper. I remember I asked her somethin', like it was, 'are you feelin' alright?' and she didn't answer back, like she was mad about somethin'. He was sendin' Blanche to the drugstore for more stuff to make Bonnie feel better. He was givin' her shots and she didn't mind. That stuff woulda made me crazy. I stayed in the cabin with him and Sis, read the comics in the paper, and then I went with Blanche to the city drugstore.

"When I got back," W.D. said, "Clyde sent me back to the restaurant for beers and food. What he done then was havin' plastered the newspaper over the window so there wasn't any way to look in, even between the crack in the blinds, and it was hotter than all get-out in that cabin. Bonnie didn't get out of bed all the time, like she was in a hospital or somethin'. I did whatever was handy, like I had to carry her into the bathroom and sit her on the toilet, and then she'd rap on the door with a stick when she'd finished and I'd go in and lift her up and carry her back to the bed where she said was the best place she'd been in a long time.

Clyde was sleeping while W.D. sat outside on the step. "I was just smokin'," he says, "and then Blanche comes along with that manager fella who wanted to get the license plate number for his records 'cause he didn't get it the night we came in, Clyde drivin' across and not goin' in the office. I went inside and Clyde was up and listenin' to the fella and Blanche outside. He made a move like tellin' me to open the door to the garage, but said only a little. The manager had written down the number and was walkin' off after shuttin' the garage door. Blanche had gone back into her and Buck's cabin. Clyde was lookin' at me, and I told him the guy had said he had to write it down on the card. Clyde didn't look like he believed that, but then he shrugged and said if he had any laws runnin' it the plates'd turn up swiped—didn't match the car, meanin' they'd know the car was swiped. I asked him what he wanted to do and he said we'd hang around a little more 'cause of how Bonnie was feelin' and then we'd get outta there."

Clyde told Buck not to go outside the cabin the next day. Because of what W.D. and Buck had done—the shooting of that sheriff while Clyde had gone to get Billie Jean—he knew the laws were on the lookout. Clyde said, "They have it fuckin' known everywhere, and they know what they're lookin' for."

W.D. said, "The laws didn't know what I looked like 'cause there wasn't any posters and stuff, but all that afternoon when I was goin' in and out of the restaurant gettin' beers and food and carryin' them back to the cabins, everythin' around the place was jittery a little, though there were a lot of folks in the restaurant. Blanche and I ate some tamale stuff and a couple of people were lookin' at us, made me worried and sure as hell not friendly. Clyde seemed okay. He was bandagin' up Bonnie's leg and wanted more beer and more sandwiches, and when I went back to fetch 'em I saw a lot of other fellas had come in and they all looked like laws, but nobody was doin' any investigatin'.

"Later on after he ate a sandwich and drank some beer, Clyde was dozin' on the wall side of the bed, that automatic rifle on the floor next to him. All day he'd monkey'd sawin' the barrel down, making it shorter. He'd given Sis another shot and she was sleepin', and except for me or him carryin' her to the toilet and bringin' her back, she never left the bed and didn't go outside the cabin door. I guess I was gettin' worried about her."

Cars were coming and going from the parking lot, and though several had arrived, the restaurant had closed. "It got quiet, late an' still hot," W.D. recalled. "I heard cars but sounded more like just the road or somethin', and I turned a little to Clyde standin' by the door to the garage. He said, 'You hear him?' I said, 'No—who?' He told me to shut up, then I hear the knockin' on Buck's door, and a fella's sayin', 'I need to talk to the boys!' and Blanche's sayin' the signal that Clyde'd worked out. She was sayin' loud, 'Just a minute, I'm gettin' dressed!' Clyde grabs up the BAR and opens the door from the cabin to the garage, and he's all like crouchin'. I peel some paper from the window and lookin' to Buck's cabin I see the guy outside, and holy cow, he's carryin' something, like big sheet of metal in front of him. Then he's waggin' his hand towards this car that's got all that same sort of sheet metal stuff on like a they'd made an armored car for themselves. Then fast: BANG! The shot from Buck's cabin and the guy with the shield goes trippin' back and falls down. At that all hell busts loose, and Clyde says, 'Get Bonnie in the car!'

"I got the car key and got her up off the bed. She feels so light, she's shakin'. Clyde's shootin' out the window 'cause there's a dozen guys out there and they're shootin' at the cabins now—both cabins 'cause Clyde shootin' and Buck's shootin'. There's shootin' all over the place. I got the car door unlocked and Bonnie inside, gettin' her slunked down so she won't get hit unless they shoot right through the door. Bullets're hittin' the garage—a window's busted, they're plunkin' at Clyde's cabin, and he's right there comin' at the car. He says, 'Get the garage open!' So I go to the latch and start pushin' it open. Clyde's been shootin' at that funny armored car with the BAR that shoots right through that metal crap and he's hit the guy behind the wheel 'cause the car's backin' off, and then here's Blanche runnin' behind Buck who's shootin' from the waist. 'Get in the car!' Clyde's yellin', and I'm gettin' in but Blanche is screamin' that Buck's hit, and I scoot up and out the rear door, grabbin' at him as she's tryin' to support him, but together we get him moved into the back seat where blood's squirtin' out of his head.

"Just a second and we're movin' like hell on fire. I've got one of the BARs Buck dropped and I'm pluggin' past the laws who're kind of runnin' after us shootin'. I hear the slugs plunkin' at the car and then one busts the back window on Blanche's side. She cries out, 'I'm hit! I'm hit!' and holdin' her hands to her face—but she's thrown back as Clyde's acceleratin' ahead like a shot-out cannon ball."

Thirty-One

He'd been in the area before. He'd driven past the same stumps and trunks of trees that blocked the sun. Over the dirt road, past thick underbrush and hard-packed hilly slopes, the front wheels of the V-8 angled from side to side as Clyde steered sharply through the deserted Dexfield Park. He could almost sense the same spot where he'd stashed another car the last time.

Buck was breathing hard from the backseat, unconscious but groaning. Before entering the park, Blanche had nodded off from exhaustion, and Bonnie asked Clyde, "Is she gonna be blind?"

"The busted glass got in the one eye," he said, "not both eyes. I gotta get a special kind of doctor's scissors at the drugstore, a point that's small and blunt so it doesn't scrape the eye. I can get the glass outta her eye if the pieces're big enough to see."

She whispered, "What about Buck?"

Clyde looked at her. "I don't know. Just keep the wound from gettin' too infected. Maybe it'll heal over. I don't know, honey...."

When the car thumped hard over a muddy ditch, Buck opened his eyes. He tried to reach up but Blanche held his hand. He said, "Where are we goin'?"

"Gonna stop in a minute," Clyde said. "We're in an empty fairgrounds north of Dexter—it's just a few miles down the road we were on. You can go back to sleep, brother. You hurtin'?"

Buck mumbled. Blanche said, "He didn't hear you say that. He's sleepin' again."

"He'll be okay," Clyde said. "Ain't nothin' to worry about." He approached a shady rise, turned off the dirt road, and came to a

266

stop. "I'm gettin' us settled here, and then headin' back to the town for food and medical supplies."

"You want me to come with you?" Bonnie asked. "I'll wait in the car—I don't know if I can walk too good."

Clyde shook his head. "Stay here."

"I'll go in with you," W.D. said.

"You stay here and get us a camp goin'," Clyde told him. "Help get Buck outta of the car and take these seats up so we got somewhere to sit."

Buck moved his hand to the back of Bonnie's seat as if to pull himself forward. He said, "Oh… This is okay, Bud." His eyes were closed. Blanche placed the towel over his wound, mopping the fluid that had leaked from his head. He tried to reach her hand, but held her wrist. "I can't see it.…" he said.

"What're you lookin' for?" Bonnie asked.

After a moment, Buck said, "I saw those trees…"

"Yes!" Blanche said, encouragingly. "You're right, honey. We're in a big park. There's woods all around, and we're gonna be campin' until you're feelin' okay." Buck said he was thirsty and Blanche looked at Bonnie, who'd turned around, then Blanche looked at the back of Clyde's head. "He isn't any better," she said. "Keeps sayin' things that most don't make sense. I'm not seein' hardly at all. I close my eye and it's like needles pushin' in the back of my head."

"I'm goin' to get grub and medicine and more painkillers for all three of you. Buck's had the last we've been usin'."

W.D. said, "That hole plumb through my side's stingin' like a son of a bitch."

Bonnie said, "Get a big bottle of aspirin, daddy, and drinkin' cups, and get some water and ice. Get hot dogs and plenty of aspirin."

"We're sure needin' more painkillers," Blanche said. "Soon as it wears off of him the pain's gonna be awful."

Clyde opened the back door, leaned in, and helped W.D. and Blanche move Buck out of the car. "He's walkin' and talkin' and next minute he's like this," Blanche said. Outside the car, Clyde moved the towel from Buck's head and looked at the wound.

"Gonna be a damn wonder," W.D. said, "gettin' him in any kind of shape to go much farther."

"You shut your trap!" Blanche hissed. "Though he looks like he can't hear you, he's hearin' you sayin' that! He hasn't got any notion about dyin' in this damn wilderness."

"He ain't hearin' a whole lot right now," Clyde said, "'cause he's out cold." He told W.D., "Get the car seat out and keep Buck off the dirt. Get what we need outta the car so I can take off. You keep that shotgun and ammo and a couple .45s. Sun's goin' down so get some sticks and branches and start a little campfire to roast hot dogs."

"Get some good buns and mustard," Bonnie said.

"See if they got marshmallows," Blanche said. "Buck's always roastin' marshmallows first chance he gets—makin' them sweet and brown."

Bonnie said, "Oh, daddy, I gotta eat somethin'. My stomach's shrinkin' on me like my leg's shrinkin' shorter than the other leg. Is there anyone patrollin' this park?"

"I haven't seen anybody," Clyde said. "This whole land's big and rollin' with hills and these woods. What the hell they gonna be lookin' for? Campers comin' sometimes, but I reckon they pick where they're gonna have a picnic, and we're so far out on this end there ain't gonna be anyone on the road we just came on. 'Sides, I figure these local folks don't wander too far in here. More they get a little campfire and be layin' and lookin' up at the stars."

"With a hole in their head?" Blanche said. "And busted glass stickin' in their eye?"

Clyde sighed. "We're takin' care of what we can, Blanche—"

"—both you and W.D. been shot," Blanche said, "and I can't see outta my eye, except the shot-up shape Buck's in that's damn near killin' me. Get whatever you can to kill pain, Clyde. And I mean pain! What're we gonna do?"

"We're gonna do as we're doin'," Clyde said. "Stay here and keep him restin', and I'll look at your eye soon as I get back with what we need to help Buck and you and Bonnie—"

"—and me," W.D. said.

"That hole in your side ain't nothin' that's gonna keep you off your feet," Clyde said. "Get some of the water that's left and mix some mud to fill in the bullet holes in the car. Won't do drivin' around these local folks in a car shot full of holes. We ain't that far from Platte City, y'know."

Soon as he'd changed his blood-stained shirt and unloaded a couple blankets from the rear of the car, Clyde drove back on the dirt road leading south to the highway that went through Dexter's main street. He'd seen the drugstore sign where he'd buy the supplies, but knew there was little he could do to mend Buck's head. Looking at the wound, he'd seen the brain swelling and pushing fluid and tissue through the two holes in his skull. The same single shot through the head would've killed anyone else. But even though Buck was tough, Clyde believed there was little he could do to keep Buck alive. Bonnie was in bad shape, he knew she was trying not to show it. The hole in W.D.'s side and the bullet Bonnie pried out of Clyde's chest would've had anybody being treated in a hospital, but things were different for the Barrows than how they were for others.

Gradually he was off the dirt road and out of Dexfield Park. He soon was on Dexter's main street and saw the meat and grocery market. Across the road from the town restaurant was the drugstore. A short distance further, he came to a clothing and furniture store, and parked the car a ways from a direct view through the store window.

The owner was at the rear in a small shoe department. He looked up, smiling as Clyde asked to see a pair of shoes. "What I'm wearin's about worn through," Clyde said.

As the merchant tried a pair of shoes on Clyde, the merchant's vest fell open, and Clyde was staring at a deputy sheriff's badge pinned to the man's shirt pocket. "I'll take the shoes like they are," Clyde said. "Don't need the box. I can use a couple white shirts I saw up front. I'm in a hurry."

With the new shoes and shirts, Clyde drove to the meat market that also served as Blohm's Indian Grill. Again, he parked a short way from the business, and went in more at ease than in the clothing store. He ordered five dinners to take with him, plus hot dogs, a block of ice, buns, and mustard. While his order was being prepared, he walked across the street to the drugstore.

"My name's Fields," he told the druggist. "I'm a veterinarian with a couple of yelpin' patients, if you get what I mean. I can use a couple tubes of morphine."

"I don't have a hypodermic," the druggist said. "Will pills do you okay?"

Clyde said, "Pills are okay. I grind 'em and put 'em in the dogs' food. They're hurtin' in a bad way, and I'd like to save 'em if I can."

He purchased the morphine, a supply of peroxide, some boric acid, two boxes of cotton, bandages, and a bottle of aspirin. Grinning, he said, "The aspirin's for me."

He examined the various medical scissors the druggist had, and selected the pair closest to what he'd described to Bonnie.

Drugstore purchases completed, Clyde crossed the street to place the supplies in the car. He then went into Blohm's to pick up the dinners, the block of ice, and hot dogs. They didn't have any marshmallows. Mrs. Blohm said, "You must have a hungry family waitin'."

"That's right," Clyde said.

He asked if he could buy some plates and silverware, but she said, "I don't sell them, but I can loan them to you if you promise to bring them back?"

"You've been very kind," Clyde said. "I'll bring 'em all back tomorrow when I'll be buyin' more meals like I've just done."

Before leaving the restaurant, Clyde bought a newspaper and two new movie magazines for Bonnie.

At the car he noticed how the mud that he'd used to hide the bullet holes was flaking off. They weren't so far from the shoot-out in Platte City that two and two couldn't be put together. He'd seen the badge on the merchant deputy. He'd looked Clyde square in the face, and if there'd been posters floating around to be seen, that lawman would've known damn well who he was fitting with a pair of shoes, and looking at eye to eye.

They stayed close to the car. Though late evening had not yet settled in, W.D. held a flashlight close on Blanche's eyes while Clyde attempted to remove any glass fragments with the surgical scissors he'd bought. He then made up a solution of water and boric acid and had her bathe her eyes.

W.D. had gathered twigs and lumps of old wood without straying far from the campsite. They lit a fire, roasted some hot dogs and ate them with the dinners Clyde had brought. W.D. wolfed his down while Blanche only nibbled the skin off a roasted wiener. Bonnie picked at the food as she thumbed through a movie magazine, illuminating pages by a second flashlight propped up on the running board of the car.

Clyde had ground up two morphine tablets, dissolved them in a thermos cap of water, and had Blanche nurse the fluid between Buck's lips.

W.D. held his flashlight as Clyde poured hydrogen peroxide into the hole in Buck's forehead, letting it run out the hole in his temple.

"I gotta tell you this is all we can do," he told Blanche. "It's gonna help keep an infection down, but his skull's busted same as he's been hit by a car. His brain tissue's comin' out the holes right now. Don't risk coverin' him up, Blanche, or gettin' him too hot, or flies or dirt in those wounds. Even bandagin' his head's maybe gonna get him infected more."

"More?" Blanche said. "You thinkin' he's got the infection already?" Clyde nodded. She said, "What in God's name we gonna do?"

"Just leave him restin' like he is," Clyde said. "He's not sufferin' any pain and won't with them pills in him. We'll keep him so he isn't hurtin' none, and keepin' this wound clean's all we can do."

Frantic, Blanche said, "If we could only get him to a hospital!"

"They'll patch him up alright," W.D. said, "then ship him to any one of three states to get him fried."

"Shut your trap!" Blanche cried.

Bonnie said, "Any one of us goin' near a hospital's enough to get

271

us shot. Buck's knowin' that the same as Clyde and all of us."

Blanche started breathing hard. She threw her head back, but didn't scream or cry. "Oh, God," she said, "what's happened? How did this happen?"

W.D. said, "I reckon we've been playin' the hands we got dealt, Blanche. Ain't that right, Bud?"

Clyde said, "I don't think Buck here's cut out to sit in any congregation, so far as I can see, and what's goin' on ain't any of God's work." He looked at W.D. and said, "Come dawn we gotta get us another car that's not shot full of holes. This one's okay where it is, but we can't keep headin' anywhere in it without gettin' spotted."

Another night of trying to sleep, with the blanket wrapped around her, Bonnie inched closer to Clyde. "I got pains shootin' through my leg and pokin' into my stomach," she said. "I don't feel it's a healin' kind of pain 'cause my thigh bone's like it's burnin'. I'm so sick with it, I'm gonna throw up."

Clyde wet a cloth and wiped her face. He gave her a morphine tablet and said, "You'll sleep better now."

She clutched his arm. "You got to sleep, daddy. You gotta go to sleep. You can't be fussin' over us and not takin' care of yourself."

"I'm takin' care of myself," he said. "Missin' you takin' care of me, but I can't sleep, honey. Eyes are burnin' and they won't stay closed. I'm okay. I'm usin' the peroxide on my chest, same as pourin' it on Buck and the hole in W.D., so shut your eyes, honey, and listen to the moon."

W.D. chuckled. "What's the moon sayin', Bud?"

Clyde said, "Moon's sayin' you're gonna get your ass kicked if you don't sit up straight and get that shotgun off your lap. You're liable to blow your fuckin' fool head off—"

"Buck's movin'," Blanche said. "He's shiftin' around and moanin'."

"Blanche," Clyde said, "Buck doesn't know he's shiftin' and moanin' around, so just go to sleep. He won't be feelin' any pain so he should stay knocked out a few hours. Soon as the sun's up we'll see how he is. Go to sleep. Just get your back against him so he don't roll off that car seat."

"His head looks so awful," Blanche said. "It makes me want to die lookin' at him."

Once again, W.D. chuckled. The shotgun was off his lap but in easy reach. He looked at Clyde and said, "I ain't sleepin', Bud. I'm layin' here listenin' to the bugs in the bushes."

"To hell with the bugs," Clyde said. "You're listenin' for feet walkin' in them bushes and not any bugs crawlin' around. I'm sleepin' for two hours and then wakin' up and you go to sleep."

By dawn, Clyde was sorting through the ammunition boxes, adjusting the guns carefully in the trunk, and, half to himself, said, "These weapons gotta be oiled and cleaned." Next he took up the hydrogen peroxide and cotton.

With his eyes open, Buck looked at him and said, "When are we goin'?"

"Buck, honey," Blanche said, "how're you feelin'? Clyde's gonna fix your head again."

"I don't know how I'm feelin'," Buck said. "I keep thinkin' I'm lookin' at smoke."

"Let me know when the dancin' girls take over," W.D. said.

"Whatever you're seein's okay," Clyde said. "Let's get your head cleaned and get you fixed. All of us gotta be movin' on out of here."

Clyde glanced at Blanche. "We're too close to where he got shot up."

"I'm hurtin' and I wanna see my momma," Bonnie said. "We go south I can see Billie Jean. Can't we go back and see our family? I want to see my mother—don't you wanna see the family?"

"I do," W.D. said. "I want to see my mom. They all think I'm gettin' plugged down like a coyote."

Clyde said nothing as he carefully poured peroxide into the hole in Buck's head, letting it seep out the second hole and be absorbed by the cotton Blanche was holding. He said, "Buck's gotta be looked at by someone knowin' more than I do about head wounds, so goin' south might be the best bet we got. Right now, Boy and me're takin' off to the other side of Dexter for another car. Bigger town that way."

W.D. and Clyde were in the car as Bonnie limped around to Clyde's window. "Daddy," she said, "I love you with my heart and soul, and I'll go anyplace, you know it. But we can find somethin' in Texas, can't we? Won't we be safe, them not findin' us like we were at the Wichita cabin?"

Clyde nodded. He kissed Bonnie's hand. "I'll be back soon," he said. "I don't like leavin' you both here with Buck as he is, but there's nobody gonna bother you. You'll be okay. I promise you that. We'll be back right away. Gotta have Boy here to bring this car back. Then we'll go, honey. We'll go to Texas and see your momma. Y'all relax and eat them hot dogs. Soon as we get another car, the boy's comin' back and I'll go get us more grub. Maybe some cake and pie, and bottles of soda pop."

Driving along the road out of Dexfield Park, Clyde was smelling his hand. He said to W.D., "Buck's head's infected. I can smell it. Didn't you smell him leakin' that infection?" W.D. shook his head. Clyde said, "I'm talkin' about my brother, boy—my flesh and kin, and he's maybe not gonna make it."

W.D. looked at him. "You thinkin' he's gonna die?"

"That's what I said. And I'm worried right now 'bout him dyin' without us there and Blanche havin' a fit. Bonnie can handle it, but we take good care of 'em."

W.D. nodded thoughtfully. "Guess we better get us a pickax and shovel, 'cause we can't be haulin' him around dead."

Thirty-Two

Clyde was awake before the sun was shining. He'd packed the second car, loaded the guns and ammunition. Bonnie and Blanche were still asleep. Buck was making sounds. Clyde knew they were the sounds of someone shot through the head that didn't die. What would he do if Buck died in the car? Could he make it back to Texas with a corpse in the car? He knew Blanche wouldn't leave him. Bonnie'd be stuck with a hysterical woman grabbing at a dead man.

W.D. was cooking the last of the hot dogs for breakfast, and asked Clyde, "You want a hot dog?" Clyde shook his head. Bonnie was up and folding the blanket. She seemed in pain. She looked sick.

Clyde said, "Honey, soon as we get outta here we're headin' south. Gonna see your momma." Bonnie had the dishes and box of flatware ready to be returned to the Dexter restaurant. She looked at Clyde, about to say something to him, but he wasn't moving. His head was turned in the direction of the woods. He said, "You hear that?"

It came in a flash—the sound of heavy feet sneaking up at the same speed through the brush. Clyde's eyes swept the tree-studded space before him and then he saw them—half a dozen, maybe more, armed with rifles and shotguns.

"Goddamn laws!" he yelled. "Everybody get in the car!"

"Our stuff's here—" Bonnie said.

"Leave it! Let's go!" Blanche and W.D. scrambled to get Buck into the rear seat of the car as Clyde grabbed a Browning Automatic Rifle (called a BAR) and fired over the heads of the approaching men. They dropped to the ground while Clyde's shots tore at the tress and branches. The first shots from the men whizzed past Clyde or hit the rear of the car. Clyde sent off another round that slowed the approach. One man was lagging behind like he'd been hit by a ricocheting blast. Two had dropped to the ground again but kept firing from prone positions. The shots busted through the back window of the car, getting Blanche screaming and hunching down over Buck.

W.D. was hit by shotgun pellets as he ran to the car, the buckshot knocking him down. He got up fast, already bleeding, helped Bonnie into the car, then went around to the driver's door. Soon as he climbed in, he tried starting the engine. He couldn't start the car.

Clyde rushed around the car, sending off another volley, then pushed W.D. over on the seat and got behind the wheel while Bonnie had scooted off the seat, her head lower than the passenger window and the top of the front seat. The laws were still firing at the car—most of them missing the target. In a second Clyde had the car accelerating away from their shots and pellets peppering them, but was suddenly receiving gunfire from another direction. He skidded to a halt, threw the gearshift into reverse, and, with wheels spinning, headed into a turn just as a bullet tore into his left arm. He couldn't control the wheel. "Grab it!" he told W.D., and as they were still turning, the car collided with a fallen log, hanging the bumper and one front wheel. Clyde climbed out and let W.D. out, who fell again, but then jumped to his feet to free the bumper from the log while Clyde raced the engine, trying to back the car out.

"It's no use!" W.D. cried.

"Get in the other car!" Clyde ordered, and the three others climbed out, Bonnie helping Blanche with Buck and ducking to avoid the gunfire. Hunkering down in front of the stuck car, they watched for a moment as a second team of laws opened fire on the second car—bursting the windshield, smashing windows, and blowing out the tires. Clyde said, "They're shootin' it out from under us. Tryin' to get us boxed in, but we gotta get in the woods—hide in the brush while I go for another car!"

They could hear dogs barking in the distance, and gripping himself where the pellets had punctured, W.D. said, "They're comin' to finish us! We're leavin' a trail of blood behind us—it's drippin' off your hand, Bud."

"We gotta get in the woods," Clyde said, grabbing Bonnie as she stumbled.

"I'm hit—they hit me," she said, gripping at her torso. "Got me with buckshot…." Clyde held her, half-carrying her as they disappeared into the woods.

Buck yelled and started to fall. "They got me again—got me in the fuckin' back!"

"Oh, God!" Blanche said. "The blood's comin' out of him!"

Sinking to his knees, Buck said, "I'm fuckin' done for. Y'all go on."

"Keep going, brother," Clyde said, pulling Buck to his feet. "Let's go!"

"He can't walk!" Blanche cried.

Clyde told W.D. to help Bonnie, then said to Blanche, "Get on that side of Buck and we'll walk him. Grab him, Blanche."

"I can't carry him," she said. "I can't see and I haven't got any strength left."

"I'm *walkin'*!" Buck said. "I'll fuckin' *run* if you want!"

"Come on, brother. You gotta hide," Clyde said. "I'm goin' over the bridge to get a car."

"Where?" Blanche said. "Where's there a car?"

"Across the river on the other side of this hill. There's farms and cars. You just keep outta sight." W.D. was half-carrying Bonnie as they made their way through the woods, both bleeding through their clothes. Clyde said, "We gotta go fast 'cause those dogs'll be on us."

Weakly helping to drag the bleeding Buck, Blanche cried, "I can't go any more! I can't lift him and if he goes much more he'll bleed to death."

"Hide here till I can get back," Clyde said. "We can't do nothin' without gettin' outta here."

Blanche sunk down onto her knees beside Buck, now on the ground. "They're gonna get us," she said. "I can't even see!"

"You gotta hide!" Clyde said, pulling Buck up while Blanche supported Buck from the other side. "Get on the other side of that clearin'. You gotta hide, Blanche, there's no more talkin'. These billies get up here, they aren't talkin'—they're shootin.'"

Buck lay on the ground, hidden behind a fallen tree trunk. "I'm done for, Clyde. Take Blanche outta here—"

"No!" Blanche cried, crouching down beside Buck. "I'm not goin' without him," she said. "No use anybody talkin.'"

Clyde told them to stay hidden as best they could. He instructed Bonnie and W.D. to burrow themselves into the underbrush. "We'll make it," he told them. Armed with only a pistol, weak from the gunshot to his left arm, he made his way to the top of the hill overlooking the narrow river. Still hearing gunshots from the direction they'd come, he scrambled down the hill, catching sight of two men at the foot of the bridge.

W.D. later said, "I saw Blanche and Buck were hidin' a ways from an old baseball field. Buck had one of the .45s with him, but if he started shootin' they'd have us for sure. We were hidden in the pricklin' brush full of stickers and thorns on some of them weeds, and Bonnie was lookin' damn near dead. I said, 'Sis, are you hearin' me?' She kind of nodded, so I said, 'I don't like bein' in a bad pickle like this—cornered like turkeys if they get up here. I'm damn scared and bleedin'.'

"There was some shootin' down by the bridge where Clyde had gone, and both of us started shakin'. She had a hard time sayin' somethin' and asked if my gun was still loaded. I said it was. She said, 'If that was Bud gettin' shot again and them laws get up here, you put one of them shots right in my head. Don't mess it up goin' in sideways or somethin'—just shoot it right in the back of my head.'

"I said, 'Sis, I ain't gonna leave you and I ain't gonna end your life. You gonna die, I'm gonna die with you, 'cause they find out who I am, I'm goin' to that electric chair.'

"We heard someone pushin' through the weeds and Bonnie was clutchin' at me, but I said, 'Sis, our prayers've been answered!' It was Clyde, crawlin' into the brush and sayin' the bridge was blocked with laws. He said they looked like farmers, only all of them had guns. They hadn't seen him, he said, and our only chance of gettin' a car was makin' it across the river, all of us bleedin' like pigs that'd been beaten near death. Bud and Sis and me made it down the hill to what's called the Raccoon River, me carryin' her like piggyback. We must've looked like shot-fucked raccoons bleedin' and leavin' trails of blood in the water as we swam across—Bonnie's arms around my neck, near chokin' me. Clyde goin' ahead with that pistol in one hand, tryin' to keep it out of the water.

"We swam across, doggy paddlin', Sis near dead when we got across. Bud got us into a cornfield where we lay on the ground gaspin' underneath all them stalks. I was thinkin' if that corn was only ripe and I had me a wad of butter. I was havin' deliriums, what it was. Clyde said, 'I'm goin' for a car, so stay here waitin' till I call you to come followin' where I've gone.' Bonnie was hearin' a dog now and she was scared, and so said to Bud, 'They comin' over here with them dogs?' He said it was a dog at the farm he was goin' to. He said, 'Stay quiet.'

"What about Buck and Blanche? I didn't know what was goin' to happen. I knew Bud would look those eyes at me that always made you feel funny when you said somethin' you were out of line sayin'. I figured he say somethin' like, 'If my brother ain't dead by now he'll be so before the sun's shinin' tomorrow.'"

The big brown barking dog was edging into the cornfield as Clyde emerged from the field, covered with blood, and the gun aimed at the dog.

A man had followed the dog to the edge of the field to see what it was barking about. Clyde said, "Get that dog back or I'll kill it."

Pulling the dog back, the man raised one hand, holding the dog's collar with the other. "Who else you got here?" Clyde asked.

"Two other fellows. One's my son. Don't shoot, mister—"

"—laws been shootin' the shit out of us. I want a car."

The man said, "We've got three but there's only one that's runnin'; a Plymouth."

"Get those other men out here so I can see what they're up to,"

Clyde said, then whistled loudly.

No sooner had the two other men showed when W.D., carrying an unconscious Bonnie in his arms, emerged from the cornfield like a blood-spattered ghost.

The youngest of the two men approached W.D. and looked at Bonnie. He said, "This girl's dead."

"She ain't dead," W.D. said.

Clyde told the young man to put Bonnie on the backseat of the Plymouth. The man gave Clyde the keys to the Plymouth, saying, "There ain't a whole lot of gas in it…."

Clyde shook his head. He took the car keys from the older man and said, "You won't be shootin' us in the back while we're tryin' to get out of here, will you?"

"No, sir," he said. "Y'all been shot up enough." The three men stood on the narrow road watching as Clyde drove away in their car.

THE END OF THE LINE,
by Bonnie Parker

You've read the story of Jesse James
Of how he lived and died.
If you're still in need;
of something to read,
here's the story of Bonnie and Clyde.

Now Bonnie and Clyde are the Barrow gang
I'm sure you all have read.
how they rob and steal;
and those who squeal,
are usually found dying or dead.

There's lots of untruths to these write-ups;
they're not as ruthless as that.
their nature is raw;
they hate all the law,
the stool pigeons, spotters and rats.

They call them cold-blooded killers
they say they are heartless and mean.
But I say this with pride
that I once knew Clyde,
when he was honest and upright and clean.

But the law fooled around;
kept taking him down,
and locking him up in a cell.
Till he said to me;
"I'll never be free,
so I'll meet a few of them in hell"

The road was so dimly lighted
there were no highway signs to guide.
But they made up their minds;
if all roads were blind,
they wouldn't give up till they died.

The road gets dimmer and dimmer
sometimes you can hardly see.
But it's fight man to man
and do all you can,
for they know they can never be free.

From heart-break some people have suffered
from weariness some people have died.
But take it all in all;
our troubles are small,
till we get like Bonnie and Clyde.

If a policeman is killed in Dallas
and they have no clue or guide.
If they can't find a fiend,
they just wipe their slate clean
and hang it on Bonnie and Clyde.

There's two crimes committed in America
not accredited to the Barrow mob.
They had no hand;
in the kidnap demand,
nor the Kansas City Depot job.

A newsboy once said to his buddy;
"I wish old Clyde would get jumped.
In these awfull hard times;
we'd make a few dimes,
if five or six cops would get bumped"

The police haven't got the report yet,
but Clyde called me up today.
He said,"Don't start any fights;
we aren't working nights,
we're joining the NRA."

From Irving to West Dallas viaduct
is known as the Great Divide.
Where the women are kin;
and the men are men,
and they won't "stool" on Bonnie and Clyde.

If they try to act like citizens
and rent them a nice little flat.
About the third night;
they're invited to fight,
by a sub-gun's rat-tat-tat.

They don't think they're too smart or desperate
they know that the law always wins.
They've been shot at before;
but they do not ignore,
that death is the wages of sin.

Some day they'll go down together
they'll bury them side by side.
To few it'll be grief,
to the law a relief
but it's death for Bonnie and Clyde.

Thirty-Three

The Plymouth started smoking bad, and W.D. said, "A cylinder's blown, Bud. We're in trouble." Clyde didn't answer, just kept the gas pedal close to the floor. W.D. looked at him. "You hear somethin' makin' a noise under us?"

Clyde glanced at him. "A fuckin' bad wheel in the rear," he said.

Their shoes and legs were caked with mud from the river they'd trudged across, Bonnie hanging to W.D.'s back while he struggled to keep his head above the water, and her head higher than his. Once he got across the river, he realized he'd lost the gun. He'd said to Clyde, "I've lost my gun!"

"Fuck it," Clyde said. "We gotta get outta here."

The only route away from the farm, where they were driving the Plymouth, ran towards the town of Panora. Clyde said they needed gas. "Grab that old blanket on the floor and cut a hole in it," he told W.D. "Stick your head through it like a Mexican, so all that mud and blood on you ain't showin'." Clyde handed him several wet bills. "You drive and I'll be in the back. Get a couple gallons of gas 'cause we're needin' another car, and get water."

"We're needin' oil, Bud. We're losin' oil all over the place."

Clyde said, "A car's what we need—a V-8's what we need, and no damn Plymouth."

Soon as W.D. got gas in the car, checked the water, then bought two soda pops, he got back into the car, saying, "My legs're still feelin' dead." Clyde had assured him when they'd staggered out of the river, that soon as the buckshot was out, he'd feel okay. It was the cold water and the buckshot, he'd said. Bad news to be wounded and

284

"soppin' around in a muck river."

He told W.D., "We'll get it out of you, boy, but I gotta get it outta Sis or we're gonna lose her. I'm glad she didn't drown." He smiled a little. "I'd've had to shoot you."

W.D. figured Clyde wouldn't shoot him, as they had no bullets for the only gun between them. Clyde kept it out of sight against his leg on the car seat. W.D. said, "I don't know what I woulda done if she'd drowned, Bud. She'd've sunk—maybe pulled me down with her."

W.D. turned around in the passenger seat and adjusted the blanket on Bonnie laying curled on the back seat. He felt her face. "She's got a fever," he said. Clyde said it was from the lead she was carrying. "She's bleedin' some more," W.D. said.

"Ain't a bad sign," Clyde replied, "long as she doesn't bleed it all out."

"Poor Sis," W.D. said. "Buckshot's got her same as me. Lucky those guns weren't right on top of us. She's conked out, but her eyes're open a little." Sitting back, he asked, "How much blood can you bleed before you croak?" Clyde didn't answer. "I feel like I got toothpicks holdin' my eyes open. How's your arm, Bud?"

Bent on bouncing the car the length of the country road, Clyde said, "We get on the other side of this town, we'll get a car or bust our butts gettin' over the line. We'll get the plate off and junk this heap in Nebraska. Get us a V-8 and we'll get where we gotta be."

W.D. said, "You think that posse's got Buck and Blanche?"

Clyde didn't answer right away, then said, "I don't know if they got 'em. They coulda got you, boy. They coulda got Sis, and maybe they did if we can't save her. You got her across that fuckin' river, Boy, and nothin' you've done's been anythin' but right for her."

"Ain't there nothin' we can do to help her until we get where we're goin'?"

"With what?" Clyde said. "We got nothin'! Haven't even got a fuckin' slug of ammo. Look't you and me—mud and blood like a pair of clowns. Everythin' we had's gone in that damn car they shot the shit out of." Turning west, he crossed a paved road, and cut sharply south onto a back road. He said, "We're the hell outta there, boy. Them hillbillies're still lookin' for us 'cause they hadn't finished shootin' by far."

"I don't want to get shot no more," W.D. said. "I feel I'm sick— like I'm full of holes. Damn slug in my chest feels like a poker. How much blood did you say you lose before you croak?" Clyde glanced at him but didn't say anything. W.D. said, "I got to look it up—see how long you live with a bunch of bullets'n' buckshot from a bunch of fuckin' hillbillies shootin' the hell out of us." He glanced at Clyde again. "How the hell they knew where we were, Bud?"

"They fuckin' knew," he said. "Those folks in Dexter called out their own damn army."

"Sorry I'm groanin'," W.D. said, "but I'm just plain sick'n' achin'. Fuckin' feel like I'm gonna die."

Grinning, Clyde said, "You're pissin' your pants 'cause you didn't eat that last hot dog. Ain't that the truth? Look me in the eye and tell me it ain't the truth."

W.D. nodded, gradually, and returned the smile. He then asked Clyde, "How's your arm?"

"Dead," he said. "No fuckin' feelin' 'cause nature's takin' her course."

"What're we gonna do?" W.D. asked.

"Get another car fast 'fore we dump this heap. Get Sis taken care of the other side of the line. Find this old dame Buck talked about. Knew her husband bein' in the Walls. Told me about her in case Blanche got knocked up."

"You mean while Buck was doin' time?"

Clyde said, "Scarin' her, he figured." W.D. was about to say something but broke into a half-choking cough. "Settle down," Clyde said. "You drank fuckin' water from that coon river. I'm gonna pull over and you get out—puke it up."

"I don't think I can puke."

"Get rid of it, boy! Put your head down and stick your fingers in your throat. Get that shit out of your guts or you'll get infected, and I got no way of fixin' that."

Clyde eased to the side of the road and W.D. got out. He leaned against a tree, choking and throwing up as best he could. "I was drained—weak," he said later. "When I turned around I said, 'Holy shit!' The fuckin' rear tire'd gone almost flat. That was the noise we'd been hearin'. Clyde got out and opened the trunk at the rear of the car. I said, 'Air's leakin' slow but we've been runnin' hard....'"

Searching into the trunk, Clyde was doubtful he'd find a spare. He wasn't surprised. No spare tire. No jack or lug wrench. Under an old blanket, he found a tire pump that seemed to work. He handed the pump to W.D., saying, "Pump this son of a bitch up so we can get us another car."

"I'm sicker'n shit," W.D. said.

"Enough pukin', boy," Clyde said, "let's pump 'fore a fuckin' cornhusker highway laws wants to help you."

"We in Nebraska?" W.D. asked.

"That's what I said. Damn *corn*huskers—bohunks. Let's pump, boy! We gotta go."

Recalling that stop on the desolate road and not knowing if Bonnie'd stay alive or was maybe already dead beneath that blanket, W.D. pumped, up-down, up-down, blood from the buckshot and slug in his chest popping blood out of his skin. "It was like bein' tortured," he says, "and knowin' you ain't in for a happy dyin'. Clyde's standin' there smokin' and lookin' around while I pumped and bled till we got that fuckin' tire full of air."

Clyde said, "Bring that pump and get in the back with Sis. Keep her okay." They rolled off onto the dirt road, picking up speed, smoke blowing out of the car. W.D. started choking, feeling like throwing up again. He said to Clyde, "It's shits not knowing if any minute the fuckin' laws'll be runnin' at us, shootin' some more. You think they got Buck and Blanche? What'll happen if they don't shoot 'em, Bud? I heard one of them old boys sayin' about bein' vigilantes."

"What the fuck!" Clyde said. "My brother's shot to shit and he ain't goin' nowhere except to be gettin' buried."

"What about Blanche? She gonna get killed, too? Bein' vigilantes, you think they'd hang her?"

"They don't hang nobody. Laws does it. If they don't shoot her, she'll get jugged. Probably rat the hell outta us."

"Tell 'em who I am?" W.D. asked. "I keep readin' in the papers them callin' me Jack or somethin'. Y'figure she'll say that name's the picture of me? All of us bein' together?"

Clyde looked at him. "How the fuck would I know? Ain't nothin' I can do if she does rat, except what I'm already doin'."

Later, W.D. discovered the dirt on the windshield was making him sick. "I could hardly see out the front or the side window, and we had no water to drink. No guns except that empty automatic. 'Wave it around,' I thought, knowin' I was dreamin' up stuff. My head was foggin' up. My throat so sore I could hardly suck air into me. It occurred I was gonna die. I kept sayin' it to myself till a chill went runnin' through me. I didn't say it to Bud 'cause he'd've got mad, maybe wantin' to kick me out, but he wouldn't 'cause he'd have so much for me to do—maybe even buryin' Bonnie in the woods if she'd croaked... So much more he didn't want to do himself like pumpin' up a fuckin' tire. I knew if he kicked me out he'd be layin' awake wonderin' if I was gonna rat, and even though he might've been thinkin' it, I wouldn't have done it. But he'd have to finish me anyway in case the laws got me singin' to save my own ass, so, sick as I was, it was a matter of me not bein' dumb. Wasn't that he had bad feelin's for me, 'cause I knew I'd fitted in and he hated lettin' go of that. Only thing I figured in that dirty Plymouth was him blowin' the car apart by hittin' a speed the car'd never seen. I hurt in every part and couldn't keep my head up straight on the end of my neck, kept thinkin' of Sis on that back seat and if she was dyin' it wouldn't bother me at all if Clyde found it fit to put a killin' bullet in me. Why not? Right then it just didn't seem to fuckin' matter, and I figured I'd be lovin' Sis the rest of my life as a dead man."

"This damn heap's dyin'," Clyde said as he drove off the road and parked behind an abandoned service station. W.D. wasn't aware that he'd slept. More like he'd been being numb and in a coma, sliding between a general ache and sharp, throbbing pains.

"What're we doin', Bud?"

Clyde said, "Get that blanket you cut a hole in and stick it over your head again. There's blood all over us, boy. I'm still bleedin', but you're gonna grab another car. There's a cemetery back a ways—a quarter mile. You see that?" W.D. nodded vaguely. "A few houses down that hill, and there's cars on the road. You get one and bring it back. Get the plate on it and stash this heap here. Get us a damned Ford, boy! We gotta get outta here."

W.D. said the walk was short—no cars came past. The cemetery was small, and he slowed down, gazing at the tombstones as he walked east on the downhill lane. He could see the cars Clyde had spotted on the short road, and he heard voices. Phonograph music. Up ahead was a tavern, an old wood frame building. Laughter and a couple women's voices. Across the graveled road and to the south, past some small, railroad houses, he saw several more cars. He walked until he came to a good-looking Ford sedan. He stared at the silver V-8 insignia on the nose of the grill.

Jittery and unsteady, he opened the car door and climbed up onto the red leather seat. He saw himself driving the Ford in downtown Dallas. Instead, here he was—not far from the graveyard. He sat wondering if he still thought he was dying. But what about Bud and Sis?

He felt a shock, a jolt, and in seconds the car engine was running smooth, W.D. making a quiet turn on the street, heading back to the road facing the cemetery.

Clyde was pissing against a broken station wall, peeing directly into the crack as the Ford slowed to a stop behind the station. W.D. got out as Clyde came to the car. "Let's go," he said. "Get her out of the heap and into the Ford, she's talkin' now. Cover her good while I get this plate on."

W.D. pulled open the rear door of the Plymouth. "Sis?" he said. "Are you okay?"

She stared up at him. "What've you got on?"

"I'm makin' myself a Mexican," he said. "Come on, we got another car. A big, beautiful seat." Still huddled, he got the blanket around her, half-sitting, and lifted her from the seat. He saw she'd lost more blood. "Can you walk?" She shook her head, and he felt a single sob jerk at his stomach.

Clyde called over, "It's gettin' fuckin' dark and cold, and she's shakin'. We gotta get where I can fix all of us. Let's go."

W.D. placed Bonnie on the rear seat of the Ford, and as she lay back breathing heavily, he asked again, "Are you okay?"

She nodded a little. "Have I been knocked out long?" Since the morning, he said, tucking the blanket around her. Clyde started the car. Getting onto the passenger seat, W.D. told him Sis seemed in pretty bad shape. Clyde said he knew, then angrily maneuvered the car around the far side of the station, accelerating onto the narrow road heading west.

"Gauge says we're full of gas," W.D. said as Clyde's speed jumped from forty to sixty, then seventy-five. Then seventy-five to eighty-five as he raced west on the highway deeper into Nebraska.

Thirty-Four

He only remembered that it was dark, that the air was turning cold and he couldn't keep his eyes open. Chuckling to himself a little, thinking how earlier he couldn't keep his eyes shut, and now he couldn't keep them open. Maybe that's what dying was all about.

They were traveling fast. He thought he heard Bonnie saying something. Was she talking to him? He said something but then wasn't sure that he had. "Open your eyes," he told himself. He couldn't. Or did he have them open and had he gone blind?

No. He caught on fast to what he was thinking. There was a big woman with white spots on her arms and the backs of her hands. She had a wide mouth and teeth larger than his own. Spaces between the upper teeth. A burning light globe was hanging above from a ragged black extension cord, but the woman was holding a flashlight on him, the beam on W.D.'s chest. She had a deep, almost man-like voice. "You got it before any infection," she said.

W.D. recalled later, "I heard those words like she was sayin' it over and kept sayin' it, but she wasn't. It was just bouncin' in my head. I remember a little, like Bud stoppin' the car, then me walkin' into a kind of office or kitchen, Bud sort of holding me up on my feet. He had me lay down on a table, and I felt how cold the wood was on my back 'cause I didn't have a shirt on. I didn't remember takin' the shirt off, but he was sayin', 'Lift your damn head up, boy, and open your mouth!' He had me drink something. Soon as I taste it I remembered he'd had me drink some in the car, and he'd had Sis drink it. She was talkin' to him but I didn't know what she said.

"I felt him pinch my arm, and then the woman, her long black

291

hair braided like big hunks of rope, shined her flashlight on my arm where Bud had a big hypodermic needle and was stickin' it into me. I could remember her sayin' to leave the bullet in 'cause it wasn't gonna do nothin' where it was—somethin' like I wasn't gonna die from it. Bud kept askin' what I was sayin' but damned if I remembered what I'd said.

"Everythin' that happened since I'd conked out in the car worryin' about bein' dead got all scrambled, and the bits of talk, like I remember Sis sayin', 'You're wrong 'cause laudanum tastes like shit!' Must've been just before I wasn't on the table anymore and Bud kickin' open a screen door, same kind of screen on my momma's house. Bud was carryin' Sis still wrapped with that blanket, and I remember hopin' she wasn't dead 'cause he had her head covered. Then I couldn't see, and I didn't know if I was dreamin' about her layin' on that table with her naked breasts and stomach all showin'. I did think I was glad that I'd warmed the cold tabletop for her, and I was talkin' but I don't know where I was in the room. I wasn't seein' good, my eyes had a damn fence over them—no, it wasn't that. I didn't know what it was. That big woman said some stuff in injun talk—to someone else in the room? Some Indian? I didn't know. Whoever it was approved of Clyde's handlin' of the bullet wound through my side, but when the subject of the hole through Buck's head came up, the man said, 'Very bad. He'll die.'

"Bud was laughin' for a minute, and then usin' the same big tweezers he'd used on me to be pullin' buckshot out of Sis's belly skin. I just saw the little holes the shots had made and him openin' the holes and goin' in with the tweezers while that big woman poured what must've been peroxide on Sis's stomach.

"Then she was still on the table, but with another sort of blanket coverin' her while Bud was pryin' at his own arm, the injun woman pourin' again, and in a moment I heard the plunk of the slug hit the bottom of a metal bucket."

W.D. would remember that night as one of the worst he'd ever passed. It wasn't over when he opened his eyes and there was still no light coming in through a little window above a door. He wasn't sure it'd been the same night or some other night. All he knew was it was dark outside. A candle stuck in an old pan was burning and he smelled cigarette smoke.

Clyde was in an old chair by the window. He was wearing blue denim pants and a kind of cowboy shirt with tin buttons. "Bud had the pistol on his lap and was pressing slugs into the clip. He pushed the magazine into the chamber, cocked it and lowered the firing pin. I asked him where he got the bullets, but all he said was to get Sis on her feet 'cause we had to get goin'.

"I was on a bed and didn't have any deep achin' like I'd had, and I smelled adhesive tape and iodine on bandages stingin' sort of on my chest. Sis was like a bundle on my right side, wrapped up in a different blanket, a puffed-up blanket with pictures of flowers on it. She was lyin' on her right side facin' the wall, and I reached to put my hand on her shoulder but my chest stung right across the front of me...."

Bonnie groaned and reached around. "My stomach's all over with tape. An' my back?"

W.D. said her back was okay. She said, "Gimme a smoke." Clyde tossed the pack of Camels and the book of matches. W.D. gave Bonnie the cigarettes, and lit a match for her.

W.D. recalled that his thoughts seemed clear but he'd never seen the room before. "An old room with a bunch of junk," he said. "A toilet in what had been a bathroom, no door on it, and a bunch of hooks on a wall to hang stuff. Looked like rags hangin' on the hooks."

"Both of you are okay," Clyde said. "We gotta get out of here, so get up. Help her up, boy. Let her do what she's gotta do in the can, and you get dressed in the car. Just wrap that blanket 'round you and get the clothes on I got in the car."

"I'm gettin' up," Bonnie said, holding on to W.D.'s arm. He lifted her and took her into the dingy bathroom. No lights. He placed her on the toilet and went back to the open doorway.

Clyde said, "We gotta go before anyone else in this town starts movin' around."

W.D. said, "Where are we?"

"Broken Bow," Clyde said. "Let's go."

W.D. remembered it was freezing cold the previous night. Clyde had replaced the Iowa plate with one from Colorado. "I got Sis on the passenger seat in front, then found the clothes on the floor under a new blanket—a couple pair of new pants like the ones Clyde had on, some dresses and a sweatshirt, some sweaters and coats with price tags on the sleeves. "I got the stuff moved over and fixed a sort of nest for Sis, but she said she didn't want to lay down. She'd stay in the front with us, she said. I said I'd sit in the rear, sleep a little. She said to hand her something to wear, so I got the girls' stuff up to her as Bud started the car.

"We were movin' and I looked around to see where we'd been, saw that old screen door I'd see him comin' through in the night. It was all too mixed-up to think about. All I knew was I didn't have the kind of hurtin' feelin's I'd had when it was day, whenever that'd been. I just got into the new duds, put on a coat, puffed up Bonnie's blanket and went to sleep."

"Following a river for a while," W.D. recalled, "then south across the line into Kansas. After runnin' the back roads, Clyde finally stopped along the highway at a roadside diner. He gave me some money from a wad I figured must've come from his night huntin', and sent me in for three orders of ham and eggs, hotcakes and coffee. There weren't any laws around, just a couple old guys with a truck, and two other fellas in the kitchen. The gal behind the counter was very pleasant and stacked up our order into a big sack. I paid her and went back to the car. Clyde had the engine goin' and nobody was lookin' after me or suspicious of anythin' goin' on. Bonnie was starvin', she said, and I gave her some my hotcakes 'cause I couldn't eat them all.

"Clyde was sayin', 'You got a bunch of tape on your chest, boy, that's holdin' a bandage. You both'll be okay in a couple days, and you'll see scabs that'll bust off and you'll have a bunch of little scars like polka dots. I got most all the shot out of you both. We left that slug in your chest, boy, 'cause it woulda been worse gettin' it out than leavin' it in, and it ain't gonna kill you.'"

Later, leaning against W.D., Bonnie slept on the front seat as they headed across the Kansas border. Clyde veered off the road and drove for minutes before finding a deserted barn. He parked behind the barn and said, "There's room on the rear seat, so Sis can be layin' down."

Shaking his head, W.D. opened the door. "I gotta go puke. I think that pill, or maybe I'm poisoned like the doc was sayin'." He got out of the car and shut the door. Clyde leaned back, his eyes closing.

"Do you think I'm ever gonna be alright?" Bonnie asked, gently massaging her leg. "Will I be crippled up for the rest of my life?"

"I don't know," Clyde said. "We'd have to go some other place— some place like Mexico, or another country, to get you worked on proper. No way to do that here without gettin' shot."

Bonnie sighed. "Right now, are they plannin' on shootin' me, too, daddy?"

Clyde nodded. "I guess so. If they're shootin' at me you're in the line of fire—if you're that close to me."

"Close to you," she said, repeating him. She then raised her head. "I saw the picture of Sittin' Bull on the doc's wall." she said. Clyde nodded. Staring through the windshield at the moon, she said, "You think he looked somethin' like Chief Sittin' Bull? Even though he told us what a half-breed means—that he isn't all Sioux."

"I don't know," Clyde said. "Things're dancin' in my head. Fuckin' pain-killin' hypos. Go back to sleep. Boy's sick. He's knocked out. He can climb on the seat back there. You stay up here and go to sleep, honey."

"What about you?" she asked. "I can stay awake."

Clyde looked at her, leaned towards her until his lips touched hers, and he said, "Go to sleep, honey. I love you."

After a few moments, she said, "Are we gonna die?"

"Does it matter?" Clyde asked.

She shook her head a little. Smiling, she said, "Not as long as we're together."

*Texas Ranger Frank Hamer in earlier days, later considered by
some to be the "cold-blooded killer of Bonnie & Clyde."*

Bonnie was often carried by Clyde. This is the last photo taken of Bonnie & Clyde alive.

*Retired but legendary, Frank Hamer was hired
to bring Bonnie & Clyde to justice.*

*Texas lawman Ted Hinton confers with Louisiana sheriff;
the road ahead is where "the outlaws will be stopped."*

Ambush site, where Hamer and posse hid in the bushes.

In approximately 12 seconds, the six lawmen had fired 167 high-caliber bullets into the car and the bodies of Bonnie & Clyde.

Killed instantly, Clyde slumped, the back of his head a mat of blood.

The aroma of Bonnie's perfume mixed with the smell of gunpowder and blood. High-caliber bullets had penetrated most of her body.

Lawmen unload Clyde's traveling arsenal. The bodies of Bonnie & Clyde, dead in the car, will remain inside until the vehicle is towed.

Guns, ammo, Clyde's saxophone, Bonnie's magazines and dresses are unloaded from the car.

Judge, jury and executioners: Frank's Hamer and his posse. Hamer, kneeling left; Ted Hinton standing second from left.

Alerted to the killing of Bonnie & Clyde, spectators crowd for a glimpse of the bodies.

Townsfolk mob the car containing the bodies of Bonnie & Clyde.

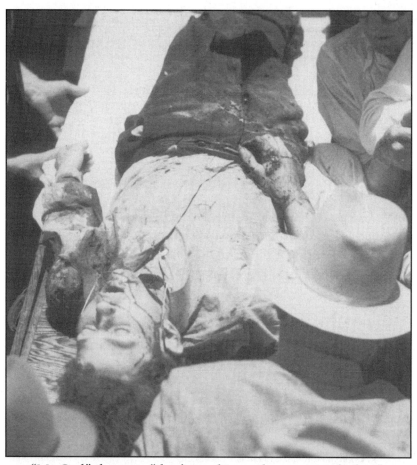

"My God," they say, "they're no bigger than a pair of tykes!"

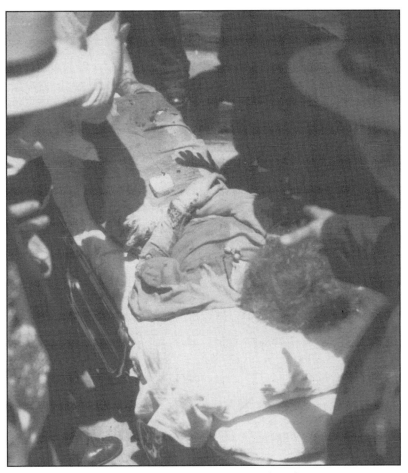

Bodies are moved to the coroner's office.

The car attracts a flock of latecomers as the town swells with visitors to see the "dead outlaws."

"More holes in that car than a hundred pounds of Swiss cheese!"

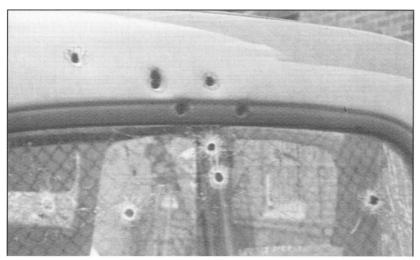

With Bonnie & Clyde dead, the car coasted to a stop as more bullets were fired through the rear window.

The car, and its occupants' personal belongings, would fetch high returns from collectors.

Clyde's jacket, removed from his body, draped on the bullet-riddled car.

Side of car opposite the firing storm. Note bullet exit hole gaping from front passenger door.

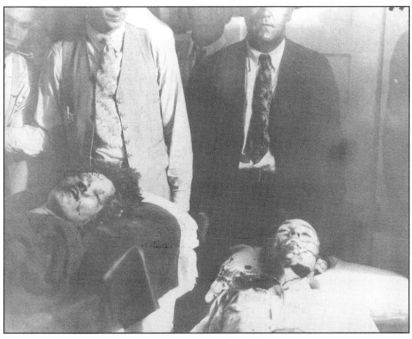

Awaiting examination by the coroner.

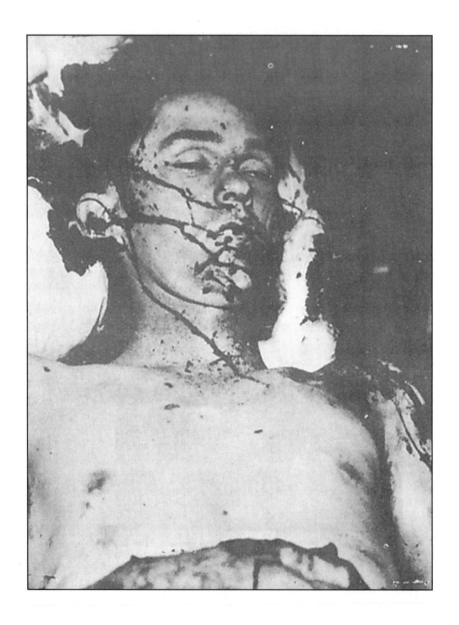

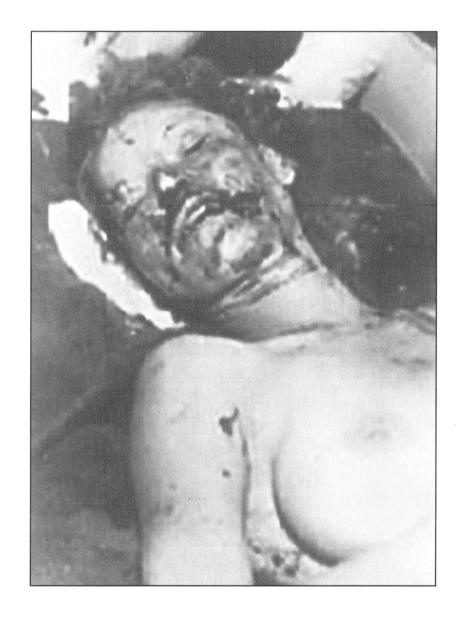

Dr. J. L. Wade
Medical Doctor and Coroner
Arcadia (Bienville parish), Louisiana - May 23, 1934

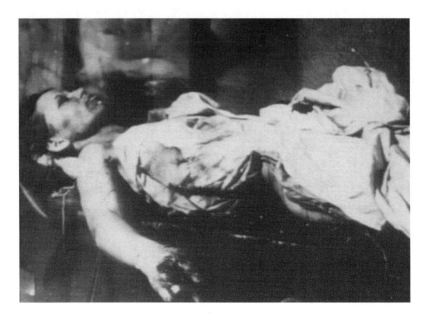

Coroner: "Close to 40 wounds to body by rifles, pistols, and shotgun."

"...shot in left breast, going into chest; shot 4" below ear; another shot, entering above the right knee; two shots front leg; two shots right leg; gunshot wound around edge of hair, 1 1/2" above the left ear; another through the mouth on left side, exiting at top of jaw; another at middle, just below left jaw; another above clavicle, left side, going into the neck; two shots about 2" below left shoulder, fracturing the bone; another wound on elbow of left arm; another, entering left chest above the heart, breaking ribs; six shots entering 3" on back region left side; five pellet wounds about the middle of left side; cuts from glass on the left ankle; cut on top of left foot, apparently from glass; cut on center of right thigh; cut 6" in length, about 3 1/2" center of right leg; eight metal fragments entering cross the front of face; exit wounds 6" on the inner side of right leg; flesh wound underside of right knee; bullet wound right leg about middle of outer right knee; wound on center of ankle about 2" above back of foot; gunshot wound to bone of first ringer; another to the middle finger; gunshot wound entering fleshy portion of left thigh; eight bullet wounds striking almost in parallel line on left side;

three parallel lines of bullets striking right side of back from base of neck to angular right scapular to middle of back bone, one striking midway of back, breaking backbone."

Coroner: "Clyde, approximately 28 bullet wounds."

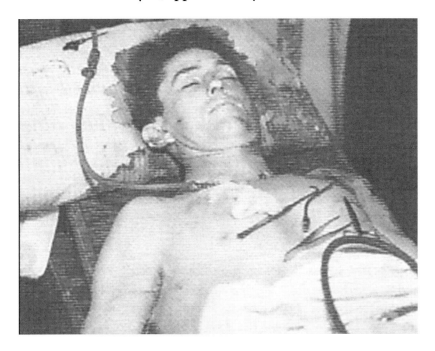

"...gunshot wound in head, center front of left ear, exiting about 2" above right ear; one entering edge of brain above left eye; several shots entering left shoulder joint; small glass cut at joint, first finger of right hand; seven small bullet wounds around middle of right knee; a number of glass wounds; bullet wound right leg, about middle of outer left knee; bullet wound on exterior ankle; wounds about face; wound 2" above back, a great hole gunshot wound, back of first finger another would, middle finger at one, entering the member."

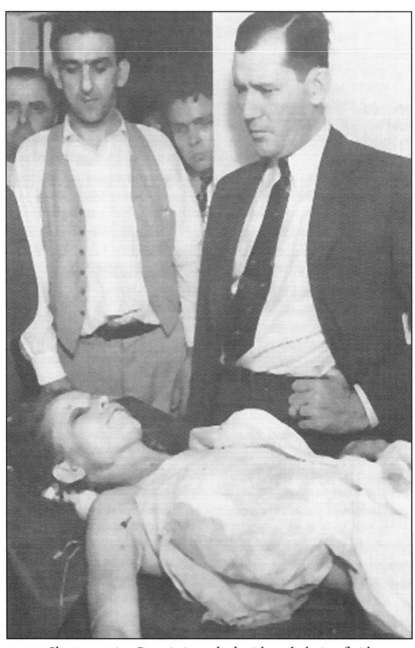

*Sheet covering Bonnie is soaked with embalming fluid
leaking from the bullet holes in her body.*

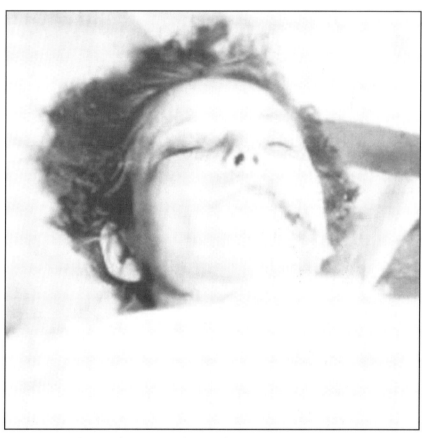

Last photo of Bonnie taken before undertaker treatment to conceal bullet hole in face.

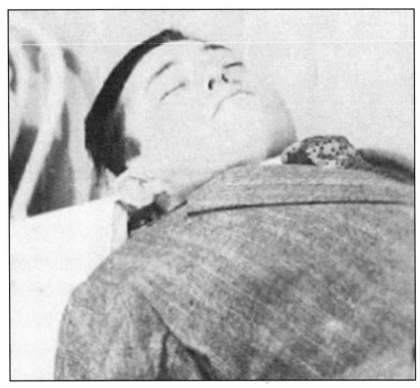

Clyde, half-embalmed, dressed in a suit, prepared for his funeral.

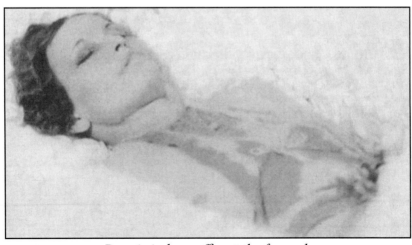

Bonnie in her coffin at the funeral.

Spectators push and shove at the McKamy-Campbell Funeral Home in Dallas.

Bonnie's casket borne by pallbearers toward a waiting hearse.

BARROW

CLYDE C.   MARVIN I.
MAR. 24, 1909   MAR. 14, 1905
MAY 23, 1934   JULY 29, 1933
Gone but not forgotten.

BONNIE PARKER

OCT. 1 1910 ⟶ MAY 23, 1934

AS THE FLOWERS ARE ALL MADE SWEETER BY
THE SUNSHINE AND THE DEW, SO THIS OLD
WORLD IS MADE BRIGHTER BY THE LIVES
OF FOLKS LIKE YOU.

Thirty-Five

Staring at the wide Mississippi River for an hour, the car parked on the bank at Clarksville, Missouri, W.D. made his decision. He'd had enough. No more bullets or shotgun pellets riddling his hide. He started the car, turned around and got the gas tank filled as Clyde had asked him to, but instead of returning to the abandoned cabin where they were hiding, W.D. drove southwest. He'd drive as far as he could, and as long as the gas held out. He'd have to ditch the car, but there were still two pistols in the trunk. He'd take them, sell one to an Indian on the highway, and keep the other as long as he could. Wouldn't do him good to be caught with it if he ran into the laws. Without it he was just another young bum "hoboin'" back to wherever he'd first lit out. Wouldn't be any good to be hauling a .45 unless he intended on defending himself. Against who? "Clyde," he'd say. He was escaping from Clyde Barrow who'd been holding him a prisoner. Chaining him to a tree at night or the back bumper of another stolen car. He'd deny playing any part in the killings. Asleep when any bad crimes were committed.

Sleeping on the near-freezing ground. He'd have permanent trouble with his bones.

The joints would work. Wouldn't bend any more. He wasn't going to change any more stinking tires or fuck with distributors. Wasn't going to steal any more batteries....

But he wouldn't be talking to Bonnie anymore. She'd be sitting with her eyes closed, almost hidden behind those rose-colored glasses. He enjoyed talking to Bonnie. He had to admit he never knew or got to know any other girl he enjoyed hearing as much as

321

Bonnie. He believed he learned things as she spoke. It was that sort of feeling he had for her.

Clyde didn't talk a lot. He was all business. But he treated them like a family. He had a job to do and did the jobs—didn't matter that it wasn't legal because he'd told W.D. if you don't live as they're telling you to live, then they say it's not legal. More than a few times Clyde said it was a war, and they were out to kill you unless you got them out of your way first. They were always there to get you—to kill you.

W.D. would say, "I never saw Clyde shoot anyone who wasn't aiming a gun at him with every intent of pullin' the trigger. He never shot any person in a bank or a store, and as for Bonnie, she never once even pulled a gun on somebody. To live with the true side of somethin's a whole lot different than the way they try and tell you how it happened.

"I didn't want to be an outlaw and be dyin'. I didn't want to get shot up no more and sleepin' on the ground. I had a choice to make and nobody'd make it except me and it didn't have nothin' to do with what I felt about Bud and Sis. It got me hard and sad to run off, but I was doin' that or dyin' a lot sooner than I had any rights to. I felt real kin to both, and knowin' what they were thinkin'—that they'd be dyin' soon and it didn't matter to 'em, the dyin' part, so long as they'd be dyin' together. Inside me, I knew I had no place in that thinkin', but if I got set on stickin' with them, I'd wind up just another hunk of baggage all shot up by the laws."

Clyde drove up a winding mountain road to a complex of rock, stopped the car and closed his eyes. Bonnie was already asleep. Nobody'd see them. There wasn't a living soul for dozens of miles. Just maybe the spirits of all the dead Indians. Clyde slept sitting behind the steering wheel until the sun came up. He opened his eyes. He knew it was time. It was moving in his bones. He couldn't sleep for the careful planning. He woke Bonnie and told her what he had to do—how it had to be, each moment of it orchestrated in precision like gears getting thrown into action.

"I'm there every minute of it," Bonnie said. "It's takin' my next breath."

His plan for the raid on Eastham had obsessed him. In dreams he felt himself pulling at the chain around his neck. He remembered every dirty detail he'd lived through, repeating and repeating every blow of a club or burn of a whip. Usually the whip was across the backs of the legs. With Ralph he'd shared the bitter memories as a brother in pain, and he'd shaped his blueprint around each galling detail like a drill bit ripping at a sheet of metal. "I can't do it without you," he'd told Ralph, "and I oughta shoot that fuckin' Ray for walkin' out on us."

Now he needed crates of ammunition. He needed partners whose hate for the head of the prison system and the steel bars was as strong as Clyde's.

Many backed away from what seemed only a crazy scheme. Lining up a gang to knock over banks was one thing—busting into a prison was "a horse of a different hue." Yet in rapid succession, Clyde brought a raiding party—two of the cons carrying memories as rotten as his own. Another, Ted Rogers, was a look-alike for Ray Hamilton, and another had been locked up with Ralph.

Clyde told Bonnie, "With the fellas I've got, we can do it, but we gotta be sure of the firepower." Two more banks were planned, in Denton, the gang hitting both at the same time. "Just like the Dalton boys of the Old West," Bonnie said.

She later told her sister that things went wrong. "Clyde's plans got wrecked," she said, because of trouble between the men. As soon as the group was ready to take the two Denton banks, they found a pair of Texas Rangers "sitting on their duffs" in front of the building. On top of that, Clyde quickly suspected other Rangers were snooping around any further jobs—seeming to know in advance whatever Clyde was targeting. Most of the men withdrew from the Eastham plan, and Clyde told Bonnie they had a "leak" in the gang—"word's gettin' to the laws ahead of us," he said.

Thirty-Six

Ray Hamilton was desperate. He'd been locked up for a year, transported often for trial after trial and wound up in Huntsville, facing almost four life sentences. He bragged—"a loud-mouth" he was called, his repeated and insisted superiority as a bank robber and gunman making him an almost laughing stock amongst the more hardened inmates. He kept insisting Clyde Barrow would soon be "bustin'" him out. The question several convicts asked was "Why should Barrow bother with a loud-mouth-stick up punk?"

Years later, Ralph Fults, also back in prison at the time, recalled the rumors about Clyde "attacking Eastham" to free a handful of "devoted killers" and bank robbers. Fults says, "Ray never shut his mouth about it, got to the point where nobody believed Barrow'd risk himself on such a far-fetched plan. Damn if it wasn't gonna happen, and since Ray was such a 'blabbermouth' no one in authority took him seriously. It was a different matter when it *did* happen, and all crap blew loose in the Texas governor's mansion all the way to Washington D.C."

Ralph knew someday in the not-too-distant future he'd be a free man—an ex-con, but free. "Gettin' busted out by Clyde would've put a lid on any idea of me bein' free. I knew damn well anyone busted out they'd be tracked without mercy. As it was, Ray was gonna be tried for murder and be gettin' the chair, and I wanted no part of it. Lee Simmons who ran the prisons was a rotten son of a bitch—a damn sadist who must've laid awake nights prayin' he'd get Clyde behind bars once again, but never once believin' Barrow'd pull such a stunt as bustin' guys out.

"Simmons made a special point of tellin' me that since Clyde and

I'd been friends, it was only a matter of time before he'd have Barrow back in Huntsville—the Walls. He said, 'There's a lot in here thinkin' Barrow's gonna be some avengin' angel, and praisin' the bastard like some king on a mountain.' He said anybody encouragin' anyone else with ideas of bustin' out were gonna find themselves in the hole until doomsday—if they lived that long. Simmons got real close to me and said nobody'd be pullin' anythin' in a Texas prison as long as he was layin' down the law."

Shortly after the meeting with Simmons, Ralph found himself moved out of Eastham and transferred back to the Walls. The first plan had been for Ray to escape with Ralph, but that idea changed when Ralph got word to Clyde that he wouldn't be able to make it, but wanted another prisoner, Hilton Bybee, to go in his place. Bybee was serving two concurrent life sentences for robbery and murder, since during a hold-up he'd shot a man between the shoulder blades "just for the fun it." He'd managed to beat the death penalty, but landed the life sentences with a twenty-five year cap tacked on.

As though in direct defiance, and with no interest in an official point of view, Clyde's plans for the assault on Eastham accelerated swiftly. Two Colt .45 automatics, plus ammunition for each, were wrapped into a cut-out hunk of old inner tube and delivered by Clyde and Bonnie to Eastham farm before dawn. On that dark, freezing Sunday morning in January of '34, Ray's brother, Floyd Hamilton, was in the car, as was Jimmy Mullins, a 48 year old ex-convict, drug addict and thug that Clyde did not like. Though Mullins had been promised $1000 to stash the guns and "work" the break-out, Clyde had told Bonnie, "I don't even like lookin' at Mullins."

Clyde drove without lights onto the Eastham farm grounds, and stopped half a mile from the prison. Floyd and Mullins got out and went on foot, following a drainage ditch until they reached a small bridge. The inner tube-wrapped guns were hidden under the bridge—less than 200 yards from the main building. After stashing the guns, Floyd and Mullins hurried back to the car.

Later that same Sunday, Floyd and his wife paid a visit to Ray, and passed on the information as to where they'd find the guns. Other on-the-run meetings and passing of information from Clyde had taken place between Floyd and the convicts in on the "break."

21-year-old Henry Methvin, a Louisiana friend of Clyde's, was serving ten years for auto theft and assault with intent to murder. Word had come back from Methvin that he was "ready for a visit."

The hidden guns were retrieved by a trustee and delivered to Joe Palmer, a 30-year-old old prisoner who suffered asthma and ill health in general. Palmer faked an asthma attack on the day before the planned raid in order to conceal the two guns beneath his mattress. Later that night, Ray picked up one of the guns from Palmer.

Both men were now armed. Clyde's obsession, as Ralph would call it, had reached its brim and was about to spill over. Ralph would later say, "That day was about as freezin' and foggy as my thinkin' had been for as far back as I could draw it up. I couldn't see it for anythin' back then, but the gettin' moved out of the farm and not bein' able to take part in Clyde's raid on Eastham was, in all ways, a blessin' that'd pay off for me in bein' granted a future to live out."

In 1986, I had a subsequent visit with retired bank robber Henry Edwards in Houston, Texas, while Edwards was visiting friends in Baytown. "Lookin' back on Barrow bustin' those boys outta Eastham prison," he said, "I could've told you those boys were gonna have a problem. Not in actually the doin' of it, but in where it was gonna go sometime thereafter. What went fast was that break-out business, 'cause Clyde and Jimmy Mullins had some heavy weaponry in those rifles, even though Clyde didn't want to do any direct shootin' at laws, but instead sendin' sprays overhead that was enough to get anyone's stomach on the ground. Idea's the same as artillery backin' up a front-line offensive—or a retreat maneuver. Keeps chasin' back what's comin' after you. Like that movie, *Kiss Tomorrow Goodbye*, where you've got the kinda break from a prison work farm, and they had that idea from what was real like what we're talkin' about.

"Ray Hamilton followed up Joe Palmer, a shooter, who got the rider—the 'boss', you'd call him—plugged him in the gut and Ray takes a shot at him, then another one at the other screw, so they've got two down—two dead, and then make their run while Clyde and Jimmy're givin' 'em cover, Bonnie blowin' that horn.

"I knew these kinda guys," Edwards told me, "knew a lot of 'em, and over the years I've kept interested in seein' what's said about stuff, same like some fellas collect stamps or broads, and havin' done time I can look at what they did an' see how it could've been better." Edwards said, "It got 'em nowhere 'cept a couple years hidin' under rocks or runnin' their asses off, and then what? Fuckin' electric chair. Nothin' else in their heads but what they're wantin' to do and shoot'n' the shit outta the world.

"What I'm sayin' now's just a sorta game I get a kick outta playin', or lookin' at old half-dead people that've had a past—had a life. I can say Clyde had the right ideas or intents to be what you'd call a 'master criminal,' like those funny-lookin' guys you had Dick Tracy in the funnies runnin' after tryin' to nail 'em. You take Clyde's brother, Buck, and it was just that where Clyde was and how he'd come outta that junkyard he was raised in, and bein' poor'n' livin' the life he'd led. You can see what I'm sayin', like for me it's a little game and you're just pushin' these play figures around."

Talking to Edwards, I was most interested in the so-called "underground telegraph" between the Walls, the Huntsville prison, and the Eastham situation. Edwards told me, "It keeps changin' from time to time, but you always gotta have someone outside. Clyde had his little sidekick with him, that Bonnie gal, and he didn't have any other friends. In the reality of things, they had each other and there was no one else playin' any fixed place in how they were— runnin' an' runnin' round in a circle in an' outta half the country like two kids cut loose in your amusement park. He was like the roadrunner—you know what I'm sayin'? With that coyote playin' the laws and thinkin' up every way to hammer 'em down but gettin' outsmarted like Clyde's not able to hit nothin' but bullseyes. An' hittin' the banks—who'd they walk away with? Joe Palmer? A sick guy with a bad personality, but faithful, y'know? Straight-shooter. Henry Methvin? Face all covered with zits'n' red like he's been dunked in the pot you're cookin' a lobster in. Hilton Bybee, like a guy that's walkin' with the devil inside him. And certainly Ray, the boy with the mouth you could stick a shoe in. But you had to chance it with that cracked nut—couldn't do nothin' right except rob a neighborhood bank until he run outta the brains to do that.

"No, Clyde wasn't a candy store robber. He was a genuine outlaw, one that's here and gone and left their mark as big as a brand. All he needed was to go it alone, no troops, no army—but you can't say he sure as hell didn't try. He busted those boys out and they hit a dozen banks, but damn near each job one of 'em was fallin' off. The general—that's Clyde—had ideas bigger than almost anyone could get their hands around. His brother couldn't even think straight. These guys like what he busted out were solo Johnnies—no one who's ever wantin' to shoulder the success of a good job that's been done workin' with somebody else. Or they got sick—they got hardons, got dope or hooked with some bone-headed cunt, got drained or shot to shit by laws or electric chairs, or a rope around their neck. There was always an end and it always ended. Clyde should've stuck on his own—should've kept on his own. His needin' to boss that gang he sprung out's what brought him down."

Thirty-Seven

Clyde rolled off Highway 114 onto a wide dirt road called Dove Lane, drove a short distance, then turned the car around. Henry sat up from the rear seat, coughed and said, "This where we meetin' your folks?" Clyde nodded and Henry slumped against the left passenger door, opened it, and got out. Following Henry out of the car, Clyde told Bonnie, "I'm gettin' in the back. Wake me when they get there. You tired?"

"I'm not tired," she said. "I'm gonna take a walk so I won't be pukin' on the floor. I feel kinda sick and I don't want to be sick when I see my mom." Clyde sat back, tipping his hat over his eyes.

Bonnie opened the car door, got out, and strolled to the edge of the road where the dirt ended and weeds began. She stretched her arms, reaching her hands above her head. The cloudless sky was cold, the color of metal. She shivered slightly. The ground was cold.

Clyde had climbed back into the front and stationed himself behind the steering wheel, his arms folded across his chest and his eyes closed. Then his eyes opened, alert.

Bonnie looked toward the highway, hearing the sound of motorcycles. More than one. She walked back to the car as three motorcycles slowed down on the highway. Two motorcycles made a turn as though heading back in the direction they'd come. Instead of continuing on the highway, the two uniformed cops turned onto Dove Lane while the third law kept going down the highway.

Bonnie grabbed Clyde's arm. "I see 'em," he said. "Highway Patrol.

You get your head down, honey. Keep it down so they don't see you."

"Nosey sons of bitches are comin' right at us," Henry said from the backseat. He reached toward the floor for the BAR.

"Hold on," Clyde said, starting the engine. "I got a better idea."

The two laws stopped their motorcycles a distance from the parked car, having yet to make out its passengers. One cop was climbing off his motorcycle when Clyde said to Henry, "Let's take 'em—" but before he could raise the shotgun to force both men into the car, Henry squeezed off a volley that blew the first patrolman backwards over his motorcycle, which fell on top of him. The second man frantically reached for his weapon—a sawed-off shotgun held in a scabbard attached to his motorcycle, but in a second went down with a second blast from Henry.

"Shit!" Clyde said. "What the hell's the matter with you!"

"Son of a bitch is still kickin'!" Henry said, jumping from the car. He ran to the downed man, rolled him over and pumped two more bullets through the man's body.

"Get back in the fuckin' car!" Clyde yelled, revving the engine, jumping ahead, and almost taking off before Henry could climb into the rear.

Henry said, "You said let's get 'em, didn't you?"

"I didn't say let's shoot 'em!"

"What the fuck," Henry said. "What's the difference?" As they left the dirt road, skidding, Clyde took the car at full throttle heading east.

While Henry drained a pint of rye, Bonnie, almost crying, said, "Our folks're gonna be there and I can't see my momma for Easter. They're gonna see what's happened—everybody's gonna see it. Dead laws layin' in the dirt."

There wasn't a lot of talking as they sped from Grapevine in a cloud of dust. Clyde drove intently, bent forward, looking straight ahead. Bonnie was thinking over what they'd left behind, and every lawman in a car or on a motorcycle or riding a horse would be loaded for bear and on Clyde's trail.

Henry was hunched over on his left side with the BAR on the floor. He grumbled, made grunting sounds. Dreaming, Bonnie thought, wondering what on earth he'd dream about. She put herself close to Clyde, her left shoulder against his right arm. He turned his head a little, glancing at her. "You okay, honey?" he asked.

"I'm okay," she said.

"Can't you sleep?"

"I still don't feel good. I'm hungry. Henry's keepin' me awake anyway."

"Sounds like a pig, doesn't he?" Clyde said. "A fuckin' hog in a mud hole."

"He makes me sick," she said. "I'm more sick right now with those two dead laws at our back. I got to forget it. I want to block it outta my head, so I'm thinkin' about my stomach. My stomach's empty, but I'm sick that's got nothin' to do with my stomach."

"We're gonna be crossin' the lake," Clyde said. "Got to get off the highway, so we'll be a while before we're stoppin'."

"I know," she said. "I know."

"Maybe we'll get you somethin' in Greenville. Maybe, I'm sayin', 'cause we gotta clear out of Texas."

Throwing a glance into the rear, Bonnie said, "Now he's shut up. Sleepin' with his mouth hangin' open like he's dead as those laws we've left layin' on the road."

"Can't be helped," Clyde said. "I had no reason to drill those fellas. 'We'll take 'em', I said. I wasn't sayin' let's shoot their asses off. Goddamn him, 'cause those fellas didn't know who we were."

"We could've had some fun tellin' stories," she said. "They weren't even goin' for their guns."

"All of it was bein' too fast," Clyde said. "He didn't heed what I said, and wasn't any time before he let loose on those fellas. I oughta pull over and throw him out. Maybe I will around one of these woods."

"Only get him pissed and he'll be liable to rat on us."

"I'd have to shut him up first," Clyde said.

"I shouldn't have been walkin' around," she said. "I should've been sleepin.'"

"What's the difference if you're sleepin' or walkin'?"

"Drinkin' in the mornin's like we've done's knocked me out," she said. "Henry was drunk—he's still drunk and sweatin' all over his face."

"Even cut that shit he's drinkin', half with factory rye," he said. "That plain moon's so strong you leak a drop without it disappearin' before it hits the ground." He patted her leg. "Go to sleep now, honey. Don't get your stomach sick and you go to sleep."

"I don't like to sleep all the time when you're drivin'."

He laughed a little. "You wanna drive?"

"I like to drive when I do."

"And you're good, too. You got a strong feel for it. Now get some sleep, honey. It won't do you any good worryin' about anybody. I'll wake you if I smell somethin' cookin'. We get to Texarkana we'll get you dinner before we see that boy about the job."

"I want to see that fancy hotel," she said. "Want to forget about today—just plain erase it from my thinkin'. Momma says they serve split pea soup in a silver-plated bowl. That's what she read in a magazine." She stared at Clyde, her eyes widening. "You think the folks showed up in Grapevine and seen those laws dead on the ground?"

Clyde said, "I don't think folks even showed. I reckon if they got there before anyone else they'd've seen what's there, but I don't believe they made it."

"That makes me sick," she said. "They'd be thinkin' we shot those laws."

"We had to get outta there," he said. "We couldn't sit around—"

"—I know. I know."

"It's just as well I don't throw Henry's ass out," he said. "Least till we're fixed up in finances. Just have to see, honey. We get the newspaper over the line and read what's happened. If the folks did show up the laws'd be jumpin' on 'em, and I sure don't relish bein' named for Henry's stupidity. I can't think of anybody who saw us there, our folks bein' the only ones knowin' we were gonna be there. I don't think Joe got word to them of the meetin' plan."

"What makes you think that?"

"Them bein' late and knowin' the law's on Joe's ass—he might not even've got across the river."

"Won't make any difference," she said, striking a match and holding it to a cigarette. "You want one?" He shook his head. She said, "They'll make us the guilty parties anyway. You and I've got no proof we didn't do it."

"Well, you're right...." Clyde said. "Technically, you're right, as they got me zeroed in whether I shot 'em or the whole state of Texas did it." He looked at Bonnie as she drew on her cigarette. "But you—" he said, "it's different with you, honey. You shootin' bean cans and soda pop bottles doesn't elect you the way they've got me nailed. You could sit in that fancy hotel with a silver soup bowl and nobody'd bother you—"

"—that's not true," she said. "Nobody payin' attention to me? I sit there long enough, the laws'll be jumpin' all over me—"

"'Cause they want you tellin' them where I'm at. But you know the story to tell 'em. You sayin' I wouldn't let you go. Holdin' you a prisoner—gonna shoot your momma if you run off."

"That worked for those hicks, but truth is I can't go even if you'd be wantin' me to. I'd just die where I was—even where I am. We don't know when it'll happen, do we? I only know in my heart it's gonna happen and we've got no say in it. Maybe even it'll happen in Texarkana—"

"Aw, don't say that, honey. Makes no difference where it happens. Only what matters is you and us bein' like we are. Get enough finances and maybe see where we go. Last night I was dreamin' about this bank—money on the walls like stacked in kinda shelves for a bunch of pigeons or hens." He shook his head. "I woke up this mornin' thinkin' there's nothin' more hateful than these damn banks, and half these people we're seein' eatin' grass or a hard old bun and some lard—"

"—or like Charlie Chaplin eatin' his shoe," she said, laughing a little. "Remember seein' that downtown? You held my hand all through the picture show and told me I smelled like a bush of jasmine."

Henry grumbled—saying something neither could make out. Bonnie looked into the backseat and shook her head. "I wish we could get rid of him."

Clyde glanced at her. "We'll be okay, honey. I don't pity those fellas back there. Well, I said to mud-ass behind us, 'We'll take 'em' and we coulda given those two laws a run like the way we're goin' right now. Could've had Henry loadin' those cycles off the road into the brush. Drivin' those laws with us. Could've let 'em off somewhere south of where we are right now, then head south ourselves so they'd get all curious and wonderin' where we'd be headin' and how we'd be out of Texas—gettin' you a fat lamb chop or turkey sandwich and gravy...."

"That sounds good, daddy." She rolled the window down a few inches and sent the cigarette into the wind. "Too bad he had to shoot like he did," she said, putting her hand out the window. "Probably would've had to anyway soon as they got a look at us."

"Not if we'd brought 'em along," Clyde said. "Could've been jokin' with those boys right now."

"They would've been too scared to think we're funny," she said. "I just felt rain." Rolling up the window, she stared ahead at the black road pulling fast beneath the car until sudden raindrops spattered across the windshield. Clyde turned on the wipers. "Rain," she said. "Rain... They're all scared of us." She folded her coat and turned to the window. Placing the rolled coat on the ledge, she tipped her head and rested it against the coat. Drawing up her knees a little, she raised her head again and looked at Clyde. "They may be all scared of us," she said, "but they're bringin' the wrath of heaven against us, aren't they, daddy? The whole heaven."

Clyde smiled. "Only heaven I'm thinkin' of is you, angel. I don't think of none other heavens. You're so sweet you're enough heaven for me, baby."

Bonnie leaned over and kissed him, then again rested her head against the folded coat.

After moments, the speed of the car pushing eighty straight into the rain, Clyde bent slightly forward to the wheel, again taking that lean position like a runner eyeing the hurdles ahead.

Thirty-Eight

Richard Cole wouldn't forget the visitors to the small, wood-frame Texarkana house he shared with his wife and son "a stone's throw from a truckin' yard."

"It was rainin' that day," says Cole. "Kicked in around evenin' and then someone was rappin' at the door. Our dog we had back then—half Lab and shepherd—started barkin' his head off, and I told him to shut up. I had a queer feelin' as I unlocked the front door and opened it a little. Clyde Barrow was standin' behind the screen, and with him was Bonnie Parker right at his side, tryin' to keep themselves out of the rain that was beatin' down all around them."

Cole had been paroled after serving four years for robbery. He says, "I made the decision to keep out of trouble, even though I had no job and it was a hell of a time. My wife was waitin' tables afternoons and evenin's until way late, and then I'd be out in the mornin' tryin' to get work. Didn't matter. Pick and shovel or whatever I could get. That's how it went, and every once in a while I'd run into guys that had big ideas—knockin' over this or that joint, and makin' big plans. I'd tell 'em thanks, but no, I'd had my fill of it.

"A guy I'd known told me he'd once run with Buck Barrow, but they'd split off, and this guy was runnin' still, the law always on his heels. He wanted me to go in with him and told me about the job in details I never wrote down, but kept in my head. While Buck Barrow was locked up in Texas, his brother Clyde wasn't, and this job was a sure cinch, he'd said, like goin' in, grabbin' and gettin' out fast. He said he'd written Buck, given him my whereabouts, sayin' I was a distant cousin, thinkin' maybe I'd go in with Clyde if the chance came up.

335

"I got a Western Union telegram sayin' somethin' like it's been a long time between cousins gettin' together and he'd pay me a visit.

"The information I had on the job was temptin' but I wasn't gonna be a party to takin' action on it—I didn't want it, but what I'd learned was with me, and then not long after that telegram, the car stopped out in front of the house.

"My blood was turnin' cold while Clyde and Bonnie were standin' on the porch. I could make out some other person in the backseat of the car, but there wasn't any resemblance with anyone I knew. It was already dark and that rain was comin' down. Times I'd seen it rushin' up on runnin' boards and slappin' around the wheels.

"I let them in. They were wet and right away Clyde's shakin' my hand like a lost pal. They had practically every cop lookin' for them, and here we all were in the same room—they were guests, and I was thinkin' I'm on damned parole, and couldn't consort with cons. My wife, God rest her, would've had a heart attack if she'd walked in.

"I'm six feet tall and they were a lot shorter and smaller, like two kids. Our dog that didn't trust strangers was waggin' its tail at both o' them, and Bonnie was pettin' the dog's head, scratchin' its ears, and that dog was lappin' it up.

"My wife knew nothin' about what had been brought up before, but I got scared because of what I knew, and here was Buck's brother, Clyde, and ten times the outlaw Buck'd ever been, face to face with me and my givin' him the rundown on a job. All the while it was like I was settin' myself up—except God takin' me by the neck and givin' me a shake, sayin', 'Wake up, boy!' My wife was pregnant again at the time, and nights I was takin' care of our one little boy.

"Our kid thought Bonnie was a little girl and he could play with her. I've remembered that clear as day. I thought it was funny how he was seein' her not as a grown girl but like she was a little kid. Even later on I asked my son, 'Why'd you think that young woman was a little girl?' He didn't know why he'd thought that, but he did, he said. So I said, she's bigger than you, and he said she was just big, that she'd grown faster than he had, so he said she was a big little girl.

"I was worryin' that a squad of laws'd come rushin' the house—

man, I could see it, and frankly it scared me shitless of bein' locked up again. I couldn't take that. If such a thing as that happened I'd hang myself soon as that door slammed shut. Done with it.

"I was embarrassed because I was scared, and I could see Clyde knew I was scared. He was armed—I could tell he was packin' a gun on one side and had an automatic on the other, down in his belt, and he's a walkin' arsenal. Bonnie had that beaded, fancy handbag or carryin' case, and damned if it didn't look as if it had some weight, like a goddamn .38 she could've been carrying.

"In short order, I sat with Clyde at the kitchen table and told him what I knew—the information I'd learned—and Bonnie was talkin' to my kid and dog, and then wantin' to pay me money. I said it was okay, wasn't necessary, though I wasn't goin' to say absolutely no. She gave my boy a couple bills and said it was to buy ice cream and a play truck—some kind of fire truck. She mentioned a toy gas truck she'd seen, and then she insisted I take money, and I said, 'Well, whatever you want and if you can't, that's alright by me.'

"Clyde said he wanted a drink of somethin'. All I had was soda pop, but he took that, and Bonnie drank some too, then he got me aside in the kitchen and was wantin' to know if I was willin' to work the job with him and another guy, 'the one's in the car,' he said. I said I couldn't, that I'd done all the time I could—and my goin' legit because of my wife and my kid and the one on the way, I couldn't go back in that line of work. The time I'd done had branded me like a goddamn steer, and I said I didn't think I was good to anyone anymore.

"Clyde said he knew that already. He said, 'Not that you aren't any good to anyone,' but that I'd done all the time I could do. He said he knew it when I opened the front door, and he wanted to know if I'd ever been to Eastham. That's where he'd done time, and I said no, I never got in dutch in Texas. I said what I'd done was Arkansas time, and no one was gonna let me forget it. I couldn't get ahead no-how, and in such a bad time with so many out of work. I couldn't be sold anythin' I'd pay for later, like folks were doin', so we didn't own the house—didn't even own most of the furniture. We owned the sofa which I said had been my mother-in-law's, and if it wasn't for her I'm sure we'd be right now sittin' on the floor.

"'I hear you, brother,' Clyde said. He needed another guy to work with, but I couldn't even help him out with that. I said I didn't have any more connections, couldn't even give him a name. Last guy I knew had been sent up again. Bonnie laughed a little, sayin' she understood everythin' I was sayin', and neither of them had any hard feelin's. She said she could see how anyone who wasn't a con was gettin' in line ahead of me, no matter how much effort I could put into makin' someone else more than I'd ever have a chance of bein'.

"Clyde said if I didn't have the kid and the one the wife was carryin', he'd convince me to ride with them, but he knew I wouldn't do it anymore, and couldn't live with myself if I did. He looked me square in the eye and said with him it was different. He didn't have any choice anymore. I said I knew that. They had killin' papers on him, and with a kind of smile, he said, 'So I got no choice.'

"He shook my hand again and said I was okay and it wasn't any skin off his nose if I didn't go 'cause I'd done him a decent turn, and he wouldn't forget it.

"The one bad thing I felt and God'll never let me forget it, was that while he was talkin' to me, his head cocked kinda and him grinnin', I thought I was lookin' face to face with a dead man. Made my skin creep up on me. One other time when I was in the jug I wasn't supposed to be talkin', but this one con was talkin' to me and I had the same feelin'—an idea that hits you like I was seein' the fella already dead except him standin' there talkin' like he was still alive.

"That's what struck me with Barrow and my shakin' his hand. He was reachin' out of a hole or a grave to pull me in if I walked out that door with him. God strike me dead if that wasn't what I was feelin'—not thinkin' it, but feelin' it plain as day; but I kept smilin'.

"They hurried out to that car where someone was sittin' in the backseat, just a dark shadow. I shut the door, sweatin' and kinda sick.

"My boy was asking me if the little girl was coming back. I said she wasn't as little as he was thinkin', but no, I told him, she wouldn't be coming back. He said, 'Not even comin' back for her dinner?' I said, 'No, sonny, not even comin' back for her dinner.'"

Thirty-Nine

Near sundown, Clyde walked into a gas station, drew his .38, and asked for the money. The attendant said, "It's been a slow day," and gave a yawn as he emptied the cash from the register.

"Been slow, huh?" Clyde said, stuffing the bills into his pocket. The attendant nodded. How could someone be so bored at gunpoint? It seemed a good idea to Clyde if they took the kid for a ride. Pocketing the gun but keeping it level, he said, "Come on out and give us some gas."

"Yes, sir!"

Clyde followed the attendant, and stood to the rear of the vehicle, watching as the kid filled the tank. "Check the oil and water."

Bonnie was sitting behind the wheel as another car pulled into the station. The young driver waved. "That's a friend of yours?" Bonnie asked the attendant. Finished filling Clyde's tank, the kid looked around and shook his head. "He's been gettin' gas a few times."

"Let's make him a friend," Clyde said. He told the attendant, "Get in the backseat next to that other fella in there. He's got a gun, too."

The attendant said, "You want me in the car?"

Clyde nodded. "Yeah, and don't be steppin' on any weapons on the floor."

As soon as the attendant climbed into the car, Clyde turned to the customer at the gas pumps. He waved for him to follow the attendant into the car. The customer looked confused. He asked, "What're you callin' me over for?" then panicked when Clyde brought the gun into view.

"Come on, boy," Clyde said. "We're goin' for a ride."

"Don't shoot—please! What do you want with me?" the boy said. Clyde motioned for him to get into the car. The customer nodded. "I'm gettin' in!" he said. "Please don't point that gun at me." Without further hesitation, he squeezed in alongside the attendant, who had placed himself uncomfortably next to Henry. "This car's full of guns," the customer said.

Bonnie slid over for Clyde to get behind the wheel. She then turned around from the front seat and looked at the new arrival. "What's your name?" she asked.

"Bob," he said.

"Well, Bob," she said, "you got nothin' to worry about, neither one of you boys, so you don't be lookin' so peaked just 'cause you're ridin' in a stolen car. This is Clyde Barrow drivin', and I'm Bonnie Parker—the gun moll terror of more states than your granny's got teeth." She smiled, watching their faces drain. Then she pointed to Henry. "That man is very mean, boys. I won't tell you what he's called, but he's with us, and these guns and boxes of bullets are the tools of our trade. What's your name?" she asked the attendant.

"I'm Wesley," he said, staring at the back of Clyde's head. "I knew that was Clyde Barrow," he said. "I knew it soon as he got outta this car, 'cause I've seen his picture in the papers. I knew it when you came in the station with that gun." He swallowed, cleared his throat and said, "I was gonna give you money when you walked in, so you didn't have to hold no gun or shoot me."

"You're a lucky fella," Clyde said. "You're actin' so casual I was thinkin', 'He's gotta be wearin' a bulletproof vest.'"

"We're supposed to be the most wanted outlaws in all tarnation," Bonnie said, her eyes gleaming. "Except maybe John Dillinger, but there's two of us to his one, and right now three of us includin' the fella next to you with the gun." Faking a serious look, she said, "I hope you boys are comin' to help us stick up a bank. That's what we're intendin' this evenin'."

"No, thanks, ma'am," Wesley said. "I don't want to stick up any bank, but thank you all the same." Bob spoke up quickly, saying he couldn't do that because he had high blood pressure. He'd only be in the way, he said. Or worse, he could have a heart attack and be bleeding right on the bank floor.

Bonnie said, "I don't think we'll be spinnin' anyone's blood— will we?"

"You never know," Clyde said.

Henry spoke up. "This here fella's lookin' peaked right now." He nudged the gun against Wesley's ribs. "You think he's needin' a transfusion?"

She looked at Clyde. "We ever been doin' any blood transfusions? Wesley's maybe needin' one—"

"—no, ma'am, I don't need any transfusion," the boy said. "That was this fella Bob here, talkin' about his blood."

"We can't do transfusions," Clyde said. "Mostly we just been spillin' it, and gettin' our pictures in the paper."

"I'm—I'm not in need of any transfusions," Bob said seriously. "I'm fairly okay right now—I mean, this minute in general, it's just I needed to get gasoline in my car."

"Well, that's a happy coincidence," Bonne said, "runnin' into us."

Shaking his head, Bob said, "Truly, Miss Bonnie, I wouldn't be any good at robbin' a bank. I've never had the experience at that sort of stuff…."

"There's nothin' to it," she said. "You boys look pale and worried. Are you worryin' about somethin'?"

"Yes, ma'am!" Wesley blurted out. "I left that station wide open when I got invited for this ride, and now this here fella's stickin' a gun in my ribs."

"And if I shoot right through you," Henry said, "I'll get your buddy at the same time, and bust a hole through your door."

Looking at Bob sympathetically, Bonnie asked, "I can see that won't be necessary. But are you worried, Bob, and not enjoyin' our repartee?"

He nodded. "I don't know what that word means, ma'am. I just needed some gas in my car."

"We've got plenty of gas in this car," Bonnie said, "since Wesley's filled the tank, and we thank you, Wesley."

"Yes, my pleasure," he said. "But I'm just thinkin' about my job—"

"—I already robbed your station," Clyde said. "You got no worry there, unless someone's swipin' tires and inner tubes."

Bonnie said, "You boys like singin'? We can all sing 'Bye Bye Blackbird'! It'll cheer us up so we won't be worryin' so much about the unpleasant side of things."

Clyde said, "I'll get my guitar outta the trunk, we can have a singin' party!"

Neither boy said anything, and minutes later on the outskirts of the town, Clyde left the highway and drove a short way on a dirt road. Slowing the car to a stop, he looked sadly into the rearview mirror at the two nervous riders. "Since you boys don't want to be robbin' a bank with us or singin' a song with Bonnie, I reckon this here's the end of the road...." When he reached into his pocket, Bob gasped and Wesley braced himself. Clyde pulled out a handful of bills. He unfolded several and gave each guest a share.

Bonnie clapped. "That should get y'all tucked safely back to the gas station, but maybe we'll be seein' you again real soon." The rear door flew open on Bob's side of the car, and both unwilling passengers scrambled out. Bonnie called, "Bye for now, Wesley, and adieu Bob! Be seein' you soon!"

A few yards from the car, both boys ran for the highway, leaving behind the laughter trailing from the car. Bonnie said, "Oh, daddy, that was fun! You think we scared the pants off those boys?"

Henry spoke up. "I don't smell any shit, but their faces turned white as a fuckin' virgin's bedsheet."

Clyde shifted gears and sped ahead. Glancing through the mirror at Henry, he said, "That's what I wanted to do with those Grapevines. Just run 'em around, havin' some fun."

Henry's eyes met Clyde's. "Just a misunderstandin'," he said. "We all make some of those misunderstandin's. I guess a body can blame God for ever creatin' the likes of us."

Forty

Between two and three o'clock in the morning, Clyde turned off Highway 66 onto a muddy dirt road running west from the highway. They were a short distance from Commerce, Oklahoma.

Henry said, "I'm awake, so you go on to sleep. She's already asleep isn't she?"

"Yeah," Clyde said.

"I'll keep my eyes open but there's nothin."

An hour and a half later, Bonnie squeezed Clyde's arm. "He's sleepin."

Clyde tipped the rearview mirror. "Stupid shit said he was awake. Coulda had our heads blown off."

"Go to sleep if you want," she said. "It's all mud here. We're sittin' in mud."

"You go on back to sleep, honey. I'll wake him soon as I want to take it easy."

"Sleep all you want 'cause I'm not shuttin' my eyes."

Clyde squeezed her hand and closed his eyes. When he opened them again the sun was shining, then dimming behind heavy cloud cover. Henry was slumped to the right side of the rear seat, and Bonnie was looking at her lips in her compact mirror. "He woke up," she said. "There's cars on the highway."

"I heard 'em," Clyde said, looking at her.

Her glance shot above the mirror. "Here they come!" she said.

Clyde instantly turned the key and started the engine. The laws' car had stopped, heading on the side road, and was blocking any passage. The doors opened and two laws stepped into the mud. Clyde threw the car into reverse and sped backwards a distance, then tried to make a turn, but he skidded, the rear wheels sliding in the mud.

"Son of a bitch!" he said. He tried to go forward but they were stuck.

Henry said, "Bastards're comin'." The older-looking law was heading for Clyde's car, unsnapping the holster, his fingers gripping the gun. The younger one had started back towards the cop's car but as soon as he saw the older one with his gun drawn, he started coming as well, trudging in the mud, getting his own gun out. The older law was yelling something at Clyde and then started crouching as he saw the barrel of the automatic rifle Henry was thrusting out the rear window. The laws fired twice—one bullet hitting the front fender, the other creasing the car door as Clyde swung it open and jumped out, followed by Henry who fired again as Clyde shot two rounds toward the other car. The younger law fired several shots, two going through the windshield. Both Clyde and Henry kept firing until the law staggered, clutching at his head, then fell in front of the car. He raised one hand as if to wave.

"Don't fire again!" Clyde told Henry. "You go get their guns, and bring these two to the car. We're takin' them soon as we get this fuckin' car outta of the mud."

Bonnie said, "Those people are all lookin' at us, they're comin' out of those houses to see what's goin' on."

The old guy was dead. Henry shrugged, left him lying, picked up the law's .38 and stuck it into his own belt. He walked carefully to the other one, whose head was bleeding. "Let loose of that pistol and get up," he told him. He pulled the law to his feet and started back to the car.

"Hurry it up!" Clyde called. "We got an audience—all these yokels. Give 'em five minutes and we'll have fuckin' militia on our necks." He looked at the law's wound. "Just glanced off your head," he said. "You're okay. Get in back and push this car outta the mud. You push it, Henry." Clyde got back behind the wheel, started the car and tried to pull ahead.

"We're just slippin' around deeper," Henry said. 'Give it more gas and we'll be gettin' nowhere."

Taking the shotgun out of the car, Clyde told Bonnie, "Get behind the wheel, see if you get it out while I run over to that house and get somethin' to pull us."

A few minutes later, Clyde returned with a pickup truck he'd convinced the owner to loan him, and a long, sturdy rope. It didn't work. The rope broke. Another car pulled off the highway onto the dirt road. Soon as Clyde saw it wasn't the law, he enlisted the driver to get behind the car with the law and Henry, and push the car out of the mud.

Frantic to get the car moving, Clyde went onto the highway, waving the shotgun and enlisting others to the task. One man in another truck had a sturdy chain, which he attached to the car, and in moments had it freed. The cop with the bleeding head was moved into the backseat along with Henry, and Clyde sped for the highway.

Bonnie opened their first-aid kit and bandaged the cop's flesh wound. She asked his name and he said, "It's Percy Boyd. I'm a cop with the Commerce Police Department, but I don't think I'll be gettin' any medals for today's job."

"Sure you will," Bonnie said. "They'll be writin' about you in the newspapers. Isn't every day someone gets taken for a ride by Clyde Barrow."

Boyd said, "I thought that's who he is."

Henry nodded. "That's who he is."

The cop looked at Bonnie. "You must be Bonnie...."

"That's me! But I don't smoke any cigars. When the newspapers are talkin' to you, you'll tell them you're sendin' a message from Bonnie Parker, and I'm not any kind of cigar-smokin' person. That was just a gag 'cause we were all takin' pictures. Bein' funny like we're real desperados."

"Aren't you?" Boyd asked.

"If we were real desperados, like John Dillinger," Bonnie said, "you probably wouldn't be ridin' with us. Nobody would've missed and skinned your head instead of blowin' your brains out."

Boyd cleared his throat. "Dillinger said he sure knows how to pick a good car. How fast you goin' now?"

Clyde said, "We're doin' ninety. Only three thousand miles on this one."

"You're sure a good driver," Boyd said.

"Gotta be," Clyde said. "If you're on the move all day and all night of every fuckin' day and night."

"I know," Boyd said. "We had no idea who was in this car. Got a call that it was sittin' all night with you all in it. Nobody knew who you were, just seein' the car sittin' there. Cal Campbell, the guy you shot, he knew right away who you were. Every state in the country must know who you are—there's four or five states lookin' for you all the time."

"I'm sorry about that old fella gettin' shot," Clyde said. "But this is a war and you kill or get killed. There ain't nothin' personal in it. He might've been a nice a guy as anyone."

Boyd said, "All that recent shootin' at Grapevine's got the whole state lookin' for you."

"We didn't have anythin' to do with that shootin'. Newspapers blamed us and you're damn right about the laws on us."

"What about the shootin' in Joplin?" Boyd asked. "Everyone keeps talkin' about that."

"That's what I was tellin' you," Clyde said. "It was the laws' fault for not runnin' off. They didn't have to be there. It was an attack, and I told you it's a war. You shoot or get shot."

They reached Fort Scott, Kansas, and Clyde sent Henry to buy newspapers and dinners. They gave Boyd a new shirt and one of Clyde's ties. Clyde wanted to give him a new suit, but it would've been too small for Boyd.

A little later that night, Clyde stopped the car a few miles south of Fort Scott. He said, "Here's where we're lettin' you out." Bonnie gave Boyd a ten-dollar bill, and Clyde told him, "Stay right here till we're behind that hill out there yonder. Gets us a little space between all those other boys out chasin' after us."

Bonnie said, "Promise me you're gonna tell the newspapers I don't smoke cigars. They got that gag picture and won't stop sayin' I'm a cigar-smokin' hellcat. But if you tell 'em, they'll believe it. You've spent a whole day and way late ridin' and eatin' with Clyde Barrow and Bonnie Parker and one of their friends. Will you do that?"

Forty-One

In 1985, I was put in contact with Evon Russo, a retired officer who'd worked with the Louisiana State Police and a former deputy of Bienville Parish, where he had been raised. He'd known the Methvin family. "Other Methvins were scattered throughout the parish," Russo said over beer and crawfish at Papa John's Restaurant in Lake Charles. "Not necessarily kin," he told me. "Later I was spendin' time in Ashland, not far from Henry's Methvin's folks, and I got to know about Henry doin' time in Texas—least 'til Clyde Barrow busted him out and a few others, all pretty rock-bottom bad guys." In his early 70s when we talked, the ex-deputy said he'd been "a couple years" older than Henry, and knew they were robbing banks and running with Clyde and Bonnie, "creatin' general hell," he said.

He became aware of a "stakeout" taking place in Bienville in the fall of 1934, "hushed up," he says, as it was related to capturing Clyde Barrow and "whoever was left of the gang he'd busted out. It was also clear," he said, "that Henry was the last of the 'hombres' left to be runnin' with Clyde."

Texas newspapers set the pace for what was to happen. Massive coverage of the Grapevine killings, offering two "eyewitness" accounts, were laying blame squarely on "a drunken Bonnie Parker, staggering to one officer wounded on the ground and emptying a shotgun into his body. Bonnie laughing as she fired, saying his head 'bounced on the road like a rubber ball.'"

The waves of sensational publicity were indelibly casting Bonnie as the maniacal murderess of the two highway patrolmen at Grapevine, labeling her a "whiskey-belting, cigar-smoking, bloodthirsty she-devil."

Though the stories were untrue, and both so-called "eyewitnesses" were ultimately discredited, the sensational publicity influenced the attitudes of government and law enforcement. When the Texas Rangers were consulted, Captain Frank Hamer said he'd read that Bonnie Parker personally had taken part in the murder spree of nine peace officers. He said he could not substantiate the information since there had never been correct murder warrants issued for Bonnie. For Clyde? Yes.

The furor reached fever-pitch with a bounty placed on Bonnie's head for her perceived role in the "bloodthirsty killings." Popular perception turned even further against her and Clyde when only five days following the Grapevine killings, Henry Methvin killed a sixty-year-old single father, Constable Cal Campbell, secretly blaming the murder on Clyde "with Bonnie at his side." Henry elaborated to his parents in Bienville that Bonnie "thought it was funny the way the old man's legs kicked as he was dying. But don't tell anyone I told you or Clyde'll find out I said it and kill me."

Bonnie and Clyde had kidnapped the city's chief of police, Percy Boyd, wounded in the same shooting, and drove for many hours, finally into Kansas where they let him go. During Boyd's conversation with the two, Clyde said he felt "bad about the old man gettin' killed," but did not indicate that he had pulled the trigger.

Chief Boyd told a reporter, "Bonnie was very good to me, took care of the bullet wound I'd got in my scalp, cleaned me up and Clyde gave me a clean shirt, even offered a suit but it was too small. I played it smart with those two, dug a little into their doin's and got them goin' over some of the activities. Soon as they freed me, what their talkin' openly did was to get their names on top of the murder warrants for Campbell's death, issued against Barrow and Parker, and with a third warrant for John Doe, as we didn't know yet who that third party was."

Russo says, "It was figured pretty quick that Henry Methvin was that third party, and the actual shooter of the constable."

In February 1934, the attorney general in Washington, D.C., notified the Department of Justice to utilize every effort possible to apprehend Clyde Barrow and associates. "The activities of Barrow and associates constitute an open defiance of the power of our law enforcement agencies."

Captain Frank Hamer had been summoned from retirement by Lee Simmons, head of the Texas State Prison systems who was infuriated over Barrow's bust-out of the Eastham farm crooks and killers. He had Hamer establish a separate post for himself: *Special Escape Investigator for the Texas Prison System*. His task, according to Simmons, was to "put Barrow on the spot and kill everyone else with him."

Hearing peripherally of the "plan," Evon quickly was in touch with a deputy of Bienville who told him the "subject's locked down tight." He said any word Evon might hear would have to come from Deputy Prentiss Oakley, or from the sheriff himself.

On that beer and crawfish afternoon in the summer of '85, Russo told me, "Of course, Oakley wasn't goin' to tell me any news, though what it had to do with was Ivy Methvin, Henry's dad, seekin' to make a deal to get Henry a pardon from Texas so he'd never have to see Eastham again. The old man got word to the sheriff that his son would kill himself if he had to go back to prison. "Henry said they're gonna put him in the hole and he'd never see sunlight again," Evon says. The try for a pardon wasn't out of the question since the governor of Texas had to sign the pardon, and Governor Miriam Ferguson was handing out pardons like candy. She'd earned the title 'The Pardon Queen,' and had been the cause of more than one devoted lawman taking an early retirement over her leniency on cons.

Evon says, "Later, I found out what was cookin', what Henry had to offer for a pardon, and that was his willingness to set up Clyde and Bonnie—betray them. That's how it worked. It went on for weeks, layin' the plan. Sheriff Henderson Jordan organized it with the Texas sheriff of Dallas county for Captain Frank Hamer to be runnin' the show...."

W.D. later learned the truth about Henry's betrayal. "Just like Judas," W.D. said, "he made his choice of goin' to the Romans to save his ass. Henry's chunk of silver was a Texas pardon for all the killin's his mangy hide had done in Texas."

"News about Barrow and Bonnie," Evon says, "runnin' loose and the failure of the law to stop them was widespread. Folks were jokin' that Clyde was in league with the Devil—*no*body could nail him. He was smarter than they were, too fast for local boys, and clever as a fox. He'd swiped hundreds of cars over a two-year period, changin' automobiles as fast some folks changin' their socks. He didn't shed a clue for the law to track. Stories about 'em were turnin' into legends as they were still on the run—some even swearin' ol' Clyde was bulletproof 'cause he'd outrun 'em even on foot. If he got hit, they'd swore he'd cut the bullet out, suck it like fixin' a snake bite and keep on runnin' till he'd disappear. 'Course, he couldn't dis*appear*, but he'd be gone—leavin' the law with its jaws hangin' open."

Catching Clyde seemed an impossibility, even with Texas, Oklahoma, Iowa and Missouri all chasing him. Nothing said "Dead or Alive" for Bonnie. She had no substantiated murder warrants out on her. "There were those sayin' she'd never fired a gun at anyone," Evon says, "and her only crime on record was transportin' a hot automobile across a state line—Clyde drivin', of course—and that wasn't any hangin' offense for her.

"Meanwhile, Henry's shittin' his pants at gettin' jugged back in Eastham. He was still runnin' with Barrow, but I imagine lookin' the other way whenever they got face to face."

Though Texas was yet ignorant of Henry's involvement in the Grapevine killings, the stakeout in Bienville Parish moved to "ambush" priority under Frank Hamer.

Half a dozen lawmen, including Sheriff Henderson Jordan and his deputy, Oakley, formed the inter-jurisdictional posse. Someone mentioned a roadblock, but that idea was cancelled out, along with dogs. "Barrow wasn't gettin' into any woods to run his ass off," one of the men said. "He'd smell hounds a mile up the road and the roadblock'll never see him."

According to Russo, "One of the six in the squad later told me they'd hide in the brush with the trees at their back, and remain crouching down on the higher shoulder of the road. They couldn't be seen from the road, even if you knew they were somewhere there and were lookin'. Hamer believed you couldn't reason with Barrow and if Bonnie was with him, no murder warrants on her wasn't goin' to make a difference. If push came to shove, the men believed she'd make a grab for a shotgun.

"There were questions of seeing a way of getting Bonnie separated from Clyde, but finally one had to face the fact: there wasn't any way. It would be rough if Clyde wouldn't surrender and aimed to shoot it out. Bonnie'd be in the line of return fire. The men believed they had no choice but to do what was necessary and demanded of them.

"One Texas lawman later told me, 'Way down on that empty dirt road runnin' through the forests, we made do with where we'd settled. The heat was awful and bugs raided every second. It was enough to make you crazy, and maybe we were, as it turned out. No one was volunteerin' to go out on that road to block Barrow's way or tell him he was under arrest. We didn't even draw straws. No one said anythin'. No one knew when it was goin' to happen, and maybe Barrow'd show or maybe he wouldn't. Maybe because of that you were wonderin' what you were doin'—sneakin' through brush waitin' to ambush a couple people, one with murder warrants floatin' and the other, the girl, no murder warrants on her. That had a bad taste when you figured maybe we were goin' to arrest that gal but if her boyfriend started shootin', you knew damn well it was all over. Near sundown we had a talk, all of us half-whisperin' as the night fell fast, sayin' the job was to mow Barrow down. Not to arrest a damn anyone.

"'None of us had any questions, a couple were thinkin' questions, but no one put any out there. No one had intention of anyone jumpin' out on that road to get killed. Your gut said he wasn't gonna surrender under any reason, and mowin' them down in cold blood could leave some legal questions, but Captain Hamer said we'd leave those matters to the lawyers since we were just there to do the job we were there to do. All agreed we wouldn't do any talkin' about any details after the job was done.

"'By sun up and a new invasion of bugs, but still no sign of Barrow, we heard an old clunker comin' north on the road. It was Ivy Methvin's old truck, the old man at the wheel. Hamer told the sheriff to stop the old man who'd agreed to aid in a decoy.

"'The old man was gripin', complainin'—didn't want nothin' to do with any shootin'. He told them Henry wasn't home that night and he might be in the car with Clyde and Bonnie. Ivy was told it was too late for any revisions in the plan and ordered out of the truck.' The old man kept whinin' that Barrow was comin'," Evon said, "and he'd kill him if he knew what was happenin'—kill him along with Henry and Henry's mother, and anyone else. Hamer tried reasonin', and Ivy Methvin got rambunctious, so Hamer said, 'This man's interferin' with the law.'"

Placing Ivy under temporary arrest, one of the posse led the old man a distance into the woods and safely out of any line of fire. He handcuffed Ivy to a tree.

"With him still yellin'," Russo said, "Ivy was quickly gagged and the men returned to their hiding places.

"'Methvin's old truck was moved to the east side of the road—the wrong side—was jacked up, the right front wheel taken off, and left on the road. One lawman kicked the wheel a yard further from the truck, narrowing the road so southbound traffic was forced nearer the opposite side of the road.'"

Back in the bushes, each man with his high-powered weapon, waited as the sun beat down on the narrow dirt road. They waited for the sound of a car approaching—traveling fast. They waited an hour. Maybe more. When a V-8 engine heading at high speed was heard, Hinton, who could recognize Barrow, raised his binoculars and focused on the approaching windshield. "This is him," he said. "It's Barrow."

Forty-Two

For several hours the previous night, Clyde sat silently staring at the black night beyond the dirty pane. His face in the glass was a mirage on a black beach with black waves creeping over the sand. As though Bonnie was reading his mind, she turned uncomfortably in the bed and said, "Do you think it's awful to be dead?"

Clyde said, "I thought you were asleep."

"I was," she said. "Now I'm awake so you come to sleep. Did you hear what I asked you?"

He shrugged. "The good thing about dyin's you don't know you're dead. If you don't know nothin' I guess it's not awful."

"So it doesn't matter," Bonnie said. "You don't know you're dead."

"You never wake up to know it," he said.

"Sleepin' without dreams," she added. "Goes on forever, doesn't it? I had that same dream so long ago. I was little. Bein' in a coffin and dressed real pretty. Sleepin' and not even catchin' a breath."

His eyes were closing. "I guess so."

"I love you, daddy. You know I'll miss you if I die."

"You won't miss nobody if you die," he said. "You won't know it."

"Do y'ever wonder what happens to your soul? Where it goes? I think about that a lot."

Clyde smiled. "Maybe your soul just stays in your bones."

Sighing, she slumped on the squeaking bed. "You think you and I will be sent to hell? Like the song I keep hearin', lovin' and goin' to hell?"

"There ain't no hell'n' there ain't no heaven," he said, impatient. "I've lost that thinkin', honey, 'cause there ain't nothin' but maybe a

353

lot of black water that's got no end. Just goes on....'"

She said, "So all we got that we're knowin' about's right here?"

"Go on to sleep now," he said. "I'll be watchin.'"

"You got to sleep too, daddy. We're okay in here, aren't we? Nobody gonna come bustin' in on us?"

He shook his head. "How can I ever know that? 'Sides, I can't s now. Just.... Somethin's not right."

"What's not right?"

"I'll wake you in a while. Maybe that singin' and music's still goin' on in my head."

"I knew some of the French words," she said. "It was sad about lovin' and then they lose the love. But you and I haven't lost any love." She closed her eyes. "Are you scared at all of bein' dead?"

He looked at her, smiling a little. "I'm not scared of it. Just tired's what I'm feelin'. I'm beat to my bones and the soles on my feet. I know you feel that way—beat through in your bones. Maybe I'm just thinkin' sometimes where's it gonna end?"

Softly, she said, "Maybe it's what I'm feelin'. I've been banged up so much I think half the time I'm almost dead. In a lookin' glass I'm sure as hell appearin' dead."

"You don't look like that," he said. "Times I'm thinkin' maybe one of 'em gets the first shot, I say make it clean, fella, shoot me between the eyes. Done'n' over. The whole fuckin' state of Texas is beatin' the weeds for us—"

"—Oklahoma and Missouri and everywhere else."

"We're okay here," he said. "Nobody in these fuckin' woods. You sleep now. I love you, baby. You believe I won't ever stop lovin' you, no matter what happens? Are you scared?"

"No, daddy. You know I'm not scared."

"You're the only idea I've got of anythin' bein' worth somethin' to me," he said. "I gotta tell you it isn't any blessin' from heaven how I'm feelin'—what we've had to do and how we've been. I can't figure it or how it came about, everythin' we've done. Just knowin' we keep goin' 'cause I don't see no other way." He turned the chair from the window and moved it closer to the bed. He said, "Baby, your momma would've seen it nice, us havin' a house like that fella in Texarkana, and you with a little squirt or two like that little bitty fella, and me havin' work to do.... All that's not any way we've been livin'—it ain't the way it's happened."

"You think it's too late to make ourselves different than what we're doin'?"

"I guess there was a time it could'a been different, so I reckon yes, honey, but none of that means I love you any less than if we were doin' somethin' your momma and the folks'd be happy about."

Clyde got up and sat on the bed beside her. He took her hands, his brow wrinkling. "It's like if you pulled a bunch of straws out of a bag sayin' you had to do this or that, an' I'm sayin' what we pulled out's what we've got. I can't be thinkin' about livin' a life we ain't got anymore'n that fella in Texarkana can haul up and be livin' another way. Don't know if he's lucky or you'n' me's the lucky ones, livin' as we're livin.'"

"Runnin' as we're runnin'," she said.

"Gettin' our butts shot, or shootin' them others 'cause that's the hand I've had as far fuckin' back as I can remember—an' I'm not enjoyin' any of it except us bein' with each other."

"Then it's the hand *I've* been dealt," she said. "I didn't have anythin' else, and it's too late, isn't it? We've gone a long ways, and it's thrilled me all the way, thrilled my heart with you. Nobody can change any of that, but now I'm thinkin' sometimes I should suicide myself an' get it done since it seems we've got no other choice."

"You're not gonna be killin' yourself!" he said. "I'm not gonna kill myself. Laws'd be all hatin' us for doin' he job they're so damned eager to be doin'. They're wantin' to put me in that electric chair, but I'm never goin' hands up to 'em so they're never gettin' the chance. An' you know I won't be locked up ever again anymore'n them puttin' me in that electric chair."

"I know that," she said. "There's nothin' on this earth that I care more about than lovin' you. There's just me'n' you, isn't it? There's nobody else."

"If we didn't have our folks it'd be different," he said. "We'd be down in Mexico livin' the life like I was sayin' and there's nobody in the world that'd ever find us down in Mexico." Bonnie didn't say anything. Looking intently at her, he said, "Now listen to me, honey, 'cause all that don't leave us a whole lot. But you can get out of it, you know, 'cause they don't have any proof you've ever done any killin' that'd show you're the same as me—"

"—but I *am* the same as you! I'm a part of you that's never gonna be surrendered."

"You're a *gal*," he said. "They'll make it easy 'cause of it. They won't be doin' any long juggin' or electrocutin' you."

She put her fingers against his mouth. "I don't think it'll make any difference my bein' a gal. We're Clyde and Bonnie and there's no separatin' us, not anymore there isn't, not with them sayin' what we've done. They'll be shavin' my head and fryin' me the same as you."

For moments he sat staring at her, again the sensation of black water flushing through his head. "You don't think sometimes if you weren't with me, if you hadn't stuck with me, you wouldn't be in all this?" She shook her head. He said, "You've wanted to be with me forever since we started lovin' each other?"

"Yes!" she said. "You know that as sure as you're breathin'."

"Chrisakes," he said, "long as I live, I'll be lovin' you, baby...." He leaned over and kissed her. "Go back to sleep, sugar. We gotta fetch Henry in the mornin' an' make a plan what we're gonna do." He touched her face. "An' you don't look like any dead girl. You look like an angel. Close your pretty eyes an' dream up the sun shinin' and maybe us bein' in Mexico on a beach of white, white sand."

She put her arms around his neck. "I don't want to live without you, daddy. Anything that happens has gotta happen to *us*, and if that's meanin' we die together, then that's what it means, and I don't mind nothin' else."

The next morning she hummed the song she could hear Clyde playing on his saxophone. Sunlight was shining through the cracked window, laying on her wet skin as she soaked in the tub smelling her rose perfume and pine sap soap. She gently washed her scarred leg that looked skinnier than her other leg, also covered with scars. Wringing the washcloth, she touched at the bullet scars and stared at her breasts, rubbing her flesh gently. The music from Clyde's playing stopped and she pulled the drain plug, then stood up reaching for a towel.

Minutes later, humming what he'd been playing, she knocked on the toilet door for Clyde to help her. He held her close and then sat her on the bed. She donned the red dress and unrolled her new stockings.

"You know, everytime I'm lookin' at my leg it make me sick," she said. "Sometimes I can't even stand up on it."

Clyde was holding his saxophone. He was staring at the floor, then looked at her. "Soon we gotta figure out what we're gonna do. You gotta make up your mind that we might have to go someplace else."

She pulled her stockings on, topped them with the elastic garters, then rolled the tops down above her knees. "You play that song slower than they do on the radio, and I like hearin' you play it better."

She edged off the bed and slipped her feet into her red shoes, then sat in the wobbly chair, brought out her writing pad and pencil and began scribbling quickly. He asked, "What're you writin'?"

"Just a note to my momma," she said. "I'm gonna write Billie Jean, too, but I'll do that later."

With half a smile, Clyde said, "You gonna be tellin' em how sad you are to be stuck in where we are with a busted sax player?"

She stared at him for a moment, then got up, went slowly to where he still sat, and cradled his head against her belly. "You're what makes me not sad, and that's how I'm gonna feel till I die."

Smiling, he put on a blue cowboy-style shirt, and got into his suit as he watched how she combed her hair. "We'll get some grub and go pick up Henry. I figure he's gotta be at his folks."

"Where do you think he ran off to?" she asked.

"We all ran off, unless the laws got him."

"Do you think we really need Henry with us? What if we don't find him and you an' me just go on to Texas?"

Clyde shrugged. "I need him for a job, honey. I got no one else now and we're only doin' this one more, so I need him for that. We'll get ourselves off for a spell, eat good and get you feelin' well and be like other folks." He stared at her. "You look so pretty and all fresh, and tomorrow we gotta buy you more presents. You just think of what'd make you happy, like you wanted those pretty shoes you're now wearin'. I'll get you ten pairs, honey."

She laughed, putting her hat on. "I'll dance my way to paradise!"

A half hour later, heading west, Clyde slowed down as they approached Gibsland. He stopped in front of Rosa Canfield's café, the local diner frequented by loggers, townsfolk, and the uneven visits of tourists. Bonnie and Clyde took stools at the far end of the counter, Clyde with his back to two loggers eating pancakes.

Bonnie drank coffee alongside with Clyde who picked at a plate of hot biscuits and gravy, and she asked, "Aren't you goin' to eat somethin' more than that?"

He shook his head. "I'm not hungry. I want to get down the road and find Henry. Let's take somethin' with us."

"That's a good idea," Bonnie said. She ordered two egg salad sandwiches "for the road." A couple of other customers stared at how she limped and hopped slightly with Clyde at her side. As they returned to the car, the waitress and both loggers had turned to watch them.

Behind the wheel, Clyde adjusted the shotgun to his left side, moved the .45 on the floor beneath Bonnie's movie magazine, then turned the key and shifted into low gear as Bonnie unwrapped one of the sandwiches. She asked, "You want part of this, daddy? You hardly ate your biscuits."

"I didn't like the gravy," he said. "Weren't at all like our mommas make. I'll eat a sandwich after we get Henry," he said. "He's probably nervous as shit waitin'. Maybe hidin' under a bed."

Clyde drove south out of Gibsland, the gravel from the dirt road rattling up in the fenders. He gathered speed on the old logging road, then veered to the right at the Mt. Lebanon crossroads. He increased his speed on the dirt road heading south to Sailes, the road narrowing as it led through the forest.

Glancing at Bonnie and and the sandwich open on her lap, the wind rattling the wax paper, he said, "You gonna eat that now, honey? It's gonna get dried out if you don't."

"Just a couple bites," she said. "I don't know why I'm so hungry, but I am."

"You're feelin' better, aren't you?" he asked.

"I guess I am," she said. "I had another hotel dream last night. I was seein' those silver sugar bowls again...." She took a deep breath. "I want to mail my letter. maybe when we get to Sailes...."

She stopped talking. Clyde was slowing down, leaning forward. Up ahead, facing north on the wrong side of the road, was the old truck that belonged to Henry's dad. Staring through the windshield, Clyde said, "There's Ivy's truck sittin' there headed the wrong way." Slowing down more, Clyde said, "He's got it jacked up and that wheel off. I don't see him. Where the hell's the old man?"

"If he got a ride," Bonnie said, "he didn't take his tire. Look at it sittin' in the road, waitin' to get run over."

Clyde shifted back into first gear, one foot holding the clutch, the right foot off the gas and easing on the brake. He pulled past the truck, wider to avoid running into the tire, almost coming to a stop as looked out the passenger window for a glimpse of the old man.

He managed to say, "I don't see him anywhere—" before the first heavy rifle bullet penetrated Clyde's head above the left ear, blowing off part of his head, then exiting the right side of his face to tear into Bonnie's breast and lungs. A split second more and a twelve-second hurricane of one-hundred and sixty-seven high-powered bullets bombarded the steel shell of the Ford, ripping through the dead bodies of Clyde and Bonnie.

ABOUT THE AUTHOR

Described by the *Sydney Morning Herald* as the "quintessential L.A. noir writer," John Gilmore has been acclaimed internationally for his true crime work, his literary fiction and Hollywood memoirs. As one of today's most controversial American writers, Gilmore's following spans the globe, from Hong Kong to his native Hollywood. He has traveled the road to fame in many guises: kid actor, stage and motion picture player, Beatnik painter, poet, screenwriter, low-budget movie director, and novelist. His work is translated into numerous languages. After heading the writing program at Antioch University in San Francisco, Gilmore taught, traveled, and lectured extensively while producing an indelible mark in crime literature with *Severed: The True Story of the Black Dahlia*, and *L.A. Despair: A Landscape of Crimes & Bad Times*. Interviewed in all media, Gilmore lives in the Hollywood Hills, where he is at work on a major novel.

Also by John Gilmore from Amok Books

L.A. DESPAIR

A Landscape of Crimes & Bad Times

John Gilmore delivers his ultimate, relentless panorama of sex, violence and death in five raw chronicles of SoCal sickness:

— Porn legend John Holmes and untouchable Hollywood crime lord and drug impresario Eddie Nash — the unvarnished story of the sex-and-coke-laced Wonderland murders

— "King of Western Swing" and early LA TV's singing cowboy phenomenon Spade Cooley walking the line of nightmare, depravity and murder

— Hollywood's fallen angel Barbara Payton — seemingly hell-bent to descend from Movie Star Sexpot to the gutters and dumpsters of real-life Tinsel Town

— From gorgeous Hollywood hooker to San Quentin's gas chamber, the infamous Ice Blonde murderous Barbara Graham

— Highway Hitchhike-Killer Billy Cook unleashing his cold-blooded hate for the human race

"John Gilmore is the best nonfiction writer of our time, the type of writer that grabs by the throat and by the heart." - *Maximum Rock'n'Roll*

ISBN 1-878923-16-1 (trade paper)

$19.95, 344 pp., illustrated

www.amokbooks.com

Also by John Gilmore from Amok Books

LAID BARE

A Memoir of Wrecked Lives and the Hollywood Death Trip

Acclaimed as a powerful chronicler of the American Nightmare through his gripping examinations of near-mythic Southern California murders (the Black Dahlia, Tate-LaBianca), author John Gilmore draws upon his own resevoir of personal experiences as he turns his sights on our morbid obsession with Celebrity and the ruinous price it exacts from those who would pursue. With caustic clarity and 20-20 hindsight, John Gilmore recounts his relationships with the likes of James Dean, Janis Joplin, Dennis Hopper, Jack Nicholson, Jane Fonda, Jean Seberg, Lenny Bruce and many other denizens of the twentieth century's dubious pantheon both on the way up and at the peaks of their notoriety.

"Beautifully written in a style somewhere between Jack Kerouac and Charles Bukowski... This is an astonishing book." - *Sight and Sound*

"John Gilmore deals with mythically familiar subjects, but not to turn them inside out. Instead he boils off the myth and shows you how things really were, and what things felt like to the people living what later became a myth. You will encounter no received ideas, no cliches, no deference to popular myths and opinions, and best of all, no lies. He's an amazing writer, and *Laid Bare* is his most astonishing book." - *Gary Indiana*

ISBN: 1-878923-08-0 (trade paper)

$16.95, 250 pp., illustrated

www.amokbooks.com

Also by John Gilmore from Amok Books

MANSON

The Unholy Trail of Charlie and the Family

Random murder and savage overkill, mind control and trips, Satanism and witchcraft, cursed glamour, Haight Ashbury, rock'n'roll, biker gangs, sexual rebellion & dune buggies tearing across Death Valley in search of the "hole in the earth..."

The persona of Charles Manson and his bizarre sway over the Family remain riveting a quarter of a century down the line. At the time of the killings, Charles Manson was instantly demonized by the media. Today he has become an icon of rebellion — "the spirit of annihilation." *Manson* is a gripping and chilling acccount of one of the most fascinating crime sagas of our time, now available in a revised and updated edition containing 36 pages of previously unpublished photos. New vectors into the kaleidoscopic tale which spins inexorably out of the slayings emerge in this updated edition with new material on killer Bobby Beausoleil and his occult alliance with experimental filmmaker Kenneth Anger.

"Fascinating!" - *Library Journal*

"A well-researched ethnography of the Manson Family more than an investigation of their crimes." - *Chicago Reader*

"A psychogeographical history of Manson and his family... Charlie considered him [Gilmore] a suitable medium for his messianic message." - *Dazed and Confused*

ISBN: 1-878923-13-7 (trade paper)

$15.95, 208 pp., illustrated

www.amokbooks.com

Also by John Gilmore from Amok Books

SEVERED

The True Story of the Black Dahlia

The Black Dahlia murder hit post-war Los Angeles like a bombshell... An impenetrable mystery—the haunting crown jewel of LAPD's "unsolved murders." Even before her savage death, beautiful 22-year-old Elizabeth Short, an aspiring starlet and nightclub habitué, was known as the Black Dahlia—now a magnetic icon in American pop culture, an almost mythical symbol of Hollywood noir. In this expanded edition John Gilmore plumbs the dark core of this terrifying story that, he argues, can never be truly solved. Here's the real Elizabeth Short—the enigmatic Black Dahlia.

"The most satisfying and disturbing conclusion to the Black Dahlia case. After reading *Severed*, I feel as if I truly know Elizabeth Short *and* her killer." - *David Lynch*

"The best book on the Black Dahlia — in fact, the only reliable book." - *Colin Wilson*

"This project stands as the only authentic true-crime book written on America's most bizarre and haunting murder case." - *Charles Higham*

ISBN: 1-878923-17-X (trade paper)

$17.95, 238 pp., illustrated